PROPERTIUS: ELEGIES BOOK I

Classical Studies series

PROPERTIUS

ELEGIES BOOK I

Text and Translation
with a Critical Analysis
of each poem

R.I.V. Hodge & R.A. Buttimore

Bristol Classical Press

This impression 2005
This edition published in 2002 by
Bristol Classical Press
an imprint of
Gerald Duckworth & Co. Ltd.
90-93 Cowcross Street, London EC1M 6BF
Tel: 020 7490 7300
Fax: 020 7490 0080
inquiries@duckworth-publishers.co.uk
www.ducknet.co.uk

First published in 1977 as *The 'Monobiblos' of Propertius*
by D.S. Brewer Ltd, Cambridge and Ipswich

A catalogue record for this book is available
from the British Library

ISBN 1-85399-651-3

PREFACE.

This book was written with two aims, which would usually have led to two separate books designed for two distinct kinds of reader. One of these readers is someone interested in poetry in general. Propertius is a great poet, difficult but immensely exciting, known by reputation, but not as widely read as he deserves. The fact that he wrote in Latin is a barrier in this relatively Latinless age, so the first need is to make his poetry more generally accessible. There are many intelligent and sensitive readers, who would need help with the Latin but have the imagination and literary experience to make use of such help. Hence the basic form of this book, a text of the poems with a close, line-for-line facing page translation, followed by essay-commentaries which try to show precisely how the language is working. Our belief is that a perceptive reader with only a small knowledge of Latin will be able to arrive at a personal possession of these poems, if we have done our job properly. It is a myth, naturally attractive to classicists, that total mastery of the language must precede any appreciation of the poetry. The relation between linguistic knowledge and critical adequacy is more complex.

The standard commentaries on Propertius are good of their kind, but they are unsatisfactory guides in some important areas, in ways they share with others of their kind. Such commentaries do not see it as their proper task to offer a critical account of a poem as a whole. But a whole is more than the sum of its parts, and the parts only find their full meaning in relation to the whole. Grasp of this whole requires more than a knowledge of the meanings of the component words and phrases. Essential also is a feel for poetic possibilities, as a context for deciding what kind of poem is at issue. Lack of this dimension in any developed form in traditional commentaries leads to characteristic defects even at the level where they ought to be strongest, the explication of words and phrases. At times, some of Propertius's boldest, most original effects are simply emended out of existence, usually replaced by an innocuous piece of 'emendese' to fill out the line. Or phrases or images will be paraphrased in a way that misses their poetic point entirely, as though the point had not been seen. Or lines which are decisive for one critical interpretation against another will be passed over without comment. There is a kind of inattention to language endemic in traditional commentaries, which can nullify many of the advantages of linguistic expertise.

If even the main traditional commentators on Propertius must be suspected of not always understanding the poems in quite basic ways, there is not just a job of popularizing to be done. Hence the second aim of the book, to argue for specific readings of the poems. With this goes a potentially different kind of reader, a Latin scholar already well acquainted with

Propertius. But these two aims are not incompatible, and a sharp opposition between the two kinds of readers comes from elitist notions that are hard to justify in this case. Wherever there is a disagreement over a meaning we try to give the terms of the dispute clearly, and the kinds of reasons that have been offered on various sides. We suppose that non-classicists will be entirely capable of following these arguments, even if they might never have initiated them, and equally capable of seeing their critical relevance. They might even disagree with our own interpretation: the materials for an opposed reading should be there. Such acts of decision should not be distractions but collaborative acts, ways of clarifying the poem and coming even closer to it. Conversely, classical scholars ought not to be impervious to arguments derived from literary critical insights. Everyone acknowledges that even Latin poems are poems as well as being in Latin.

The main purpose of the translations is to mediate between texts and essays, literal enough to indicate what every word of the Latin is doing, while trying to convey more general poetic qualities as well, such as tone, form, movement. This makes them one way of testing the claims of the essays, to demonstrate that the words can carry the interpretation we give them in the essay and cohere in a possible English poem. But though it is hoped that they are easy and pleasant to read, they are of course no substitutes for the originals, especially originals as rich and multi-layered and irreducibly Latin as Propertius's elegies.

This project has been collaborative from its inception, but the final form of the introduction and notes has been the responsibility of Buttimore, the translations and essays of Hodge. We have received invaluable criticism of various parts of the book from Guy Lee, of St. John's College, Cambridge, Dr. R.O.A.M. Lyne, of Balliol College, Oxford, and Dr. Mike Long, of Churchill College, Cambridge.

INTRODUCTION

I

The life of Propertius and the biographical question.

We have very little external evidence for the life of Propertius, as is the case with most ancient poets. However, although he is not often clearly and anecdotally biographical in the manner of Horace, some information can be securely derived from the poems themselves. The date of his birth can be established within limits from what he says of himself in IV i 120 ff. There he implies that when he assumed the 'toga virilis' he had already lost part of his paternal estates in the confiscations of 41—40 B.C. The toga virilis was not usually taken after the age of 17, so the earliest date for the poet's birth would then be about 57 B.C. In the same passage in Book IV he says that he lost his father in boyhood and his mother in early manhood. He also implies that his family was of equestrian standing, a social advantage which distinguishes him from his contemporaries Horace and Vergil. He was born in Umbria probably near Assisi (see I xxii and IV i 121—6). He was still alive in 16 B.C., since the eleventh poem of Book IV celebrates a Cornelia who died in that year. But by A.D. 2 he had died, since Ovid speaks of him in the past tense in the Remedia Amoris (line 763), which belongs to that year.

Some of the experiences implied by this sketchy history clearly enter into his poetry and colour the tone of his relationships. This is particularly obvious in the case of those poems addressed to Tullus in the first book (see below on VI, XIV, XXII). The experience of the confiscations, the consciousness of having been on the wrong side in the civil wars, a feeling of loyalty to his dead cousin (XXI, XXII), all these are significant factors in his relationship to Tullus, an Italian of consular family who happened to be on the winning side. This kind of interaction between poetry and life is relatively easy to perceive, but for other aspects of Propertius's biography, and particularly for the affair with Cynthia, two problems face the scholar and critic. The first is the elusive nature of the evidence where the source is largely poems, the second, a sense that all such speculation is in any case irrelevant to the study of the poems as poems. Clearly if the second is felt to be the case, the first problem ceases to be of any critical importance. This is essentially the position argued by A.W. Allen in an influential article.[1] Allen, however, concentrated on a particular target, the speculative biography that derives from Barth and Lachmann, which is an attempt to establish a chronology of the affair with Cynthia from scattered references in the poems. Allen conclusively demolishes such theories, showing in detail how this attempt is doomed to failure because of the nature of the evidence. All proponents of particular schemes have been guilty of going wildly beyond the literal meaning of the evidence and of wilfully ignoring what goes against

(1)   'Sunt qui Propertium malint': in Sullivan 'Essays' pp.130 ff.

their own thesis.

But not even Allen seems to have realised how trivial and perverse an enquiry these scholars have engaged in. To seek to reduce a long and involved relationship to a series of dates is the extreme of pedantic irrelevance. Such a list of dates is hardly likely to help the understanding of any of the poems. Conversely, the failure to establish a chronology from the poems alone proves much less than Allen thinks about Propertius's life or poetic intentions. The poems are certainly not arranged in chronological sequence, but not every narrative begins at the beginning and plods through to the end. This may irritate scholars, but we can hardly blame Propertius.

There is in fact a danger here of over reacting against the apparently lightweight and unintellectual nature of the biographical knowledge sought; at best it may seem gossip, even if it is obtainable. But it is especially true of Propertius's poetry that the connections between literature and life, between the pressures of experience and the exact literary form, are too important to be ignored, however difficult they are to follow. If they are so ignored, a gravely impoverished reading of the poems results. Propertius's poems are supremely allusive; some of the allusions are to other literature and scholars pursue these where they can: others are to his unique personal experience, and the scholar is bound to follow these as well, again as far as he can.

Propertius's poems in Book I are distinctively written out of a specific situation which itself is a stage in the single relationship that dominated his life. This supremely important and highly complex relationship is, however, very rarely displayed directly. It becomes the invisible centre of most of the poems, indicated with a brevity disproportionate to its structural importance. The principle of composition here could be termed eccentric, since the real centre is outside the poem, a real experience that can be communicated only imperfectly and must be supplemented by the reader's own experience. This is not an anachronistic view — Propertius saw his only comprehending audience as lovers, especially a 'neglectus amator' like himself (I vii 13). An analogy can be taken from sculpture: this used to be thought of as a matter of solids receiving shape, but now it can be seen as a system of voids and volumes. In these terms, the 'voids' in some of Propertius's poems, the precise but compressed indications of an immensely important experience outside the occasion of the poem, are their most significant feature. Some works of art aspire to autonomy: these poems are not like this and are arguably greater because of this fact. They are not self-contained and can hardly be understood solely by a contemplation of their words in isolation.

So it is clear what kind of knowledge we need and how we should use it. The knowledge is of two kinds, neither of which has the inert quality of dates: (a) facts that help us to understand the dynamics of the key relationship, the pressures that lie behind the tensions and quarrels that Propertius writes out of but so rarely about; (b) something of the background of the addressees, Cynthia of course, but the others as well. It is true that the character of the addressee usually emerges in broad outline simply from a close attention to an individual poem, but even so it is hard for a poem to interact closely with a construct derived solely from itself. The poems gain in definition and dramatic force when the addressee is felt as a real person whose presence has modified the poem crucially, but who still remains to some degree independent of it.

So what do we know about Cynthia? The single solid fact that used to be taken for granted was that she was a 'meretrix', a high class courtesan, whose name was Hostia.[2] G. Williams however has recently shown that the arguments for the meretrix belief are wholly inadequate.[3] He maintains a different view, that she was of high social standing and probably married. The traditional case rests primarily on inference from II vii. In this poem Propertius refers to the repeal of a law that would have impeded their relationship. He is not explicit, however, and the law does not survive. The meretrix case hypothesises that there were provisions in the lost law that would have forced him to marry and prevented him from marrying Cynthia. She must have belonged to a forbidden class, so the speculation goes, because she was a courtesan. Williams exposes the tenuous nature of this speculation, pointing out that an adulterous union would very likely have been forbidden and is a more probably source for Cynthia's concern. This at least nullifies the value of this particular piece of evidence, even if it does not itself prove anything. In support of Williams's thesis is II xxiii which unmistakeably talks as though Cynthia is married (see line 20), and Propertius is tired of the problems involved in an adulterous relationship. No other poem so explicitly describes her as a courtesan (charges of promiscuity are, of course, a very different matter). The general caveat against using poems as evidence remains: this may be merely a literary performance on a conventional theme, quite unrelated to Cynthia's real position. However, supporters of the meretrix case must sound unconvincing when dealing with this poem: Butler and Barber say on line 20: 'Ostensibly the husband of his mistress . . But on the natural assumption that Propertius is describing the difficulties besetting his liaison with Cynthia and in view of the fact that she is a courtesan and unmarried, we must regard the 'husband' as being the successful lover by whom she is kept for the time being'. They merely accept the traditional case without question; otherwise they would have seen the inadequacy of their account here. None of the evidence that Williams puts forward proves his case beyond a shadow of doubt, but it is a much stronger case than the alternative. It is also a more satisfactory account of the relationship behind the poems, a more powerful and illuminating explanation of the tensions involved in general and even also in particular details.

Adultery is a much more subversive kind of relationship, though asso-

(2) The evidence for the name is Apuleius Apologia 10: there is no obvious reason for disbelieving him.

(3) Pp. 529 f.

ciation with prostitutes may be more undignified. The popularity of the meretrix case may have something to do with the fact that it would have been less offensive to Victorian morality. Prostitution has been described as a safety valve required to preserve marriage;[4] adultery is the destruction of marriage. Moreover, Propertius never suggests that he is at all degraded by the relationship, and he is not conscious of himself as having betrayed a high social position. On the contrary, he seems inferior in status to both Tullus (see e.g. VI 19–20) and Gallus (see e.g. V 23–4), his two principal male addressees in this book. He may also have been Cynthia/Hostia's social inferior: that would have added to the tensions of the relationship more than if she had been a relatively lowly if promiscuous prostitute. In two poems at most of this first book, II and possibly XV, Cynthia is talked of as though she is a prostitute, but at other times she seems a kind of wife (see e.g. III, XVII). If she was in fact a prostitute, the implications of II and XV would be true, and these other poems would be a representation of a pathetic wish to create a quasi-marriage relationship in an area where society disapproved. The barrier to this desired union would be his real acceptance of social sanctions against it, added perhaps to a recognition that Cynthia could not be trusted.

However, if she was really married, both sets of implications are false, and the poet's position is inherently self-contradictory. He aspires after a relationship with all the permanency and total commitment of an ideal marriage, but this can only be created out of the destruction of an already existing marriage. Cynthia must be a harlot to her husband to be a wife to Propertius, and this dual character is central to their union. The poet's anxiety and love are polarising reactions to Cynthia's two aspects. He makes extreme demands on her and extreme accusations, both unreal.

So the accusations (always implicit) of harlotry gain a different significance and serve a different poetic function. Their truth is subjective — they are expressions of Propertius's acute anxiety. So poem II's force is not 'You are a prostitute, but for Heaven's sake don't show everyone' but 'you are behaving in a manner unworthy of you, like the prostitute I have made you'. The ambiguous quality of feeling in that poem can be seen as basically a response to the ambiguities of his own position as an adulterous mate demanding total fidelity from the wife he has seduced. In II vi the polarisation of Cynthia as wife and harlot is more acute. He begins by comparing her house to those of the legendary prostitutes, Lais, Thais, and Phryne, but finishes hoping for 'loyalty' from her and swearing 'semper amica mihi semper et uxor eris' (II vi 42 'You will be my mistress for ever and for ever my wife'). It is a lesser poem that I ii but more explicit about Cynthia's paradoxical status, and Propertius's vulnerability in face of it.

Book I is full of poems of departure, to which Propertius seems resigned in strange ways. The difficulties especially concern VIII and XI, where Cynthia proposes to depart or has departed. If Cynthia was a professional

(4) Consonant with Cato's view as recounted by Horace Satires I ii 31–35.

8

prostitute at a place as notorious as Baiae, as in poem XI, the poet's doubts about her fidelity ought to have been certainties. A girl has to live, and Propertius seems to have been able to provide only poems. Poem VIII is a more interesting case. A rival is referred to in line 3 as 'quicumque est' ('whoever he is'), and is then apparently forgotten and assumed irrelevant. This is strange, unless he had proved himself irrelevant over some period of time. Only the cuckold husband could be as 'safe' as this. A detail later in the poem also seems inexplicable (or simply irrelevant) unless this is her husband. She is said to prefer Propertius and Rome to 'the ancient realm that was Hippodamia's dower and all the wealth that Elis won by its steeds' (lines 35–6). If this involved and specific allusion means anything at all, it can only suggest that for Propertius's sake she has rejected both her dowry and the wealth she has acquired from other lovers or admirers: that is, wealth committed to a parentally arranged marriage plus the spoils of her own conquests. This would make her a married woman of great wealth and position, as well as character and beauty. Propertius offers her poems instead of wealth, and the eternal devotion of a lover-husband, but if she had the reality of everything that he could offer only in simulacrum, it is no wonder he felt insecure.

II

The dating of poems in Book I

The latest probably dateable reference in Book I is in poem VI, which refers to the pro-consulship of Lucius Volcacius Tullus, the uncle of the addressee. This was in 30–29 B.C., when he went to take up the governorship of the province of Asia. The book as a whole must have been published after that, though how soon is difficult to say (and what exactly was involved in ancient publication is difficult anyway). Enk argues that the publication must have been fairly soon afterwards, since Book II contains a poem, XXXI, which, he claims, refers to the dedication of the temple of Apollo on the Palatine on the 9th October, 28 B.C.[5] But as Rothstein argues on this passage, it is not at all certain that it is the dedication of the temple that is being referred to, but possibly merely the opening of a section of it for public use after the decoration had been completed. So this date is not very useful. But in II x, Octavian is referred to as Augustus, which dates this poem as later than 27 B.C. Another poem which is significant in this respect is II xxiv, where Cornelius Gallus is said to have died lately and this implies a date around 27–6 B.C. It is on the whole likely then that Book I was completed before 27 B.C. and not earlier than 30 B.C. It is impossible to be more specific than that.

If this were all, it would not perhaps be very important, but there is also evidence of an internal kind in Book I which suggests a dating of the

(5) Pp. 16 f. of his edition of Book I.

poems relative to each other. It has long been noticed that the percentage of pentameters ending in a polysyllable decreases from Book I to Book IV, and in particular there is a fairly marked decrease between the first two books from about 36% to about 9%. A tendency towards a more consistent use of disyllabic endings is consequently a feature of his developing style. In Book I itself there is a fairly wide variation between individual poems in this respect – the figures are as follows: I 37%, II 44%, III 61%, IV 21%, V 13%, VI 39%, VII 31%, VIII 22%, IX 6%, X 13%, XI–XII 36%, XIII 6%, XIV 50%, XV 67%, XVI 75%, XVII 21%, XVIII 25%, XIX 8%, XX 54%, XXI 60%, XXII 60%. On the basis of these figures, one may reasonably divide the poems into three main groups: early poems (75%–50%) XVI, XV, III, XXI, XXII, XX, XIV: Middle (a) (44%–30%) II, VI, I, XI–XII, VII; (b) (25%–21%) XVIII, VIII, XVII, IV: late (13%–6%) V, X, XIX, IX, XIII. It is not on general principles very likely that a difference of less than 10% is very signicant, so some poems are on the borders between groups; the central point one may make is that most of the poems in each of these three groups were written before most of those of any later group.

The evidence of the pentameter endings has to be used circumspectly. Where it confirms conclusions of relative dating reached on other grounds, it performs a useful corroborative function. The most obvious case is that of poems VII and IX, where the latter is clearly the sequel to the former. Here the pentameter test is confirmatory, though the question was not one admitting of much doubt. More significant and useful information is given by the fact that the last three poems of the book all fall into the earliest group. One might suspect on other grounds that these poems, all of which are new and interesting treatments of Hellenistic genres and are therefore probably experimental, are early; the language of XX shows qualities of strain and the poem is not perhaps fully realised (see our discussion). Here the evidence of the pentameter endings provides an important kind of confirmation. But this evidence by itself may be misleading. For example, it seems to us that poem XV is probably later than II (for the arguments see our discussion below) although the percentages here are 67% for XV and 44% for II. Other types of evidence which validate themselves in more purely rational ways than the numerical must weigh more heavily than the pentameter endings. However this is another tool which a critic can use, so long as its limitations are respected.[6]

It has become fashionable recently to suppose that the poems of Book I are arranged in a particular kind of symmetrical pattern. In fact Courtney[7] specifically says 'An elaborately symmetrical arrangement . . . . is now establi-

(6) It is surprising that the pentameter endings have not been used before as a means of relative dating. Camps (p. 10 note 1 of his edition of Book I) comes close to doing so without being explicit.

(7) P. 251 'Cl. Phil.' 1968. The other principal articles discussing this feature of the poems are E. Solmsen, 'Cl. Phil.' LVII (1962), O. Skutsch 'Cl. Phil.' LVIII (1963), and Brooks Otis 'H.S. Cl. Phil.' 70 (1965).

shed as Propertius's deliberate intention'. No voices have been raised in protest, and so the basis of this orthodoxy demands careful scrutiny.

The theory in its strongest form, as e.g. presented in Courtney's article, argues that poems I–XIX are arranged chiastically in four blocks; A^1 (I–V), B^1 (VI–IX), B^2 (X–XIV), A2 (XV–XIX), and in this version B^1 and B^2 even have an identical number of lines. The Mss unfortunately give us 142 lines in B^1 and 140 in B^2: to achieve symmetry, Courtney transposes VII 23–4, which, he says, is logically out of place. But there are notoriously many couplets in Propertius whose logical connections with their context are not immediately clear. Before transposing, one ought to try to look for some other kind of connection, perhaps not exactly logical, that may exist. This couplet is not especially difficult to account for in its place, but the real danger here is that a Courtney might accept one's argument and the tradition on VII 23–4, and remove another couplet instead. He might then turn his attention to A^1 and prune its 176 lines to 172 to match A^2. The theory in this extreme form is a Procrustean bed.

Weaker forms of the theory at least accept the transmitted text. Of these, however, it must be said at the beginning that the idea itself is implausible and almost entirely gratuitous, adding little to the value or significance of the poems or of the book as a whole. The book was probably composed over a period of time, and no-one claims that most of the poems were written to fill out some symmetrical scheme. The only proposition at all plausible is that the poet arranged them in this order, in many cases long after they had been written for quite different reasons. The only parallel for the symmetry that has been adduced is Ovid Tristia V: but even if the case were true for that book, Ovid is later, a much more prolific and artificial poet, and this work is only a small proportion of his large output. All arguments from parallels are weak, and this is a weak parallel. The case must be proved for Propertius independently.

But the scheme which has won acceptance does not stand up to close examination. Firstly it does not include all the poems of this book – XX–XXII are normally treaded as addenda. If Propertius did not take the schema seriously enough to extend it throughout the whole book, doubts must arise as to whether it was really important to him. But the basic objection to these schemes is that they rely not on one ordering principle but on two. These are said to "complement" each other, but in practice this means that they are invoked intermittently and arbitrarily in support of such symmetries as can be found. The first principle is objective – the choice of addressee: this gives a pattern for VI–XIV as follows:

Tullus
Ponticus
Cynthia
Ponticus

Gallus
Cynthia
Gallus
Tullus

This is neat enough, although too few poems are involved for it to be unmistakeably the product of design not chance. Outside these poems, however, this principle not only needs to be "complemented" by an alternative, largely subjective principle, but is also on many occasions overridden by it. Ponticus is not addressed elsewhere in the book, but Gallus, Tullus and Cynthia are. The pattern that emerges for the book as a whole, or up to XIX, to accept that unsatisfactory expedient for saving the theory, is untidy and unsymmetrical. Poems I, V, and XIV, to Tullus, would be connected; so would V, X and XIII, to Gallus (and XX, also to Gallus, clamours to rejoin the rest of the work, with XXII putting in its claim also with Tullus as its addressee). Poems II, VIII, XI, XV, XIX to Cynthia also ought to be connected. The pattern now looks random, suggesting that the apparent patterning of VI–XIV was in fact fortuitous.

Tullus
Cynthia
?
Bassus
Gallus
Tullus
Ponticus
Cynthia
Ponticus
Gallus
Cynthia
Gallus
Tullus
Cynthia
?
?
?
Cynthia
Gallus
?
Tullus

The ordering principle invoked instead of this relies on a perceived similarity of subject in pairs of poems. This principle has the merit of allowing interesting things to be said about individual poems, but it is far too subjective to support any rigid theory of order. To take the most interesting example, Brooks Otis's connection between II and XV illuminates both poems. Otis has done a useful service in pointing it out, but there are innumerable other connections that could be made. The setting of XV, for example, is Propertius's imminent departure; as such it contrasts with VI (to Tullus) where Propertius is refusing to go, and with VIII and XI, where Cynthia is the one proposing to go or has actually already gone. Again in XVII he seems to have gone on a voyage himself and to have regretted doing so. There are innumerable connections of this kind that can be made, far too many to be fitted into a tidy symmetrical scheme, unless for some prior reason it has been decided to notice only connections that give rise to a symmetrical scheme – but that would be arguing in a circle. The fact is that the two ordering principles conflict in several cases, and poems I and XIX have neither theme nor addressee in common.

So the arguments that can be brought forward to support this theory are entirely inadequate. It is most unlikely that such a scheme exists for this book and the theory can do nothing but harm. It attaches undue importance to certain connections which coincide with the scheme, at the expense of the innumerable points of contact the poems naturally have with each other. This web of interconnections is far richer and more satisfying than any straightened symmetry, whose only merit is to gratify an undisciplined desire for tidiness.

IV

Propertius' Language

The normal preconceptions about the language of poetry with which scholars set out to study Propertius have been inadequate and misleading. The prime assumption is included in the belief that all Latin poetry is rhetorical. Ancient prose is rhetorical, and much ancient verse is rhetorical, but not all. Nor is it sufficient to assume that any particular poet is rhetorical: this is something that has to be shown in each individual case. In practice, what is generally meant by saying that a poet is rhetorical is that he uses words as equivalents of their synonyms. This is the usual assumption of the commentaries and it is normal for a word in the text to be glossed by a more usual word in the note. The serious critical consequence of this is that all strange locutions of the poet come to be seen as simply 'metri gratia', as devices for filling up the line. Any striking qualities the language may have are simply normalised out of existence by this procedure, and Latin poetry becomes in the eyes of the critic a sort of superior crossword puzzle, composed in the same way as modern scholars compose Latin verses. This is the implicit assumption of most commentaries. Nowadays, attempts are made to break free from this assumption, but it is very difficult to do so, since all early training with the use of standard editions has unconsciously drilled it into the basic mental procedures of most Latinists. The disease is not always recognised and it has in fact been instrumental in the overvaluing of Horace as compared to Propertius, since if the process of writing poetry is the fitting of unexceptional statements into complicated metres, then the more complicated the metre, the better the poet.

Rhetorical assumptions are equally in evidence when it comes to the treatment by commentators of the mythological exempla employed by Roman poets. These are often dismissed as simply decorative, though in recent years a rather closer attention has been paid to them than in the past.[9] The same point may be made as was made in respect of language: that one ought not to assume that myth passages are simply ornamental until one has examined the other possibilities very closely. Propertius's employment of myth is functional, and though it may be difficult to discover completely the significance of a particular exemplum, it is usually clear that it has some significance and is not simply detachable from its context. The importance of being aware of the story from which the exemplum is derived is easy to see, for example, in the myth section in poem II. There the poet draws attention by the language he uses to elements not explicitly mentioned. The works 'succendit', 'discordia'. 'patriis, 'falso' (lines 15–19) all warn the reader to be alert for nuances of tone that arise out of the background of these stories.[10]

So mythological elements in Propertius are not like extended Homeric similies; they do not contain simply one point of comparison. This is usually unrecognised even nowadays, and it is customary to note one obvious point of comparison in the myth passages and ignore what is not immediately obvious. The point is that in this area, as well as in the wider area of use of language, the conscious or unconscious assumption that Propertius is 'rhetorical' totally inhibits serious criticism.

A different kind of mistaken criticism arises out of a critical virtue, namely a rational approach. But the extreme rationalism of critics like Housman (and a sterile rationalism of the type he represents is wholly inimical to the criticism of poetry) refused to contemplate the possibility of an argument proceding by any means other than the strictly rational. Consequently they were led frequently to emend, since they could not tolerate what they regarded as anomalies in the text of so subtle and complex a poet as Propertius. But a poem may develop its own logic by which to validate its argument. An obvious example is the famous crux 'persuadent' in II 13, where the word is so much the mot juste, so appropriate and brilliant in its context, that it is inconceivable that such felicity should have been arrived

(9) Cp. Allen, in the article already cited.

(10) For a full discussion, see below.

at through scribal error. The basic point is that the skills required in understanding a poet's language are the skills of literary criticism and so the criteria for establishing the text, given the tradition, are predominantly literary critical also.

In Propertius's case, there are two major sources of difficulty. One is the erudition he demands from his reader. He calls Cynthia 'docta puella' ('well-educated girl') and she needed to be if she was to catch the full range of his often oblique allusions. But most of his poems are not even addressed to Cynthia, but to a set of male friends, a highly sophisticated and literate group. He claimed to Ponticus, aspiring writer of epics, that he was 'more slave to sorrow than skill' ('nec tantum ingenio quantum servire dolori', VII 7), but he was a very self-conscious poetic craftsman, aware that his poetic virtuosity reflected credit on his mistress and himself. But the virtuosity was never simply to impress, an end in itself. The other source of difficulty with Propertius's poetry comes from the reality and complexity of the experience out of which it grew, a highly intelligent and cultivated young Roman's encounter with the deeply problematic and often contradictory emotions generated by his relationship with Cynthia.

I

Cynthia prima suis miserum me cepit ocellis,
    contactum nullis ante cupidinibus:
tum mihi constantis deiecit lumina fastus
    et caput impositis pressit Amor pedibus,
donec me docuit castas odisse puellas   5
    improbus, et nullo uiuere consilio.
et mihi iam toto furor hic non deficit anno,
    cum tamen aduersos cogor habere deos.

Milanion nullos fugiendo, Tulle, labores
    saeuitiam durae contudit Iasidos.   10
nam modo Partheniis amens errabat in antris,
    ibat et hirsutas ille uidere feras;
ille etiam Hylaei percussus uulnere rami
    saucius Arcadiis rupibus ingemuit.
ergo uelocem potuit domuisse puellam: 15
    tantum in amore preces et bene facta ualent.

in me tardus Amor non ullas cogitat artis,
    nec meminit notas, ut prius, ire uias.
at uos, deductae quibus est fallacia lunae
    et labor in magicis sacra piare focis,   20
en agedum dominae mentem conuertite nostrae,
    et facite illa meo palleat ore magis!
tunc ego crediderim uobis et sidera et amnis
    posse Cytinaeis ducere carminibus.

et uos, qui sero lapsum reuocatis, amici,   25
    quaerite non sani pectoris auxilia.
fortiter et ferrum saeuos patiemur et ignis,
    sit modo libertas quae uelit ira loqui.
ferte per extremas gentis et ferte per undas,
    qua non ulla meum femina norit iter: 30
uos remanete, quibus facili deus annuit aure,
    sitis et in tuto semper amore pares.
in me nostra Venus noctes exercet amaras,
    et nullo uacuus tempore defit Amor.
hoc, moneo, uitate malum: sua quemque moretur   35
    cura, neque assueto mutet amore locum.
quod si quis monitis tardas aduerterit auris,
    heu referet quanto uerba dolore mea!

POEM I

Cynthia captured me first, to my cost, with those eyes —
    I'd never before been struck by lust's disease:
my gaze, once firmly arrogant, bent to the ground,
    and Love's triumphant foot pressed on my head,
till now he has taught me to loathe respectable girls,   5
    depraved god! and to lead this senseless life.
The madness has raged in its course for a year on end,
    but the gods I'm forced to worship oppose my suit.

No, Tullus, it wasn't by running away from ordeals
    that Milanion crushed cruel Atalanta's rage: 10
he wandered deranged through caves in the Virgin Mountain,
    and ventured where hairy beasts affronted his eyes,
and once he was struck and wounded by Hylaeus' bow,
    and groaned as he lay in pain by Arcadia's cliffs.
And hence he was able to tame that fleet-footed maiden: 15
    prayers and good deeds like his work wonders in love.

But Love runs slowly in me, and devises no schemes,
    and forgets to use the methods he once knew well.
So you, who pretend you eclipse the moon from the sky,
    performing your magic rites on hallowed hearths,   20
here is your chance, come, change my mistress's heart,
    eclipse the light of her cheeks, fainter than mine!
I'll believe in your claims then, that Thessalian spells have power
    to drain the sea of its floods and stars of their light.

And you, friends, who at this late stage still urge me to stand,   25
    find me something to help a heart that's sick.
I'd suffer the knife or savage cautery bravely,
    to win the freedom to talk as my fury craves.
Send me to some far out-post, over the ocean,
    where none of her sex would know the route I took: 30
but remain in Rome, if the god is kind and has heard you,
    be always carefully matched in a safe affair.
That passion in me is the cause of nights of anguish,
    my lack of love is present every hour.
Fly from this peril, I warn you: let everyone hold   35
    to his own, not shift an inch from a well-tried love.
Should anyone listen too late to this warning I give,
    alas! he'll echo my words with endless grief.

II

Quid iuuat ornato procedere, uita, capillo
    et tenuis Coa ueste mouere sinus,
aut quid Orontea crinis perfundere murra,
    teque peregrinis uendere muneribus,
naturaeque decus mercato perdere cultu,   5
    nec sinere in propriis membra nitere bonis?

crede mihi, non ulla tua est medicina figurae:
    nudus Amor formae non amat artificem.
aspice quos summittat humus formosa colores,
    ut ueniant hederae sponte sua melius,   10
surgat et in solis formosius arbutus antris,
    et sciat indocilis currere lympha uias.
litora natiuis persuadent picta lapillis,
    et uolucres nulla dulcius arte canunt.

non sic Leucippis succendit Castora Phoebe,   15
    Pollucem cultu non Hilaira soror;
non, Idae et cupido quondam discordia Phoebo,
    Eueni patriis filia litoribus;
nec Phrygium falso traxit candore maritum
    auecta externis Hippodamia rotis: 20
sed facies aderat nullis obnoxia gemmis,
    qualis Apelleis est color in tabulis.

non illis studium uulgo conquirere amantis:
    illis ampla satis forma pudicitia.
non ego nunc uereor ne sim tibi uilior istis: 25
    uni si qua placet, culta puella sat est;
cum tibi praesertim Phoebus sua carmina donet
    Aoniamque libens Calliopea lyram,
unica nec desit iucundis gratia uerbis,
    omnia quaeque Venus, quaeque Minerua probat.   30
his tu semper eris nostrae gratissima uitae,
    taedia dum miserae sint tibi luxuriae.

POEM II

How pointless, my life, to parade with your hair adorned,
    and flutter tight-pursed hearts with your silks from Cos,
or anoint your curls till they drip with Orontean myrrh,
    selling your gift-wrapped self with foreign goods:
you squander Nature's finery for grace from a shop —   5
    your body's parts are your assets, let them shine!

Believe me, dressings applied to beauty are worthless!
    Love is unclothed, and hates contrivers of charm.
For look at the colours the beautiful soil produces,
    how ivy is better winding where it will: 10
arbutes are most beautiful springing in lonely hollows;
    without a tutor streams can follow a course:
shores persuade with the tropes of their coloured stones,
    and art can teach the birds no sweeter song.

And Phoebe relied on no arts to kindle Castor,   15
    her sister without refinements fired his twin:
nor did Evenus's daughter, the prize when Idas
    and lustful Phoebus fought by her father's shores:
no spurious glitter attracted Hippodamia's
    Phrygian husband, who won her with alien wheels,   20
but a face not vilely owing its beauty to gems,
    and a colour bright as Apelles' finest work.

They made no efforts to conquer masses of lovers:
    they found discretion and virtue beauty enough.
And I'm sure you value my favour more than all theirs: 25
    and a girl is refined enough if she find one man —
and you supremely, for Phoebus composes you poems,
    Calliope freely gives her Aonian lyre;
and a singular grace abounds in your words of delight,
    where nature and art, wisdom and love combine;   30
and you so adorned will add grace to our days for ever —
    for just so long as cheap excesses sicken you.

III

Qualis Thesea iacuit cedente carina
  languida desertis Cnosia litoribus;
qualis et accubuit primo Cepheia somno
  libera iam duris cotibus Andromede;
nec minus assiduis Edonis fessa choreis   5
  qualis in herboso concidit Apidano:
talis uisa mihi mollem spirare quietem
  Cynthia non certis nixa caput manibus,
ebria cum multo traherem uestigia Baccho,
  et quaterent sera nocte facem pueri.   10

hánc ego, nondum etiam sensus deperditus omnis,
  molliter impresso conor adire toro;
et quamuis duplici correptum ardore iuberent
  hac Amor hac Liber, durus uterque deus,
subiecto leuiter positam temptare lacerto   15
  osculaque admota sumere et arma manu,
non tamen ausus eram dominae turbare quietem,
  expertae metuens iurgia saeuitiae.

sed sic intentis haerebam fixus ocellis,
  Argus ut ignotis cornibus Inachidos: 20
et modo soluebam nostra de fronte corollas
  ponebamque tuis, Cynthia, temporibus;
et modo gaudebam lapsós formare capillos,
  nunc furtiua cauis poma dabam manibus;
omniaque ingrato largibar munera somno,   25
  munera de prono saepe uoluta sinu.

et quotiens raro duxit suspiria motu,
  obstupui uano credulus auspicio,
ne qua tibi insolitos portarent uisa timores,
  neue quis inuitam cogeret esse suam: 30
donec diuersas praecurrens luna fenestras,
  luna moraturis sedula luminibus,
compositos leuibus radiis patefecit ocellos.
  sic ait in molli fixa toro cubitum:

POEM III

Just so did she lie while Theseus' keel slipped out,
    Ariadne limp on the empty shore:
just so did Cepheus' daughter Andromeda drowse
    unloosed, in her first sleep on the flinty crag:
no less exhausted by constant dancing a Bacchante   5
    might drop in Apidanus' bed, still grassy and safe:
she seemed to my eyes to breathe the same soft peacefulness,
    Cynthia, resting her head on unsteady hands,
as I entered on drunken footsteps, heavy with Bacchus;
    and late though it was, my Boy's torch flared into flame.   10

My senses not wholly destroyed as yet, I tried
    to approach where her form softly moulded the couch.
And though urged by a double passion, commanded by Love
    and wine this way and that, hard gods both,
to gently assault the sleeper, to slide in under her,   15
    presenting kisses and arms with active hands,
I wouldn't have dared to consider disturbing her rest,
    fearing the lash of that rage I knew so well.

So I stood quite motionless, staring intensely as Argus
    gazed, transfixed, on Io's ominous horns: 20
and then I slowly dismantled the wreaths on my brow,
    my Cynthia, putting them round your temples instead,
and then with delight I tidjed some curls that had strayed,
    and then gave pilfered apples from hollowed hands,
with all of my gifts being lavished on thankless sleep,   25
    gifts that had poured from my breast as I stooped above.

And sometimes she heaved a sigh, just moving her limbs,
    and I'd freeze, believing a foolish omen there,
that a vision provoked you, my love, to extravagant fears,
    that a ghost had made you his own against your will.   30
Till the moon, running on past windows of myriad kinds,
    industrious moon! paused with his lingering beams,
and opened those settled eyes with his gossamer rays.
    She then spoke, her elbow propped on the soft couch:

'tandem te nostro referens iniuria lecto   35
    alterius clausis expulit e foribus?
namque ubi longa meae consumpsti tempora noctis,
    languidus exactis, ei mihi, sideribus?
o utinam talis perducas, improbe, noctes,
    me miseram qualis semper habere iubes!   40
nam modo purpureo fallebam stamine somnum,
    rursus et Orpheae carmine, fessa, lyrae;
interdum leuiter mecum deserta querebar
    externo longas saepe in amore moras: ·
dum me iucundis lapsam sopor impulit alis.   45
    illa fuit lacrimis ultima cura meis.'

POEM III (continued)

"So at last your offence to our bed has brought you home   35
    by throwing you out, locking her doors in your face?
Where else would you squander the night that ought to be mine?
    returning limp, as the lamps of night expire?
You lecher, I wish that you had to endure such nights
    as I, poor fool, must suffer on your command.   40
For a while I tricked Sleep, by spinning a purple thread,
    and then, more tired, with songs on my Orphean lyre:
and sometimes, bereft, I gently complained to myself
    at how long and often you stay with this other love:
till I slipped, and Slumber with wings of delight mastered me: 45
    I cried with worry at that as I fell asleep."

IV

Quid mihi tam multas laudando, Basse, puellas
    mutatum domina cogis abire mea?
quid me non pateris uitae quodcumque sequetur
    hoc magis assueto ducere seruitio?
tu licet Antiopae formam Nycteidos, et tu   5
    Spartanae referas laudibus Hermionae,
et quascumque tulit formosi temporis aetas;
    Cynthia non illas nomen habere sinat:
nedum, si leuibus fuerit collata figuris,
    inferior duro iudice turpis eat.   10

haec sed forma mei pars est extrema furoris;
    sunt maiora, quibus, Basse, perire iuuat:
ingenuus color et multis decus artibus, et quae
    gaudia sub tacita dicere ueste libet.
quo magis et nostros contendis soluere amores,   15
    hoc magis accepta fallit uterque fide.

non impune feres: sciet haec insana puella
    et tibi non tacitis uocibus hostis erit;
nec tibi me post haec committet Cynthia nec te
    quaeret; erit tanti criminis illa memor,   20
et te circum omnis alias irata puellas
    differet: heu nullo limine carus eris.
nullas illa suis contemnet fletibus aras,
    et quicumque sacer qualis ubique lapis.
non ullo grauius temptatur Cynthia damno   25
    quam sibi cum rapto cessat amore deus.

praecipue nostri maneat, sic semper adoro,
    nec quicquam ex illa quod querar inueniam!

POEM IV

Bassus, I'm tired of you lauding innumerable beauties,
  to force me to change and leave the mistress I love.
Allow me instead to spend whatever is left
  of life enslaved in these well-worn bonds of mine.
The praise of a poet like you can recall the beauty   5
  of Dirce's victim Antiopa, Spartan Hermione,
and all whom the prime of that Age of beauty produced:
  but Cynthia stops all mention of their names.
And match her with trivial beauties, how could a judge
  dismiss her harshly, vanquished and ugly with shame.   10

But this beauty is only the tip of what drives me mad,
  Bassus: I'd gladly die for the sake of the rest —
the glow of her skin, enhanced by arts of adornment,
  and under her mute gown, joys that I love to praise.
The harder you strive to untwist our intricate love,   15
  the deeper your error, foiled by our mutual vows.

Your attempt has its dangers: my love will know and in fury
  she'll assail you directly, loudly, naming the names:
never would Cynthia trust me again to your company,
  nor seek you out: she'll remember so great a crime,   20
and angrily broadcast scandal about you to all
  Rome's girls — no door, alas! will welcome you then.
And her indiscriminate tears will wet Rome's altars,
  and every sacred stone of any kind.
No loss distresses my Cynthia more than if someone   25
  steals her lover, and Love stands idly by.

I incessantly pray she'll remain so vehemently mine:
  I hope I'll never uncover reasons to grieve!

24

V

Inuide, tu tandem uoces compesce molestas
  et sine nos cursu, quo sumus, ire pares!
quid tibi uis, insane? meos sentire furores?
  infelix, properas ultima nosse mala,
et miser ignotos uestigia ferre per ignis,   5
  et bibere e tota toxica Thessalia.
non est illa uagis similis collata puellis:
  molliter irasci non solet illa tibi.

quod si forte ruis, non est contraria nostris,
  at tibi curarum milia quanta dabit!   10
non tibi iam somnos, non illa relinquet ocellos:
  illa feros animis alligat una uiros.
a, mea contemptus quotiens ad limina curres,
  cum tibi singultu fortia uerba cadent,
et tremulus maestis orietur fletibus horror,   15
  et timor informem ducet in ore notam,
et quaecumque uoles fugient tibi uerba querenti,
  nec poteris, qui sis aut ubi, nosse miser!

tum graue seruitium nostrae cogere puellae
  discere et exclusum quid sit abire domum;   20
nec iam pallorem totiens mirabere nostrum,
  aut cur sim toto corpore nullus ego.
nec tibi nobilitas poterit succurrere amanti:
  nescit amor priscis cedere imaginibus.
quod si parua tuae dederis uestigia culpae,   25
  quam cito de tanto nomine rumor eris!
non ego tum potero solacia ferre roganti,
  cum mihi nulla mei sit medicina mali;
sed pariter miseri socio cogemur amore
  alter in alterius mutua flere sinu.   30

quare, quid possit mea Cynthia, desine, Galle,
  quaerere: non impune illa rogata uenit.

POEM V

You're jealous! But curb your disastrous tongue in time,
    and leave us to tread our present path, yoke-mates.
What do you want, you madman? To feel my stings?
    Poor fool, eager to know the ultimate ill,
and trail your desperate footprints through unknown fires,   5
    and drain Thessalia dry of poisoned charms!
She's not like the flirts you know, it's unwise to compare her:
    her rage is usually ungentle, and will be to you.

Yet if you rush on, she's not averse to my friends,
    but her generous gift will include thousands of cares.   10
She'll deprive you of sleep, she'll even deprive you of eyes:
    alone she can bind a horde of fierce-willed males.
And when you're rejected! How often you'll run to my door,
    your brave words failing you, turned to sobs.
A trembling horror will grow as you sadly weep,   15
    and fear leave marks on your cheeks, ugly, obscure,
the words you want to lament with eluding you, wretched,
    unable to tell your name, or where you are.

So then you'll be forced to learn her heavy conditions
    of service, returning home from her bolted doors.   20
No more will you wonder incessantly why I'm so pale,
    or why my body has wholly shrunk away:
and your noble birth will be powerless to help you in love;
    Love won't notice or yield to your rows of busts.
Yet if you betray the slightest sign that you're straying,   25
    that noble name will ensure that the gossip spreads.
I won't have potent palliatives then, if you ask,
    since nothing I have can cure my own disease,
but yoked by our sorrow in Love's community, each
    will be forced to weep on the other's sobbing breast.   30

So what my Cynthia's powers are, Gallus, cease
    to inquire: she's not unlethal and comes when called.

VI

Non ego nunc Hadriae uereor mare noscere tecum,
    Tulle, neque Aegaeo ducere uela salo,
cum quo Rhipaeos possim conscendere montis
    ulteriusque domos uadere Memnonias;
sed me complexae remorantur uerba puellae,   5
    mutatoque graues saepe colore preces.
illa mihi totis argutat noctibus ignis,
    et queritur nullos esse relicta deos;
illa meam mihi iam se denegat, illa minatur,
    quae solet irato tristis amica uiro.   10

his ego non horam possum durare querelis:
    a pereat, si quis lentus amare potest!
an mihi sit tanti doctas cognoscere Athenas
    atque Asiae ueteres cernere diuitias,
ut mihi deducta faciat conuicia puppi   15
    Cynthia et insanis ora notet manibus,
osculaque opposito dicat sibi debita uento,
    et nihil infido durius esse uiro?

tu patrui meritas conare anteire securis,
    et uetera oblitis iura refer sociis.   20
nam tua non aetas umquam cessauit amori,
    semper at armatae cura fuit patriae;
et tibi non umquam nostros puer iste labores
    afferat et lacrimis omnia nota meis!
me sine, quem semper uoluit fortuna iacere,   25
    hanc animam extremae reddere nequitiae.
multi longinquo periere in amore libenter,
    in quorum numero me quoque terra tegat.
non ego sum laudi, non natus idoneus armis:
    hanc me militiam fata subire uolunt.   30

at tu seu mollis qua tendit Ionia, seu qua
    Lydia Pactoli tingit arata liquor;
seu pedibus terras seu pontum carpere remis
    ibis, et accepti pars eris imperii:
tum tibi si qua mei ueniet non immemor hora,   35
    uiuere me duro sidere certus eris.

POEM VI

I'm still not afraid to gaze on the Adriatic,
    Tullus, with you, and sail the Aegean main;
with you I would scale the ice-capped peaks of the north,
    and push much further south than negroes dwell:
but she holds me back with her words, and clutches me tight,   5
    her colour comes and goes with her urgent pleas;
her passion is shrilly manifest nights at a time,
    she cries that now she's deserted, the gods are false,
denies that she's mine to my face, or makes that threat:
    what a desperate girl will say to her angry love.   10

I couldn't survive an hour of pleading like that:
    death to the man who dares to be slow in love!
For what would I gain from deep knowledge of learned Athens,
    or seeing the sights of Asia, her ancient wealth,
with Cynthia making a scene as my ship moved off,   15
    writing her grief on her cheeks with maddened nails,
claiming I only kissed her to fill in the time,
    saying nothing's more cruel than a faithless man.

Your uncle deserves his high office, yet strive to surpass him;
    restore the ancient laws where our allies have lapsed.   20
For the prime of your manhood never had time for love –
    you only cared for your steel-clad mistress, Rome –
and I pray that Cupid will never impose such hardships
    as mine on you, all that I've wept to know.
But leave me to lie here, abject, as Fate has decreed,   25
    to render my soul to the death of a worthless life.
Yet many would choose such a lingering dying in love;
    and as one of this host, may the earth cover my corpse.
I was born ill-suited to glory, unfit for arms;
    the Fates decreed I serve in another campaign.   30

Yet once there, where easy Ionia stretches, or golden
    Pactolus tinges Lydia's rich ploughed lands,
whether you cover the land in your stride, or the sea
    with oars, part of a rule that all approve,
if ever you spare me a thought in an idle hour,   35
    you'll know my life is ruled by a hostile star.

VII

Dum tibi Cadmeae dicuntur, Pontice, Thebae
    armaque fraternae tristia militiae,
atque, ita sim felix, primo contendis Homero,
    (sint modo fata tuis mollia carminibus:)
nos, ut consuemus, nostros agitamus amores,   5
    atque aliquid duram quaerimus in dominam;
nec tantum ingenio quantum seruire dolori
    cogor et aetatis tempora dura queri.

hic mihi conteritur uitae modus, haec mea fama est,
    hinc cupio nomen carminis ire mei.   10
me laudent doctae solum placuisse puellae,
    Pontice, et iniustas saepe tulisse minas;
me legat assidue post haec neglectus amator,
    et prosint illi cognita nostra mala.

te quoque si certo puer hic concusserit arcu   15
    (quod nolim nostros euiolasse deos),
longe castra tibi, longe miser agmina septem
    flebis in aeterno surda iacere situ;
et frustra cupies mollem componere uersum,
    nec tibi subiciet carmina serus amor.   20
tum me non humilem mirabere saepe poetam,
    tunc ego Romanis praeferar ingeniis;
nec poterunt iuuenes nostro reticere sepulcro
    'Ardoris nostri magne poeta, iaces.'

tu caue nostra tuo contemnas carmina fastu: 25
    saepe uenit magno faenore tardus amor.

POEM VII

While Cadmaean Thebes, my Ponticus, grows in your lines,
    the sad strife of the war two brothers waged,
and you challenge (really I mean it) the earlier Homer —
    if only a gentle Fate may spare your songs! —
I'm still as I always was, immersed in my love,   5
    in search of something to sway her obdurate heart,
compelled to attend to my sorrows and not to skill,
    my theme, the pains of youth, that unhappy age.

This is the life that consumes me: but this is my glory,
    I long for my verse to win renown from this.   10
Then girls of refinement will praise me, sole giver of pleasure,
    who suffered, Ponticus, many an unjust threat;
and rejected lovers in turn will avidly read me,
    observe their sickness deeply known, and thrive.

You too, if Cupid's unerring weapon should stun you,   15
    (not that I'd want my gods to shatter a friend) —
far from your wars you'll weep, distressed, while the Seven's
    battalions lie for ever deaf and unmoved,
and you'll long to compose a tender couplet, but fail,
    for rusty Love will refuse to yield you songs: 20
and my status then will amaze you, no lowly poet
    then but the choice of the finest minds in Rome;
and youths will burst into sighs when they see our tomb:
    "Our Passion's mighty Poet, here you lie!"

So beware of arrogant scorn for verses like mine: 25
    if love comes late, his interest rates are high.

30

VIII

Tune igitur demens, nec te mea cura moratur?
    an tibi sum gelida uilior Illyria?
et tibi iam tanti, quicumque est, iste uidetur,
    ut sine me uento quolibet ire uelis?
tune audire potes uesani murmura ponti   5
    fortis, et in dura naue iacere potes?
tu pedibus teneris positas fulcire pruinas,
    tu potes insolitas, Cynthia, ferre niues?

o utinam hibernae duplicentur tempora brumae,
    et sit iners tardis nauita Vergiliis,   10
nec tibi Tyrrhena soluatur funis harena,
    neue inimica meas eleuet aura preces!
atque ego non uideam talis subsidere uentos,
    cum tibi prouectas auferet unda ratis,
ut me defixum uacua patiatur in ora   15
    crudelem infesta saepe uocare manu!

sed quocumque modo de me, periura, mereris,
    sit Galatea tuae non aliena uiae:
ut te felici praeuecta Ceraunia remo
    accipiat placidis Oricos aequoribus.   20
nam me non ullae poterunt corrumpere de te,
    quin ego, uita, tuo limine uerba querar;
nec me deficiet nautas rogitare citatos
    'Dicite, quo portu clausa puella mea est?',

et dicam 'Licet Atraciis considat in oris,   25
    et licet Hylaeis, illa futura mea est.
Hic erit! hic iurata manet! rumpantur iniqui!
    uicimus: assiduas non tulit illa preces.
falsa licet cupidus deponat gaudia liuor:
    destitit ire nouas Cynthia nostra uias.   30
illa carus ego et per me carissima Roma
    dicitur, et sine me dulcia regna negat.
illa uel angusto mecum requiescere lecto
    et quocumque modo maluit esse mea,
quam sibi dotatae regnum uetus Hippodamiae,   35
    et quas Elis opes ante pararat equis.

POEM VIII

Are you mad, then? Doesn't concern for me hold you back?
    or is cold Illyria a better lover than me?
And your old man: whatever his rank, do you rate him so high
    that you'd leave me to sail with the first fresh breeze?
Do you think you could bear the roar of a maddened sea   5
    unflinching, and lie on a ship's hard deck?
Could your delicate feet support thick layers of frost,
    your sun-loving body, Cynthia, stand the snow?

O double the length of the brumal Winter season,
    let sailors idly wait while Spring delays!   10
May the sand of our native shore still grip your cables,
    (and may no hostile winds scatter my prayers!)
And I pray that I'll see those gusts continue to blow
    when the surge has swept your speeding ship away,
and left me standing transfixed on the empty shore,   15
    repeatedly calling you cruel, shaking my fist.

But whatever I really owe you for breaking your vows,
    may the nymph who spurned Polyphemus guard your ways;
may you round Ceraunia safely with fortunate oars,
    till Orico's placid waters welcome you home.   20
For never will other women corrupt me, or stop me
    mourning your absence, my life, here by your door:
and I'll endlessly pester the sailors hurrying past:
    "Tell me what haven holds that girl of mine!"

"Alright", I'll reply, "so she's staying at Atrax now,   25
    or maybe Hylaeus: but still in the end she's mine!
Here where she swore she abides — so laugh till you burst! —
    we've won: she didn't resist my ceaseless prayers.
Let leering envy renounce its abortive delight:
    Cynthia's ours, she's ceased her wandering ways.   30
She loves me, and Rome for my sake is her best-loved town
    she says, and swears that without me kingdoms pall.
She'd rather lie resting with me on a narrow bed,
    whatever our style of life, so long as she's mine,
than own a fabulous kingdom like Hippodamia's   35
    dowry, plus all her defeated suitors gave.

VIII (continued)

quamuis magna daret, quamuis maiora daturus,
    non tamen illa meos fugit auara sinus.
hanc ego non auro, non Indis flectere conchis,
    sed potui blandi carminis obsequio.   40
sunt igitur Musae, neque amanti tardus Apollo,
    quis ego fretus amo: Cynthia rara mea est!

nunc mihi summa licet contingere sidera plantis:
    siue dies seu nox uenerit, illa mea est!
nec mihi riualis certos subducit amores: 45
    ista meam norit gloria canitiem.'

POEM VIII (continued)

Although he had given huge gifts, with better to come,
    she's not been driven by greed from my breast's riches.
I needed no gold or Indian pearl to persuade her,
    but urged my suit with moving verses alone.   40
It's the Muses, then, and Apollo who speeds for a lover
    whom I trust in love: and matchless Cynthia's mine!

I can touch the highest star now with the soles of my feet;
    and day and night have ceased to matter, she's mine!
My love is too sure for a rival to take it away: 45
    that boast will live to see my hair turn white."

IX

Dicebam tibi uenturos, irrisor, amores,
    nec tibi perpetuo libera uerba fore·
ecce iaces supplexque uenis ad iura puellae,
    et tibi nunc quaeuis imperat empta modo.
non me Chaoniae uincant in amore columbae   5
    dicere, quos iuuenes quaeque puella domet.
me dolor et lacrimae merito fecere peritum:
    atque utinam posito dicar amore rudis!

quid tibi nunc misero prodest graue dicere carmen
    aut Amphioniae moenia flere lyrae?   10
plus in amore ualet Mimnermi uersus Homero:
    carmina mansuetus lenia quaerit Amor.
i quaeso et tristis istos compone libellos,
    et cane quod quaeuis nosse puella uelit!
quid si non esset facilis tibi copia? nunc tu   15
    insanus medio flumine quaeris aquam.
necdum etiam palles, uero nec tangeris igni·
    haec est uenturi prima fauilla mali.
tum magis Armenias cupies accedere tigris
    et magis infernae uincula nosse rotae,   20
quam pueri totiens arcum sentire medullis
    et nihil iratae posse negare tuae.

nullus Amor cuiquam facilis ita praebuit alas,
    ut non alterna presserit ille manu.
nec te decipiat, quod sit satis illa parata: 25
    acrius illa subit, Pontice, si qua tua est,
quippe ubi non liceat uacuos seducere ocellos,
    nec uigilare alio nomine cedat Amor.
qui non ante patet, donec manus attigit ossa·
    quisquis es, assiduas aufuge blanditias!   30
illis et silices et possint cedere quercus,
    nedum tu possis, spiritus iste leuis.

quare, si pudor est, quam primum errata fatere:
    dicere quo pereas saepe in amore leuat.

POEM IX

I used to reply, when you mocked me, that Love would come,
    you'd not be free for ever to talk in that vein:
and look at you! kneeling and abject, slave to the sex,
    and yesterday's common whore is today your queen.
Where Love is concerned, no doves of Dodona surpass me   5
    at telling which youths a given girl will tame.
I won my title of expert by anguish and tears —
    O to be still called novice, that love were dead!

What use to you now to recite your sonorous verses,
    or weep for those walls built by Amphion's lyre?   10
For lovers, one line by Mimnermus outweighs all Homer:
    a love assuaged requires a polished style.
So go and compose sad lyrics, the mode you despised,
    and sing what any girl would want to be told.
You worry you might lack matter? That's as insane   15
    as to stand in a river's midst and cry for drink:
and you're not even pale yet, not touched by genuine fires —
    and this is only a spark from the ills to come.
You'd rather wrestle Armenian tigresses then,
    and rattle hellish chains on Ixion's wheel,   20
than feel Love's bow strike to the marrow so often,
    be helpless against her fury, denying her nothing.

For Love may offer you effortless flight with his one hand,
    but every time his other will pull you back.
So don't be deceived, if a girl seems ready enough: 25
    she'll strike you even deeper, when once she's yours,
and you won't be allowed to stray with your heart or eyes,
    nor wait at another's door, Love will forbid it
who works unseen till his hand has pierced to the bone.
    Fly his relentless allure, whoever you are!   30
If flintstone and oak might find it hard to resist,
    your windy epic grandeur would prove too weak.

So reform, confess your errors as soon as you can:
    naming his murderess can lessen a lover's pains.

X

O iucunda quies, primo cum testis amori
   affueram uestris conscius in lacrimis!
o noctem meminisse mihi iucunda uoluptas,
   o quotiens uotis illa uocanda meis,
cum te complexa morientem, Galle, puella   5
   uidimus et longa ducere uerba mora!
quamuis labentis premeret mihi somnus ocellos
   et mediis caelo Luna ruberet equis,
non tamen a uestro potui secedere lusu:
   tantus in alternis uocibus ardor erat.   10

sed quoniam non es ueritus concedere nobis,
   accipe commissae munera laetitiae:
non solum uestros didici reticere dolores,
   est quiddam in nobis maius, amice, fide.
possum ego diuersos iterum coniungere amantis,   15
   et dominae tardas possum aperire fores;
et possum alterius curas sanare recentis,
   nec leuis in uerbis est medicina meis.

Cynthia me docuit semper quaecumque petenda
   quaeque cauenda forent: non nihil egit amor.   20
tu caue ne tristi cupias pugnare puellae,
   neue superba loqui, neue tacere diu,
neu, si quid petiit, ingrata fronte negaris,
   neu tibi pro uano uerba benigna cadant.
irritata uenit, quando contemnitur illa,   25
   nec meminit iustas ponere laesa minas:
at quo sis humilis magis et subiectus amori,
   hoc magis effecto saepe fruare bono.
is poterit felix una remanere puella,
   qui numquam uacuo pectore liber erit.   30

POEM X

The exquisite peace! when I'd witnessed the start of your love,
    so close that I almost wept the tears that you shed.
That night! the memory to me is exquisite joy —
    how often I have to summon it back with prayers —
when I saw you engulfed in her arms, near dead with longing   5
    Gallus, jerking out words as she still delayed.
Even with sleep oppressing my drooping eyes,
    and the moon though riding high an ominous red,
I stayed there powerless, unable to leave your sport,
    the whispers passing between you were still so hot . . .   10

Well: you admit my pre-eminence now; that's brave:
    so accept these gifts for the joy that night began.
I'm expert at hiding the grief of a lover like you,
    and I've something stronger than loyal silence, friend.
I've power to heal the divorce when lovers quarrel,   15
    power to open a mistress' stubborn doors,
and power to cure love's wounds (with others at least) —
    no trifling medicine this that my words contain.

For I've learnt my skills in Cynthia's school, these do's
    and don'ts for lovers: Love has at least done that.   20
The don'ts: wanting to fight when she's feeling morose;
    arrogant speech — or silence that lasts too long;
a boorish refusal, whatever she deigns to ask you;
    a lack of response to her every gracious word;
she throws a terrible tantrum at any affront,   25
    and never forgets her claim to righteous revenge.
But the more you abase yourself as the slave of love,
    the more often this good you've done will yield you fruit.
A man can remain with a single mistress and thrive
    by never escaping passion, never being free.   30

37

XI

Ecquid te mediis cessantem, Cynthia, Bais,
    qua iacet Herculeis semita litoribus,
et modo Thesproti mirantem subdita regno
    proxima Misenis aequora nobilibus,
nostri cura subit memores adducere noctes?   5
    ecquis in extremo restat amore locus?
an te nescio quis simulatis ignibus hostis
    sustulit e nostris, Cynthia, carminibus?

atque utinam mage te remis confisa minutis
    paruula Lucrina cumba moretur aqua,   10
aut teneat clausam tenui Teuthrantis in unda
    alternae facilis cedere lympha manu,
quam uacet alterius blandos audire susurros
    molliter in tacito litore compositam! –
ut solet amota labi custode puella,   15
    perfida communis nec meminisse deos.

non quia perspecta non es mihi cognita fama,
    sed quod in hac omnis parte timetur amor.
ignosces igitur, si quid tibi triste libelli
    attulerint nostri: culpa timoris erit.   20
an mihi non maior carae custodia matris?
    aut sine te uitae cura sit ulla meae?
tu mihi sola domus, tu, Cynthia, sola parentes,
    omnia tu nostrae tempora laetitiae.
seu tristis ueniam seu contra laetus amicis,   25
    quicquid ero, dicam 'Cynthia causa fuit.'

tu modo quam primum corruptas desere Baias:
    multis ista dabunt litora discidium,
litora quae fuerant castis inimica puellis:
    a pereant Baiae, crimen amoris, aquae!   30
quid mihi desidiae non cessas fingere crimen,
    quod faciat nobis conscia Roma moram?
tam multa illa meo diuisa est milia lecto,
    quantum Hypanis Veneto dissidet Eridano;
nec mihi consuetos amplexu nutrit amores   35
    Cynthia, nec nostra dulcis in aure sonat.

XII)

5)

POEM XI

Cynthia, say: as you laze in the centre of Baia,
    where the path lies that leads to Hercules' shores,
then sail on the bay that extends below the Thesprotian
    realm, down from the hero Misenus's cape —
does our love reach you and woo you to nights of remembering?   5
    Is somewhere sacred to us on the edge of your heart?
Surely no nameless enemy, feigning his passion,
    has snatched you, Cynthia, out of our songs' embrace?

But I'd rather suppose that a tiny canoe, relying
    on pixie oars, confined you in Lake Locrine,   10
or that delicate Teuthras's waves were clasping you tight
    as the easy Nymph gave way to your swimming hands,
than think of you listening at leisure to whispered enticements,
    softly propped on a mute collusive shore —
for a girl is likely to lapse with her chaperone gone,   15
    forget the gods she swore by, betray her vows.

I'm sorry! I'm not unaware of your famous virtue:
    but every love in Baia generates fear.
So pardon me any distress these poems of ours
    inflict on your ears; my fear must take the blame.   20
For my dear dead mother is guarded more closely than you,
    yet what would I want in life, if you were gone?
O Cynthia, home and family, all I possess,
    every hour of our joy is embodied in you!
So whether I'm sad when I meet my friends, or delighted,   25
    whatever my state I'll say: "The Cause was Cynthia"

But waste no time in leaving Baia's depravity:
    many will cite those shores as grounds for divorce,
you shores that of old assaulted virtuous girls —
    death to you, Baian waters, for crimes of love!   30
And stop pretending I'm guilty of crimes of sloth,
    that Rome shares in my guilt and holds me back.
My love is too far from my bed, as far as Hypanis
    on the Black Sea is from Venice's river Po.
No longer does Cynthia daily nourish my love   35
    with embraces: her sweetness sounds in my ear no more.

XI (Cont'd)

<table>
<tr><td>(XII)</td><td>olim gratus eram: non illo tempore cuiquam
    contigit ut simili posset amare fide.</td><td></td></tr>
<tr><td></td><td>inuidiae·fuimus: non me deus obruit? an quae</td><td></td></tr>
<tr><td>(10)</td><td>   lecta Prometheis diuidit herba iugis?</td><td>40</td></tr>
<tr><td></td><td>non sum ego qui fueram: mutat uia longa puellas.
    quantus in exiguo tempore fugit amor!
nunc primum longas solus cognoscere noctes
    cogor et ipse meis auribus esse grauis.</td><td></td></tr>
<tr><td>(15)</td><td>felix, qui potuit praesenti flere puellae;</td><td>45</td></tr>
<tr><td></td><td>   non nihil aspersis gaudet Amor lacrimis:
aut si despectus potuit mutare calores,
    sunt quoque translato gaudia seruitio.
mi neque amare aliam neque ab hac desistere fas est:</td><td></td></tr>
<tr><td>(20)</td><td>   Cynthia prima fuit, Cynthia finis erit.</td><td>50</td></tr>
</table>

POEM XI (Cont'd)

<table>
<tr><td></td><td>But once I pleased her. As long as that lasted, no-one
    was lucky enough to love with a faith like mine.
Too lucky: some envious god destroyed us, some herb</td><td></td></tr>
<tr><td>(10)</td><td>   picked on Prometheus' mountain drove us apart.</td><td>40</td></tr>
<tr><td></td><td>I'm no longer my self; and a long trip changes a girl:
    how great a love has fled in so short a time!
So my new self must live through tedious nights alone
    for the first time, myself all that I hear.</td><td></td></tr>
<tr><td>(15)</td><td>Happy the man that can weep to his mistress's face,</td><td>45</td></tr>
<tr><td></td><td>   for Love has great delight in offerings of tears:
and happy the slighted lover who burns for another,
    for slaves have some delight in swapping their chains.
But how could I love another, or love her less?</td><td></td></tr>
<tr><td>(20)</td><td>   My life began in Cynthia, there it will end.</td><td>50</td></tr>
</table>

XIII

Tu, quod saepe soles, nostro laetabere casu,
    Galle, quod abrepto solus amore uacem.
at non ipse tuas imitabor, perfide, uoces:
    fallere te numquam, Galle, puella uelit.

dum tibi deceptis augetur fama puellis,   5
    certus et in nullo quaeris amore moram,
perditus in quadam tardis pallescere curis
    incipis, et primo lapsus adire gradu.
haec erit illarum contempti poena doloris:
    multarum miseras exiget una uices.   10
haec tibi uulgaris istos compescet amores,
    nec noua quaerendo semper amicus eris.

haec ego non rumore malo, non augure doctus;
    uidi ego: me quaeso teste negare potes?
uidi ego te toto uinctum languescere collo   15
    et flere iniectis, Galle, diu manibus,
et cupere optatis animam deponere uerbis,
    et quae deinde meus celat, amice, pudor.
non ego complexus potui diducere uestros:
    tantus erat demens inter utrosque furor.   20

non sic Haemonio Salmonida mixtus Enipeo
    Taenarius facili pressit amore deus,
nec sic caelestem flagrans amor Herculis Heben
    sensit in Oetaeis gaudia prima iugis.
una dies omnis potuit praecurrere amantis: 25
    nam tibi non tepidas subdidit illa faces,
nec tibi praeteritos passa est succedere fastus,
    nec sinet abduci: te tuus ardor aget.

nec mirum, cum sit Ioue digna et proxima Ledae
    et Ledae partu gratior, una tribus;   30
illa sit Inachiis et blandior heroinis,
    illa suis uerbis cogat amare Iouem.

tu uero quoniam semel es periturus amore,
    utere. non alio limine dignus eras.
quae tibi sit felix, quoniam nouus incidit error;   35
    et, quodcumque uoles, una sit ista tibi.

POEM XIII

You'll rejoice as usual, call it my lucky break,
    Gallus, that Cynthia's gone, I'm alone, and free;
but, traitor! I'll not be adopting a tone like yours:
    never may Gallus be tricked by the girl he loves.

For just as your fame for deceiving girls has been growing,   5
    and you're sure you'd never want a lingering affair,
you're lost, you care for someone at last, love's pallor
    begins: your first stumble advanced you in love.
The griefs you despised in those others will find their Avenger:
    the wretched fate of many, one will requite.   10
She'll prune your desires from straying to commoner loves,
    you'll lose your fondness for seeking constant change.

I know this is true, and not from gossip or omens:
    I saw it myself; my witness can't be denied.
I saw you, your neck encircled, engulfed, and you swooned.   15
    Gallus, in tears that her hands claimed you so long,
and you yearned to pour out your life for the words you desired.
    What happened next shouldn't be talked of, friend,
but all my strength was unable to prise you apart,
    so mad a frenzy raged between you both.   20

The god of the ocean pervaded Enipeus' stream
    no less, when he covered Tyro with easy love:
Hercules burnt on his pyre with less heat for immortal
    Hebe, that moment he felt his joys begin.
A single such day can surpass a lifetime's loving: 25
    the torch she set to your heart has no weak flame.
She conquered your pride, refused to allow it a chance,
    and will ban its return: your love will drive you on.

No wonder: She's worthy of Jove, the equal of Leda,
    whose daughters, three combined, please less than this one: 30
her ways are more winning than Io's, and all the Danaids,
    her words would bind the ruler of heaven to love.
So since you are now about to perish in love,
    enjoy it: your worth deserves no lesser door.
I hope she'll be kind, for you've entered a strange, dark maze: 35
    may all you desire be found in only that one.

XIV

Tu licet abiectus Tiberina molliter unda
    Lesbia Mentoreo uina bibas opere,
et modo tam celeres mireris currere lintres
    et modo tam tardas funibus ire ratis;
et nemus omne satas intendat uertice siluas,   5
    urgetur quantis Caucasus arboribus;
non tamen ista meo ualeant contendere amori:
    nescit amor magnis cedere diuitiis.

nam siue optatam mecum trahit illa quietem,
    seu facili totum ducit amore diem,   10
tum mihi Pactoli ueniunt sub tecta liquores,
    et legitur Rubris gemma sub aequoribus;
tum mihi cessuros spondent mea gaudia reges:
    quae maneant, dum me fata perire uolent!
nam quis diuitiis aduerso gaudet Amore?   15
    nulla mihi tristi praemia sint Venere!

illa potest magnas heroum infringere uires,
    illa etiam duris mentibus esse dolor:
illa neque Arabium metuit transcendere limen
    nec timet ostrino, Tulle, subire toro,   20
et miserum toto iuuenem uersare cubili:
    quid releuant uariis serica textilibus?
quae mihi dum placata aderit, non ulla uerebor
    regna uel Alcinoi munera despicere.

POEM XIV

A Tullus can languidly lie by the Tiber's verge,
    swilling Lesbian wine from a Mentor cup,
observing with pleasure how quickly the punts can go,
    (and as pleasant, how slow the laden barges come!)
while your grove covers the hill with its hand-sown trees   5
    their trunks as huge as Caucasus endures:
but pleasures like those would hardly compete with my love;
    Love disdains to yield to enormous wealth.

For when she's beside me, delaying our longed-for repose,
    or spending a day entirely in easy love,   10
Pactolus comes to my room with its liquid gold,
    and pearls lie there to be plucked from a glowing sea,
and my joys assure me that kings will kneel at my feet –
    long may it last, till Fate decrees that I die –
for who has delight in wealth when his love has turned sour?   15
    Nothing would cover my loss if Venus frowned.

She's able to cripple a hero's enormous strength,
    and even in hardened minds is a source of pain;
she crosses a threshold of marble and feels no fear,
    nor dread at approaching, Tullus, a purpled couch   20
and tossing the helpless youth about on his bed:
    will a fine collection of silks then help him rest?
So as long as she's with me and kindly disposed I'll fearlessly
    scorn whole kingdoms, and with them Alcinous' gifts.

44

Saepe ego multa tuae leuitatis dura timebam,
    hac tamen excepta, Cynthia, perfidia.
aspice me quanto rapiat fortuna periclo!
    tu tamen in nostro lenta timore uenis;
et potes hesternos manibus componere crinis   5
    et longa faciem quaerere desidia,
nec minus Eois pectus uariare lapillis,
    ut formosa nouo quae parat ire uiro.

at non sic Ithaci digressu mota Calypso
    desertis olim fleuerat aequoribus: 10
multos illa dies incomptis maesta capillis
    sederat, iniusto multa locuta salo,
et quamuis numquam post haec uisura, dolebat
    illa tamen, longae conscia laetitiae.
Alphesiboea suos ulta est pro coniuge fratres,   15
    sanguinis et cari uincula rupit amor.
nec sic Aesoniden rapientibus anxia uentis
    Hypsipyle uacuo constitit in thalamo:
Hypsipyle nullos post illos sensit amores,
    ut semel Haemonio tabuit hospitio.   20
coniugis Euadne miseros elata per ignis
    occidit, Argiuae fama pudicitiae.

quarum nulla tuos potuit conuertere mores,
    tu quoque uti fieres nobilis historia.
desine iam reuocare tuis periuria uerbis,   25
    Cynthia, et oblitos parce mouere deos;
audax a nimium, nostro dolitura periclo,
    si quid forte tibi durius inciderit!
multa prius uasto labentur flumina ponto,
    annus et inuersas duxerit ante uices,   30
quam tua sub nostro mutetur pectore cura:
    sis quodcumque uoles, non aliena tamen.

POEM XV

How often I feared you'd wound me deeply with shallowness,
    but Cynthia, not betrayal, nothing like this!
For look at me, hurried away by a dangerous fate,
    but still in our hour of fear you are slow to come,
so cool you can tidy your hair from last night's ravages,   5
    squandering hours in search of a beautiful face,
your breast now a shifting pattern of orient gems
    like a beauty decked to go to another mate.

How different in myth: for Calypso, moved at the Ithacan's
    going, wept by the empty, tranquil sea,   10
and day after day with her hair neglected in grief
    she sat, pleading his case to the hostile waves;
and still she lamented, for though she saw him no more,
    the joy they'd shared so long still lived in her mind.
And Alphesiboea to avenge her husband killed   15
    her brothers; Love annulled the bond of blood.
Hypsipyle too: distressed when the winds had carried
    her Jason off, she stayed in their empty room;
and that was the last Hypsipyle felt of love;
    she died with longing to tend to his needs again.   20
And Evadne, exalted, was killed by the grievous fires
    of her husband's pyre, and Argos cherished her name.

But none of these famous examples could change your ways,
    to make you worthy of note in any tale,
so stop protesting your love – you recall your perjury,   25
    Cynthia – don't arouse the gods you forgot.
You thoughtless fool! you'll grieve for my danger in earnest
    if something happened to hurt you, as well it might.
For rivers would sooner return from the boundless ocean,
    the seasons go in reverse for a year on end,   30
before this love that I guard in my breast would alter:
    be whatever you wish, still never apart!

tam tibi ne uiles isti uideantur ocelli,
    per quos saepe mihi credita perfidia est!
hos tu iurabas, si quid mentita fuisses,   35
    ut tibi suppositis exciderent manibus:
et contra magnum potes hos attollere Solem,
    nec tremis admissae conscia nequitiae?
quis te cogebat multos pallere colores
    et fletum inuitis ducere luminibus?   40
quis ego nunc pereo, similis moniturus amantis
    'O nullis tutum credere blanditiis!'

POEM XV (continued)

So value those lovely eyes at their proper worth,
    those pledges that often made me trust betrayal;
you'd swear in their name that if you ever deceived me   35
    they'd fall from their sockets, drop in your waiting hands:
so how can you lift them to gaze at the mighty Sun?
    doesn't a guilty conscience make you tremble?
Is it me who forces your cheek to change its colour,
    and makes you drag those tears from reluctant eyes? —
which now destroy me — so lovers like me take note,
    trust at your peril kisses and vows of Love.

'Quae fueram magnis olim patefacta triumphis,
    ianua Tarpeiae nota pudicitiae;
cuius inaurati celebrarunt limina currus,
    captorum lacrimis umida supplicibus;
nunc ego, nocturnis potorum saucia rixis,   5
    pulsata indignis saepe queror manibus,
et mihi non desunt turpes pendere corollae
    semper et exclusis signa iacere faces.

nec possum infamis dominae defendere noctes,
    nobilis obscenis tradita carminibus;   10
nec tamen illa suae reuocatur parcere famae,
    turpior et saecli uiuere luxuria.
has inter grauibus cogor deflere querelis,
    supplicis a longis tristior excubiis.
ille meos numquam patitur requiescere postis,   15
    arguta referens carmina blanditia:

"Ianua uel domina penitus crudelior ipsa,
    quid mihi tam duris clausa taces foribus?
cur numquam reserata meos admittis amores,
    nescia furtiuas reddere mota preces?   20
nullane finis erit nostro concessa dolori,
    turpis et in tepido limine somnus erit?
me mediae noctes, me sidera plena iacentem,
    frigidaque Eoo me dolet aura gelu:
tu sola humanos numquam miserata dolores   25
    respondes tacitis mutua cardinibus.

o utinam traiecta caua mea uocula rima
    percussas dominae uertat in auriculas!
sit licet et saxo patientior illa Sicano,
    sit licet et ferro durior et chalybe,   30
non tamen illa suos poterit compescere ocellos,
    surget et inuitis spiritus in lacrimis.

POEM XVI

In the glorious past I have opened for splendid processions,
    a door like chaste Tarpeia's — welcoming all.
Chariots crusted with gold have thronged past my threshold,
    which dripped with captives' tears begging compassion.
But now! — I'm wounded in drunkards' nocturnal battles,   5
    and often groan, pounded by vulgar fists:
no garlands, rich only in filthy bouquets that hang here,
    and prostrate torches, banners of routed Love.

I'm too weak to fight off my mistress's scandalous nights,
    my noble frame surrendered to scurrilous rhymes: 10
yet still she's lost to herself, and neglects her good name,
    and lives a viler life than this profligate age.
Surrounded by this I'm constrained to bitter complaints,
    made sadder by one who has urged his suit so long,
for he never allows my hinges to rest in peace,   15
    but applies the piercing sweetness of his verse:

"O Door, you are crueller at heart than the mistress within:
    Why are you silent, hard, and shut so tight?
Why are you never unbarred to receive my love,
    too dull to be moved so prayers could steal inside?   20
Will nothing be granted ever to end my pain,
    but a filthy sleep on this half-warmed slab of stone?
When Night rides high with the stars at their prime, I'm prostrate;
    I'm pitied by breezes icy with frosts of dawn,
and alone in the world you're indifferent to human distress,   25
    your hinges' duo of silence your sole response.

But oh that my voice could contract and push through a chink,
    and strike on her lovely ears, and wind in deep.
Maybe Sicilian agate's more yielding than her,
    she's harder perhaps than iron or tempered steel,   30
but still she couldn't restrain those beautiful eyes,
    her soul would rise in sighs and force her to weep.

nunc iacet alterius felici nixa lacerto,
  at mea nocturno uerba cadunt Zephyro.
sed tu sola mei tu maxima causa doloris,   35
  uicta meis numquam, ianua, muneribus.
te non ulla meae laesit petulantia linguae,
  quae solet irato dicere tota loco,
ut me tam longa raucum patiare querela
  sollicitas triuio peruigilare moras.   40
at tibi saepe nouo deduxi carmina uersu,
  osculaque impressis nixa dedi gradibus.
ante tuos quotiens uerti me, perfida, postis,
  debitaque occultis uota tuli manibus!"

haec ille et si quae miseri nouistis amantes,   45
  et matutinis obstrepit alitibus.
sic ego nunc dominae uitiis et semper amantis
  fletibus aeterna differor inuidia.'

POEM XVI (continued)

She leans on a rival's fortunate shoulder, now,
  and my pleas are wasted on air and night alone.
But the sole cause of my woes, or the greatest, is you,   35
  door, you remained unconquered by all my gifts.
But why? I never assailed you with reckless tongue —
  the vehement things that are said to quarrelsome doors —
to warrant your leaving me, hoarse from lamenting so long,
  to wait for anxious hours in a public street.   40
The contrary — I've often woven you poems, originals,
  leant on my lips to kiss your soft-pressed steps,
and circled so often, traitress! around your hinges,
  bringing my gifts with hands reverently veiled."

Things of that kind, and all that you wretched lovers   45
  know, he croaks to the birds that herald dawn.
So now, with my mistress's sins and her lover's ceaseless
  weeping, I'm doomed to eternal hatred and shame.

XVII

Et merito, quoniam potui fugisse puellam,
    nunc ego desertas alloquor alcyonas.
nec mihi Cassiope solito uisura carinam,
    omniaque ingrato litore uota cadunt.
quin etiam absenti prosunt tibi, Cynthia, uenti: 5
    aspice, quam saeuas increpat aura minas.
nullane placatae ueniet fortuna procellae?
    haecine parua meum furius harena teget?

tu tamen in melius saeuas conuerte querelas:
    sat tibi sit poenae nox et iniqua uada.   10
an poteris siccis mea fata reponere ocellis,
    ossaque nulla tuo nostra tenere sinu?
a pereat, quicumque ratis et uela parauit
    primus et inuito gurgite fecit iter!
nonne fuit leuius dominae peruincere mores   15
    (quamuis dura, tamen rara puella fuit),
quam sic ignotis circumdata litora siluis
    cernere et optatos quaerere Tyndaridas?

illic si qua meum sepelissent fata dolorem,
    ultimus et posito staret amore lapis,   20
illa meo caros donasset funere crinis,
    molliter et tenera poneret ossa rosa;
illa meum extremo clamasset puluere nomen,
    ut mihi non ullo pondere terra foret.
at uos, aequoreae formosa Doride natae,   25
    candida felici soluite uela choro:
si quando uestras labens Amor attigit undas,
    mansuetis socio parcite litoribus.

POEM XVII

Yes, I've deserved this: I dared to desert my mistress,
    and now to weeping Halcyons plead for calm.
Stars that shine gently for others look blind on my bark,
    and all my prayers fall void on this hostile shore.
In spite of your absence, Cynthia, the winds are your allies;   5
    see how the gusts rattle their savage threats.
Will my luck not change? Will nothing placate this storm?
    or here will a little sand conceal my end?

But transpose your savage complaints to a gentler key:
    a night and voyage like this is enough revenge.   10
For you couldn't rehearse my end with your sweet eyes dry,
    hugging my unreal bones to your living breast –
death to that unknown madman, the first inventor
    of ships and sails to traverse the sullen deep!
Easier far to master her feminine ways –
    she's hard to please, perhaps, but precious, unique –
than to scan this beach surrounded with nameless forests,
    or look for the lovely Gemini, not her eyes.

But if some kind fate had buried my griefs in Rome,
    and the final stone was standing where Love was laid,   20
my love would have offered her precious locks at my end,
    gently wrapping my bones with tender roses,
and over the final dust she'd have called my name,
    praying I felt no weight from the earth above.
But Sea-Nymphs, you gentle daughters of lovely Doris,   25
    Break out our sweet white sails and dance us home:
if ever Love as he glides has touched your waves,
    spare me, his friend, by taming those obdurate shores.

XVIII

Haec certe deserta loca et taciturna querenti,
　et uacuum Zephyri possidet aura nemus.
hic licet occultos proferre impune dolores,
　si modo sola queant saxa tenere fidem.

unde tuos primum repetam, mea Cynthia, fastus?　　　　5
　quod mihi das flendi, Cynthia, principium?
qui modo felices inter numerabar amantis,
　nunc in amore tuo cogor habere notam.
quid tantum merui? quae te mihi carmina mutant?
　an noua tristitiae causa puella tuae?　　　　　10
sic mihi te referas, leuis, ut non altera nostro ˋ
　limine formosos intulit ulla pedes.
quamuis multa tibi dolor hic meus aspera debet,
　non ita saeua tamen uenerit ira mea,
ut tibi sim merito semper furor, et tua flendo　　　　15
　lumina deiectis turpia sint lacrimis.

an quia parua damus mutato signa colore,
　et non ulla meo clamat in ore fides?
uos eritis testes, si quos habet arbor amores,
　fagus et Arcadio pinus amica deo.　　　　　20
a quotiens teneras resonant mea uerba sub umbras,
　scribitur et uestris Cynthia corticibus!

an tua quod peperit nobis iniuria curas,
　quae solum tacitis cognita sunt foribus?
omnia consueui timidus perferre superbae　　　　25
　iussa neque arguto facta dolore queri.

pro quo, diuini fontes, et frigida rupes
　et datur inculto tramite dura quies;
et quodcumque meae possunt narrare querelae,
　cogor ad argutas dicere solus auis.　　　　　30
sed qualiscumque es resonent mihi 'Cynthia' siluae,
　nec deserta tuo nomine saxa uacent.

POEM XVIII

I'm sure this spot is deserted, and won't tell tales,
    and a Zephyr's breath possesses the empty grove.
Perhaps I can safely mention my hidden griefs —
    these rocks have no-one to talk to, they should be safe.

Where shall I look for the source of your cruelty, Cynthia?   5
    Cynthia, what was the primary cause of my tears?
I, who was numbered with fortunate lovers once
    must wear this brand of shame in your love's constraint.
Have I deserved this? What spells in verse have changed you?
    Perhaps the thought of a rival causes this pique?   10
As I hope you'll return, you flirt, no other
    has stepped with a pretty foot across our doorway.
Though I owe you that and worse for the pain you've caused me,
    my anger would never exact the drastic revenge
that I've earnt, an endless rage that would make your glowing   15
    eyes go ugly with weeping cascades of tears.

Or perhaps my changes of colour are smallish proofs,
    my "faith" not loud and frequent enough on my lips?
You be my witness (if trees have a kind of love)
    O beech and pine, you friends of Arcadia's god,   20
how often your gentle shades have rung with my cries,
    and your bark is cut to carry Cynthia's name.

Or perhaps your anxiety comes from a sense of guilt,
    for things that only your silent door-posts know?
Don't worry: I'm abject, accustomed to bear your tyrannical   25
    orders, not shrilly lamenting the things you've done.

So therefore, o sacred fountains, my fate is these icy
    crags, and a stony rest by rough hewn tracks.
And whatever complaints I can manage in lucid order,
    I'm forced to tell them only to shrill-voiced birds.   30
But whatever you are the woods respond with "Cynthia",
    no rock is so deserted it lacks your name.

XIX

Non ego nunc tristis uereor, mea Cynthia, Manis,
    nec moror extremo debita fata rogo;
sed ne forte tuo careat mihi funus amore,
    hic timor est ipsis durior exsequiis.
non adeo leuiter noster puer haesit ocellis,   5
    ut meus oblito puluis amore uacet.

illic Phylacides iucundae coniugis heros
    non potuit caecis immemor esse locis,
sed cupidus falsis attingere gaudia palmis
    Thessalus antiquam uenerat umbra domum.   10
illic quidquid ero, semper tua dicar imago:
    traicit et fati litora magnus amor.
illic formosae ueniant chorus heroinae,
    quas dedit Argiuis Dardana praeda uiris –
quarum nulla tua fuerit mihi, Cynthia, forma   15
    gratior; et (Tellus hoc ita iusta sinat)
quamuis te longae remorentur fata senectae,
    cara tamen lacrimis ossa futura meis.
quae tu uiua mea possis sentire fauilla!
    tum mihi non ullo mors sit amara loco.   20

quam uereor, ne te contempto, Cynthia, busto
    abstrahat e nostro puluere iniquus amor,
cogat et inuitam lacrimas siccare cadentis!
    flectitur assisuis certa puella minis.
quare, dum licet, inter nos laetemur amantes: 25
    non satis est ullo tempore longus amor.

POEM XIX

No Cynthia, I don't fear gloomy shadows of Hades,
    nor care for my fate, what I owe the final fire:
but maybe I'll lack your love as I go to the grave,
    that's more frightening than pacing behind a corpse.
This Cupid of ours has clung too close to your eyes   5
    for my dust to forget love, and be not possessed.

Down there the hero Protesilaus couldn't
    not think of his joyful bride in the sightless realms,
but greedy to touch his delight with unreal hands
    had come to his ancient home — as just a Shade.   10
Whatever I'll be down there, I'll be known as your spectre;
    the shores of fate are no bar to mighty Love.
Down there they can come, that troupe of legendary beauties,
    booty from Troy assigned to the Argive chiefs:
no beauty of theirs will please me, Cynthia, more   15
    than your own: and (Mother Earth I pray be just)
though the Fates may hinder your coming with tedious age,
    I'll cherish your bones-to-be, and weep for your death.
If only you saw this, alive, in my still hot ashes,
    then Death would lose its sharpness, wherever I was.   20

O but I'm troubled, my grave may be slighted, Cynthia,
    and hostile Love may drag you out of my dust
and force you — resisting — to dry your tears as they fall:
    persistent threats can sway a constant maid.
So as long as we can, let our mutual love delight us —   25
    Love is too brief to last the shortest time.

XX

Hoc pro continuo te, Galle, monemus amore,
    (id tibi ne uacuo defluat ex animo)
saepe imprudenti fortuna occurrit amanti:
    crudelis Minyis dixerat Ascanius.

est tibi non infra speciem, non nomine dispar,   5
    Theiodamanteo proximus ardor Hylae:
hunc tu, siue leges umbrosae flumina siluae,
    siue Aniena tuos tinxerit unda pedes,
siue Gigantea spatiabere litoris ora,
    siue ubicumque uago fluminis hospitio,   10
Nympharum semper cupidas defende rapinas
    (non minor Ausoniis est amor Adryasin);
ne tibi sint duri montes et frigida saxa,
    Galle, neque expertos semper adire lacus:
quae miser ignotis error perpessus in oris.   15
    Herculis indomito fleuerat Ascanio.

namque ferunt olim Pagasae naualibus Argon
    egressam longe Phasidos isse uiam,
et iam praeteritis labentem Athamantidos undis
    Mysorum scopulis applicuisse ratem.   20
hic manus heroum, placidis ut constitit oris,
    mollia composita litora fronde tegit.
at comes inuicti iuuenis processerat ultra
    raram sepositi quaerere fontis aquam.
hunc duo sectati fratres, Aquilonia proles,   25
    hunc super et Zetes, hunc super et Calais,
oscula suspensis instabant carpere palmis,
    oscula et alterna ferre supina fuga.
ille sub extrema pendens secluditur ala
    et uolucres ramo summouet insidias.   30

POEM XX

Because of our long, deep friendship, Gallus, I'm warning you,
    (watch that it doesn't slip from your empty mind)
things can happen to lovers who don't take care,
    as cruel Ascanius told the Argo's crew.

Your love's not inferior in beauty, unequal in name   5
    to Hylas, Theiodamas' child — they're very alike:
so whether you coast along rivers in shadowy woods,
    or whether Anio's waters whiten your feet,
or you stride the gigantic shores of Giants' Bay,
    or wherever a river's wandering welcome glides,   10
protect him always from lustful assaults by the Nymphs
    (our local Dryads love no less than others!)
or you'll have to endure hard mountains and frozen crags,
    Gallus, and endless journeys to blank pools:
the sufferings of Hercules' wanderings by unknown shores,   15
    the pains he told with tears to wild Ascanius.

For they say that of old the Argo, leaving her docks
    at Pagasa far behind on the way to Phasis,
still gliding along with the Hellespont dropping away,
    moored her vessel at last by Mysia's rocks.   20
The cove was peaceful, so here the warrior band
    covered the sandy softness with woven fronds.
But our conquering hero's lover had gone beyond,
    to seek a sequestered fountain's precious drink.
Two brothers pursued him, the twins whom the North Wind bore;25
    Zetes above him now and now Calais
kissing his hovering hands as they pressed their attack,
    kissing his upturned lips as they fled in turn.
But he crouched, closed in on himself, framed by their wings,
    and scattered the flying ambush by waving a branch.   30

iam Pandioniae cessit genus Orithyiae:
    a dolor! ibat Hylas, ibat Hamadryasin.
hic erat Arganthi Pege sub uertice montis
    grata domus Nymphis umida Thyniasin,
quam supra nullae pendebant debita curae   35
    roscida desertis poma sub arboribus,
et circum irriguo surgebant lilia prato
    candida purpureis mixta papaueribus.
quae modo decerpens tenero pueriliter ungui
    proposito florem praetulit officio,   40
et modo formosis incumbens nescius undis
    errorem blandis tardat imaginibus.
tandem haurire parat demissis flumina palmis
    innixus dextro plena trahens umero.

cuius ut accensae Dryades candore puellae   45
    miratae solitos destituere choros,
prolapsum leuiter facili traxere liquore:
    tum sonitum rapto corpore fecit Hylas.
cui procul Alcides iterat responsa, sed illi
    nomen ab extremis fontibus aura refert.   50

his, o Galle, tuos monitus seruabis amores,
    formosum Nymphis credere uisus Hylan.

So those brothers, descended from Pandion through Orithyia, left,
and Hylas, alas! went on to meet his Nymphs.
For near Arganthus's crest was the fountain of Pege,
agreeably liquid home of the Thynian nymphs;
and suspended above were some dewy apples, tended   35
by no-one, available, under the solitary trees,
and lilies were springing around in the water-logged field,
whiteness and purity mixed with the poppies' stain.
So at first he plucked them with tender nails, like a child,
preferring a flower to his self-appointed task;
then mindlessly, lay in the prettily rippling stream,
and sweet reflections delayed his wandering return.
But ready at last to drain the river, he dipped
his hands, his shoulder leaning to take the strain.

The nymphs of the fountain, inflamed by his pure white flesh,   45
paused from their usual dance to gaze in wonder,
and lightly they pulled him prone through the yielding stream.
Then, with his body ravished, he made some sound,
and distant Hercules answered, repeating his name:
but a breeze brought "Hylas" back from the fountain's edge.   50

I hope you'll be warned, friend Gallus, and look to your love,
for you seemed to entrust fair Hylas to the Nymphs.

XXI

'Tu, qui consortem properas euadere casum,
    miles ab Etruscis saucius aggeribus,
quid nostro gemitu turgentia lumina torques?
    pars ego sum uestrae proxima militiae.
sic te seruato possint gaudere parentes: 5
    ne soror acta tuis sentiat e lacrimis,
Gallum, per medios ereptum Caesaris ensis,
    effugere ignotas non potuisse manus;
et quaecumque super dispersa inuenerit ossa
    montibus Etruscis, haec sciat esse mea.'   10

POEM XXI

"YOU, there! you're eager to fly from our kinsman, Death,
    soldier, you're wounded, the town you fought for lost;
but why do you swivel your eyeballs at hearing me groan —
    I'm only what happens next in your own campaign.
But look to your life, so the parents can have some joy: 5
    and tell our sister gently, and not by tears,
that Gallus, preserved in the midst of Caesar's swords,
    failed to escape the hands of nameless men:
and whatever bones she discovers, scattered all over
    Etruscan hills, tell her that these are mine."   10

XXII

Qualis et unde genus, qui sint mihi, Tulle, Penates,
    quaeris pro nostra semper amicitia.
si Perusina tibi patriae sunt nota sepulcra,
    Italiae duris funera temporibus,
cum Romana suos egit discordia ciuis   5
    (sit mihi praecipue, puluis Etrusca, dolor:
tu proiecta mei perpessa es membra propinqui,
    tu nullo miseri contegis ossa solo)
proxima supposito contingens Vmbria campo
    me genuit terris fertilis uberibus.   10

POEM XXII

Status-rank-ancestors-place-of-origin —
    You're always at me, Tullus, "for friendship's sake".
Have you heard of Perugia's — our country's — cemetery?
    Italy's graveyard it was in those hard times,
when factions in Rome affected all her citizens —   5
    dust of Etruria, sting me to special grief,
for you groan with the weight of my cousin's scattered limbs,
    you shield his wretched bones but not with soil: —
Umbria's sheltered plain just bordering those hills
    bore me, a rich place with fertile ground.   10

POEM I

A Roman would have found this an intriguing and slightly disquieting introduction to the volume. It is almost accidentally suitable to stand first. It was probably composed early,[1] when most of the poems that follow did not exist, yet it has a retrospective air, as though summing up the whole relationship. It seems a more public poem than most in this book, as though it was addressed to the general reader, but it is strangely opaque, always hinting at a private dilemma which he seems unable to talk about directly. In it Propertius generalises about Love more than usual, but he is not expounding his Philosophy of Love. The successive statements come across as oblique expressions of an inner disturbance. Individually they are elliptical and obscure, over-all they follow no clear logical progression. The poem itself divides into sections that remain discrete: it gives a sense of having evolved by accretion. In the earlier poems the addressee usually gives one kind of unity to his poems, but here Tullus appears belatedly at line 9, and has only an insecure place in the poem. He merges into the plural 'vos amici' at line 25, and is supplanted by others at line 31. The result is an elusive poem, dense, impacted, intricate, registering subterranean tensions through the movement of the verse and the quality of the language. Those first Roman readers would have been uneasily impressed but they would not have been sure quite what was to follow.

The first four lines make a clear enough statement. They are unusually impersonal and undramatic for Propertius, and the basic image is conventional. Its immediate source in this case is probably an epigram by Meleager.[2] Propertius gives a new complexity and seriousness to the stock images, however. The movement of his verse is carefully controlled, and the precise positioning of each word contributes subtly to the overall effect. 'Cynthia prima' appropriately begins the poem and the whole volume, 'prima' here perhaps having something of the force of "excellent, rare", as well as its more basic adverbial meaning.[3] Then 'miserium me' follows, enclosed mimetically by 'suis ocellis', the instruments of his capture. The affectionate diminutive 'ocellis' makes the process seem pleasant. 'Miserum me' is the self-pitying sigh of the stock lover. So far there is nothing really surprising, but the structure already hints that the poet will be taking the materials of the convention unusually seriously.

The same enclosing structure determines the next three lines, where lines 2 and 3 about Propertius are contained by lines where first Cynthia and then Amor is the subject. Cynthia and Amor are closely identified: in fact over these two couplets Cynthia seems to transform into the abstract Love, the

(1)   The percentage of pentameters which end with a word of more than two syllables is 37; see introduction pp. 9, 11 etc.

(2)   Palatine Anthology XII ci 1–4, cited by most commentators.

(3)   For 'prima' applied in this way to a girl, cp. Terence, Eunuch 567 'primam dices, scio, si videris'.

woman disappearing as the force takes over. This crucial transformation is embodied in the syntax, through a transient ambiguity over 'deiecit'.[4] The subject of this verb would naturally be taken to be Cynthia till line 4 reveals that the true subject is Amor.

The painful side of love, which was latent in the first line, becomes more evident in the second. 'Contactum' is stronger than Meleager's ʼατρωτον ποθοις suggesting that love is a disease as well as an arrow. 'Cupidinibus', especially in the plural, suggests the emotion rather than the god ('Cupido' is not normally a god for Propertius). The word does not carry such pejorative overtones as the English "lust", but in conjunction with 'contactum' it has a definite negative charge, communicating an unelegiac hostility towards the dominant emotion of the genre.

Line 3 proceeds through a series of slight shifts in the evaluation of Love. 'Constantis' was a morally positive word, normally used of virtues persisted in resolutely by good Romans. 'Fastus', which it qualifies, was not, however, usually a virtue. It represented·a kind of arrogant and contemptuous independence disapproved of by the Romans, and invariably criticised by Propertius where it occurs in others.[5] So to eliminate this quality could be a virtuous action, though there is a violence about the remedy suggested by 'deiecit' that might seem excessive. 'Lumina' binds this line to the first through the contrast with 'ocellis', his bold gaze dashed to the ground, her feminine eyes so much more powerful in their effect.

So far the poem could have seemed only a highly-wrought version of a familiar notion. The fifth line, however, would have been more startling. 'Castus' is a strongly positive word, meaning someone untouched by scandal, above reproach. So for Propertius to say that he hates ('odisse') such girls is outrageous: and in spite of the uneasiness of commentators, 'odisse' cannot with any authority be reduced to mild aversion or simply lack of interest.[6] 'Improbus' right at the beginning of the next line is exactly the word a Roman would use of someone who hated irreproachable women. However, Propertius uses it of Love, turning the accusation away from himself and endorsing it against the god or the emotion. In the space of four words he has repudiated both Roman morality and the repudiation itself. Such a self-

(4) See M.W. Edwards, esp. pp. 132 ff (for full ref. see Bibliography).

(5) For the meaning of 'fastus', see O.L.D.; for Propertius's usage cp e.g. III xii 9–10 'Haec etiam clausas expugnant arma pudicas,/ quaeque gerunt fastus, Icarioti, tuos', where the word is a criticism of aristocratic snobbery.

(6) Camps e.g. wishes to translate 'castas odisse puellas' as 'to have no use for women who are not free with their favours'. This involves a considerable reduction in the meaning of two words, 'odisse' and 'castas', in a context which is obviously (and by Camps's own admission) emotionally highly wrought. So the context gives no justification for this reduction and the dictionaries give little justification for the first (in the case of a personal object) and none for the second. Our account of this couplet is in general agreement with that of J. Fontenrose.

contradiction is of course not offered as a moral stance, but there is genuine moral feeling behind it. This is not the cheeky amorality of the elegiac lover, but a resentful, compulsive rejection of the prevailing morality.

The final lesson of Love inverts the normal aim of education. Propertius is reduced to living 'nullo consilio', 'with no rational scheme'. 'Consilium' is the practical use of the intelligence, the ability to devise means of getting what one wants. With a cruel irony Love makes him want the wrong things, then leaves him powerless to obtain them. Lines 17–18 will also lament that perversity.

Lines 7–8 emphasise the pains of his state. 'Furor' is an intense emotional state, a kind of madness. This has lasted a whole year, however, and Propertius emphasises that there has been not a moment's respite. The case of 'toto anno' is significant. This is the ablative of a point of time: the whole year is considered as a single unbroken unit.

Line 8 again brings out the cruel irony of his position. The gods are opposed to his love, he reveals for the first time. But the line implies more than this sad but commonplace fate. Commentators and translators tend to treat 'cogor habere' as equivalent to 'habeo', no doubt thinking that Propertius has suffered enough already in having the gods against him. But 'cogor' represents part of his condition, and is not redundant. 'Habere deos' on its own means to be subject to gods[7] – in this case, Amor and Venus. Propertius, however, has not willingly chosen this fate. He has been compelled (cogor) to be in love, and hence to rely on these gods, who then of course refuse to help him. 'Cogor' juxtaposed with 'adversos' brings out his helplessness before the contradictory forces acting on him. His inner need and the forces that oppose fulfilment are both conceived of as external to him, and the source of both is ultimately the same, the contradictory nature of the state he is in.

There is a sharp break in the poem at this point. Tullus is introduced as an addressee, and Milanion's example is invoked for no apparent reason. The negative 'nullos fugiendo labores' seems to be a response to some previous advice from Tullus, of the form: Why not get away from her then, go to Athens, or to some pleasant country retreat? Tullus was especially likely among Propertius's friends to recommend this obvious kind of solution: in I vi he seems to have invited Propertius to accompany him to Asia, in I xiv to join him at his Tiber estate.[8] Propertius refuses both times. In both poems Tullus emerges as a public-spirited man of ample means, simple-mindedly and inappropriately generous towards Propertius, worthy in ways that the poet could respect but not imitate. His form of benevolent incomprehension makes him a suitable recipient of the present poem, represen-

(7) Cp. e.g. Prop. III vii 18 'non habet unda deos'; III xx 22 'non habet ultores nox vigilanda deos', and IV xi 13 'non minus immitis habuit Cornelia Parcas', etc.

(8) See the discussions of these poems below.

tative of the other friends who would like to reclaim Propertius in line 25.

But the tone and function of this exemplum is not easy to determine. At first we might think of it as mythic authority for the course Propertius proposes to follow, but later he complains that Love does not work like this in his case. Nor is it simply the ideal that Love ought to aspire to, for by the time the conclusion is reached the authority of the exemplum has been subverted. The language is highly wrought, elevated in diction and strained in syntax, but as the passage progresses the triviality of Milanion's exploits deflates it into mock-heroic. Milanion, the exemplary lover, emerges as ludicrous by the heroic standards evoked by the grand style. But the final effect of the passage is again to convey an ambivalent attitude to love. Milanion may be ridiculous, but at least he is successful.

The first couplet of this section (lines 9–10) opens at a high pitch. 'Labores' connects Milanion's efforts with heroic labours such as those of Hercules.[9] 'Contudit' is an epic word for a violent act such as a hero would perform. The object of this doughty blow is not an opponent's head, but Atalanta's cruelty. The substitution of this abstract, 'saevitiam', for a physical object makes the syntax remote from normal speech. 'Iasis', the patronymic instead of the name Atalanta, also heightens the style.[10]

The narrative that follows is highly allusive. 'Iasidos', for instance, is meaningless except to well-informed readers who knew that Jasus was Atalanta's father. So a detailed prior knowledge of the Atalanta myth seems to be required. The myth had a number of variant forms, but the details in Propertius point to a version similar to that given by Apollodorus. Apollodorus gives the suitor's name as Milanion not Hippomenes, and names Jasus as her father, Hylaeus as the Centaur who attacks her, and the Parthenian mountains as her birthplace.[11] But the best-known feature of the Atalanta story was the famous race. It was common to all extant versions of the myth. In Propertius, this is only briefly and indirectly alluded to in line 15, through 'velocem'. Till then it might have been thought that Propertius was following a different version, in which Milanion won Atalanta by other means. Commentators have in fact supposed this, treating 'velocem' as an inert relic of the dominant version of the myth. This, however, is hardly plausible. After Propertius had written so allusively that a particular version of the myth needed to be recalled, and had then followed one version in detail after detail, it would have been extraordinarily perverse in him to have first omitted the most famous element in the myth, and then forgotten that he had left it out.

The Milanion of myth won Atalanta by cunning. He relied on her greed for the golden apples Aphrodite had given him. Propertius's Milanion behaves

(9)   Cp. E. Burck, esp. p. 176, on 'labores'.

(10)   On the stylistic qualities of the language here, see H. Tränkle, pp.12 ff.

(11) See Apollodorus III ix 2.

far more like the standard lover of the elegiac convention. The expectations aroused by 'contudit' are not fulfilled at all. First Milanion wanders deranged around Atalanta's birthplace. 'Partheniis' may recall its Greek meaning, "the maiden's", especially here since it is used adjectivally in connection with such a famous virgin. If so, it might give erotic overtones to the caves and hollows ('antris') through which he gropes his way. Line 12 is the closest this Milanion gets to heroism, but it is not in fact very close. Some commentators have tried to make 'videre' describe a positive action, but the word cannot be strong enough on its own.[12] This leaves Milanion a mere spectator of hairy wild animals. Even this may be brave for a lover, but it hardly counts as heroism.

Nor does he come out too well in the battle with the Centaurs. In Apollodorus, it is Atalanta who defeats them. Propertius says nothing to suggest otherwise for his Milanion. His only addition to the myth is to have Milanion present as an ineffectual participant, who is wounded and makes loud groans. Again the diction is elevated and the syntax strained, an absurdly inflated context for Milanion's inept contribution. The syntax of 'Hylaei percussus vulnere rami' in particular is so tortuous that the meaning is obscure. 'Rami' is usually interpreted as a club, since that is the most common metonymy. However, Apollodorus, whom Propertius otherwise follows so closely, attributes bows and arrows to the Centaurs. Ovid's otherwise close imitation of this passage uses 'arcu'.[13] 'Percussus' usually implies penetration, which would be more proper for a bow than a club. So there are a number of reasons for supposing that 'rami' here refers to a bow (which was made out of a bough) and not the more usual club. Strictly it is the arrow that would strike, not the bow: but Propertius uses that metonymy at I vii 15. The point would be to make a closer parallel between Milanion's sufferings and the sufferings of a lover at the hands of Love the archer. Milanion's groans of line 14 are certainly more like the laments of a lover than the fortitude of a hero.

So 'ergo' of line 15 is pseudo-logical. 'Velocem puellam' recalls Atalanta's defeat in the famous race. 'Preces et bene facta' were certainly not the immediate causes of the mythical Milanion's success. The elegiac Milanion has not been notable for either of these, of course. (Housman, followed by others, postulated a missing couplet to supply this lack.) But the moral has been stated only to be subverted by the preceding verses. Success in love is not a simple matter of good deeds rewarded and prayers answered. The mythic Milanion triumphed by cunning manipulation of feminine greed. It is this latent moral that the next couplet (lines 17–18) picks up. Love refuses to inspire Propertius with the necessary guile (or provide him with the equiva-

(12) We agree with Shackleton Bailey, p. 3, that 'videre' means simply 'to look upon', and that 'this makes Milanion no hero'.

(13) Ovid, The Art of Love, II 185–191.

ıent of golden apples). 'Tardus' makes the connection with the race of the unstated myth most clearly, and 'artis' recalls Milanion's guile. Milanion was too slow for Atalanta, but made up for it with trickery. Love in Propertius is even slower, but is stupid as well.

The whole section is obscure and complex. Propertius has substituted an elegiac lover and elegiac behaviour for the mythic Milanion, but told the story in strained language that indirectly recalled the traditional myth. So the myth is available to provide the moral, and is also a standard that makes the behaviour of the elegiac lover seems ludicrously unheroic. There is some wit in the execution of all this, directed ultimately at himself, but the thought is as devious, intricate and recondite as the language itself. Any laughter that survived all this would not be uproarious.

At line 19 the poem changes direction sharply again. This time Propertius invokes witches' aid. 'Labor' of line 20 ironically echoes 'labores' of line 9 to connect the witches' activities with those of the lover Milanion. 'Fallacia' indicates Propertius's scepticism from the beginning.[14]

The meaning of the next line is obscure. Sandbach suggests that 'sacra piare' = 'to expiate a religious offence'. This would fit in well with what Propertius thinks of his relationship with the gods Venus and Amor and with the god-like Cynthia. He has in some sense offended and an appeal to some kind of magical purification would be appropriate. The alternative explana-tion (i.e. 'to make sacrifices for the sake of appeasing the gods') would have the same sort of connection with Propertius's position.[15]   In fact the point of these 6 lines is an elaborately worked out parallel between heaven and earth, the moon and Cynthia, which may have been motivated in the firs place by the connection between the goddess Cynthia and the moon.[16] 'Deductae lunae' looks strange, but is a standard way of describing an eclipse of the moon.[17] The literal significance of 'deducere', to draw down a hea venly body, will make it easier for Propertius to refer it to Cynthia.

In the two couplets that follow (lines 21–24) he sets these witches a test: if they can win over Cynthia he will acknowledge their powers ove Nature. This challenge is made less arbitrary by the Cynthia-moon parallel

(14) 'Fallacia' implies a deception, and so Propertius does not suggest that the witches can in fact draw down the moon.

(15) The precise meaning of this phrase does not make any real difference to the validity of our overall account of the poem. For the discussion see Sandbach (see biblio graphy) and Enk and Shackleton Bailey on this passage.

(16) Though Cynthia is not applied overtly to the moon before Ov. Her. XVIII 74 Diana (=Cynthia) is: see O.L.D. under 'Diana' b. On the connection betweer Cynthia and the moon in this and other passages in Propertius, see E. O'Neil

(17) Cp. Verg. Bucolics VIII 69 'carmina vel caelo possunt deducere lunam'; and cp the scholiast to Apollonius Rhodius III 533 (cited by Enk) –

'Palleat' can be used of eclipses as well as for the pallor of a lover. As used of eclipses it suggests a general loss of luminosity rather than simple pallor, so his wish here might recall his own 'dejecta lumina' of line 3, which were her effect on him.[18] The parallel is worked out more extensively in lines 23–24. The trick of causing eclipses is repeated in 'sidera/ducere', but this time the phrase is made much more difficult by the insertion of 'amnes', which creates an extremely harsh zeugma. '(de) ducere sidera' could have remained a dead metaphor without this, but 'ducere amnes' must employ the normal sense of 'ducere'. One effect of this is to insist on the literal meaning of the phrase: he wants Cynthia brought down. The currents or streams ('amnes') which are brought into prominence by this curious syntactical role and by their position in the line, may have their analogue in the tears that he hopes Cynthia will be induced to weep.[19] If 'amnes' refers to tears, the zeugma will be less harsh, since tears and stars can both be brought down, but the magic spell to do with streams ought to draw them upwards, against the current. 'De' cannot be understood with this construction. The point of all this is probably Cynthia's semi-divine status, as something like a force of nature, but the strain on language involved, especially in the last couplet, may be felt to be excessive.

In line 25 Propertius turns back to his conventional friends, into whose number Tullus has been absorbed. 'Sero' here is usually taken with 'revocatis' ('you reclaim me too late') but such despair is premature and out of place here. It is more satisfactory to take it with 'lapsum', where the sentiment would recall lines 1–2, implying something like I vii 26 ('venit magno faenore tardus amor'). In this poem Propertius wants to emphasise his resistence to love and his wish to return to his former habitual state. So in line 26 he accepts the view of himself as sick, as did 'contactum' of line 2, and he offers himself for a painful cure by surgery and cautery. But he cannot unequivocally wish to be reclaimed any more. 'Ignes' is qualified by 'saevos' a word with almost a technical meaning in elegy (as in 'saevitiam' of line 10). 'Ignes' of course often refers to the fires of love.[20] Through this double sense in the image he is asking for the disease again at the very moment he seems to be requesting a cure.

Line 28 is even more equivocal and obscure. What is a 'libertas quae velit ira loqui'? He seems to want to express anger, an emotion that has not been mentioned previously, though it has been felt as a powerful undercurrent throughout the poem. In this curious phrase 'velit' has the effect of

(18) 'Palleo' is the normal word used for eclipses of the sun; it is first so used of the moon in Luc. VI 500 and then again in Claud. 'Cons. Mall. Theod.' 40.

(19) For the woman's tears signifying longing cp. Ter. Heaut. 304–7. 'Ubi dicimus redisse te . . . mulier . . . continuo et lacrimis opplet os totum sibi ut facile scires desiderio id fieri'.

(20) Cp. for example Verg. Aeneid. IV 2 'caeco carpitur igni' (of Dido).

69

half-personifying anger: rage like love is seen as an external and potentially tyrannous force. The freedom Propertius craves is a limited one at best, freedom of speech not emotional freedom.

The mention of 'libertas'[21] also reflects back on the images of the previous line. The escaped slave who was recovered was branded and chained up. The images of fire and steel could then gain a different kind of significance. To be reclaimed by his friends would then be seen as a return to a kind of slavery. Again this would represent an extremely equivocal judgement on love and normality. Each is a kind of slavery from the other's point of view. The desperate request of the next couplet, lines 29–30, is for escape from both civilization and love.

The people whom he now addresses (line 31) seem to have changed slightly. These are lovers, but successful ones. Propertius gives them some advice which has an equivocal edge to it. He urges constancy ('semper') equality ('pares') and above all safety, but the tense quality of this "safety" comes out in lines 35–6. 'Vitate' implies movement away, but the lover will avoid the danger by staying exactly where he is.

Propertius's description of his own condition, in lines 33–4, again brings out the self-contradictory nature of his love. 'Venus noctes exercet' on its own would refer to nights of making love. 'Nostra' generalises this Venus to include the lovers of line 31 ('vos'), but 'in me' distinguishes his unhappy experience from their success.[22] 'Amaras' coming at the end of the line then effectively negates the sentence. His venereal activity is the bitterness of not making love for night after night. The next line repeats that sentiment even more tortuously. 'Vacuus' indicates idleness, lack of activity. 'Vacuus Amor' must be a stronger form of 'tardus Amor' of line 17. Love is now not simply slow, it is wholly inactive on his behalf. But this complete ineffectiveness is an unremitting presence. 'Nullo tempore defit' recalls 'toto furor hic non deficit anno' of line 7. Love is always working at not working for him: lack of love is always present.

The poem closes with a warning, and insists on the penalties that await someone who does not heed it. The warning itself, however, is obscure and hard to profit by. The 'malum' to be avoided is not simply love, for the way to avoid it is by desperate adherence to a well-tried conventional love. The

(21) 'Libertas' is a very unusual word in elegy. It is used also in II xxiii 23 by Propertius, but apart from that occurs only once elsewhere, at Tib. II iv 2. Propertius uses other cognates of the word 'liber' fairly frequently also, which tend to emphasise the paradox of the independent man in the constraints of love.

(22) On this line we agree with B & B etc. as against Enk. The contrast is not between an implied 'vestra' and 'nostra': in fact the obvious contrast underlined by the positioning of the words is between 'vos' and 'in me', and for this contrast to be properly understood, the same force must be operating in both cases to produce the different effects; therefore, 'nostra Venus' cannot possibly mean 'my Venus' but must mean 'our Venus',

true evil is Propertius's present condition, alienation from both love and society. Conventional notions of love have proved as inapplicable as conventional morality. The final line carries a sense of the incommunicability of the experience. 'Referet' is stronger than "to remember",closer to "re-enact".[23]

So the poem concludes having failed to understand the distressing experience at its core, still not having talked about it directly. The failure has been re-enacted by the poem itself. Its power comes from the sense it gives that even the difficulties and obscurities are essential to convey the texture of the experience. There is no conclusion, but there could be none. Inconclusiveness is a primary quality of the poem, though in tension with this is an urgent need to understand. His attempts to generalise constantly break down, as he is unable to tell how general his experience is, or who he is talking to. Yet the refusal to be explicit could seem like a way of escaping from his private hell, not a strategy for understanding it. The obscurity may come, partly at least, from a deep reluctance to confront the insoluble. The result is a powerful and darkly troubled poem, but not a wise one, and only just a unity. The transitions are abrupt and there are vertiginous shifts of addressee. It is a poem of disorientation, a missing centre, shifting perspectives. From line 3, when Cynthia merged into Amor, the person who could have held it in a single focus has disappeared.

(23) There are several meanings of 'refero' in a transferred sense; of these the most important here are those in Lewis and Short B 2: viz. e.g. 'to repeat, renew . . ; to reproduce; to call to mind'. This indicates that the word implies something rather more active than the simple act of memory.

POEM II

Initially this poem seems an argument on the somewhat trite theme that "Beauty unadorned is best adorned".[1] Propertius starts by arguing that Cynthia should rely on her natural beauty, not on false adornment. He pursues this argument through a series of oppositions between art and nature often witty and ingenious in detail but fundamentally serious and extremely interesting. Probably this aspect of the poem accounts for his placing it second in the volume. I i comes first, as the fullest statement of the nature of Propertian love, but he may have regarded this poem as his most interesting statement about his art. The first poem of Book II, written after the Monobiblos had made his reputation, is more obviously a programmatic poem. It seems to echo this one at a number of key points, as though Propertius was using it to gloss its less explicit precursor.[2]

But this is a love poem, not a treatise. The argument twists and turns in response to emotional pressures, his anxiety warring against his love. So he starts by praising the beauty of nature but finishes urging the beauty of faithfulness, which is not at all the same, in spite of the ingenuity Propertius expends to make the connection. The doubts are not acute in this poem, but they are real. The poem is a magnificent performance, witty and intelligent, passionate and rich, but all its energy and variety cannot fully exorcise the underlying tension.

The first six lines are highly formal in structure. So are lines 9–14. Such a display of art may seem paradoxical, especially since he is most elaborately formal when he is arguing most strongly for the virtues of Nature. His delight in his own art and the sheer richness of the forms he can create is a witty counterstatement to the ostensible praise of Nature, part of his resolution of the opposition between Nature and Art.

Lines 1–6 are built around a repeated syntactic form. They all consist of an infinitive and an ablative governed by the opening 'Quid iuuat'. This basic form, elegantly varied and sustained so long, seems highly mannered and self-conscious, but it is essentially simple. The infinitives of decoration just accumulate as the poet itemises the excesses of which Cynthia is guilty.

The poem does not start with outright hostility to adornment. There is nothing inherently pejorative in the central description of line 1, 'ornato procedere . . . capillo'. 'Procedere' suggests a progress confident of its attractive powers.[3] There is nothing self-evidently wrong with dressing one's

---

(1) See B & B on this poem.

(2) II i 5–6 and II i 58 seem fairly definite echoes of I ii 2 and 8: II i 3–4 and 9–10 may echo I ii 27–8 (see our discussion below); II i 7–8 may more remotely recollect I ii 1 and 3.

(3) Enk's note seems to us to show this, and Shackleton Bailey, though he disputes this reading of 'procedere', does not impugn the validity of Enk's examples.

hair, either. However, the opening 'Quid iuuat' brusquely questions the value of that and everything that Cynthia does in the next six lines. The pragmatic note it introduces will connect with the purely mercenary values that Propertius is to attribute to Cynthia. Even in those terms she is foolish, he tries to maintain. The interposed vocative, 'vita', life, subtly sets up the opposing set of values. The word is more than an inert term of endearment.[4] The absence of 'mea' makes it even more striking. The word here reminds Cynthia of her significance for Propertius, what ought to be her significance for herself. Life is not a simple opposite to Art in Propertius's poem, but its affinities are with Nature.

The second line is usually read as "and move the fine folds of your Coan dress", and would have to refer to an unduly suggestive manner of walking. However, this reading involves some linguistic oddities which individually would not be remarkable, but cumulatively are rather unsatisfactory. It breaks from the pattern established so strongly in this opening section, where the ablatives are of an instrumental kind.[5] Moreover, 'Coa veste' would have to be a very unusual kind of ablative, perhaps an ablative of material, if such a thing exists.[6] To make this even more awkward, 'vestis' never elsewhere refers to a material: it always means a garment, or by extension a cover.[7] For this phrase to be attached loosely to 'sinus' creates a further strain. These usually refer to the folds over the breast: obviously these are part of the garment, not vice versa.[8] There is no apparent poetic reason for such lexical

(4) It is difficult to assess exactly how far this word may have been more or less inert in general, but certainly Propertius seems to use it frequently with some kind of punning on its real meaning; Cp. 'num tibi nascenti primis, mea vita, diebus / candidus argutum sternuit omen Amor?' II iii 23 and '(iuro) me tibi ad extremas mansurum, vita, tenebras: / ambos una fides auferet, una dies' II xx 17. Altogether he uses it nine times as against four in Catullus, none in Tibullus and two in Ovid. It usually has a possessive in comedy, always in Catullus and Ovid.

(5) The ablatives, even if not all strictly instrumental, certainly belong to the instrumental group of functions: cp. Hofman Szantyr par. 76, 82, 'In propriis bonis' is the one departure from the pattern; for an explanation of this, see our discussion below.

(6) For this suggestion, see Rothstein and Camps; Enk describes the ablative as 'liberior', but the parallels he offers are not apposite since they all involve ablative plurals.

(7) See Lewis & Short.

(8) Ovid Heroides, XIII 36 seems to use 'sinus' (pl.) = 'dress', but such usage is rare. 'Sinus' could refer to folds in a Coan dress (A.G. Lee). This is the most plausible account along the traditional lines: its only linguistic difficulty is to leave 'tenuis' rather functionless, but that would be a small enough matter. The sense it yields, however, is less satisfactory, since it requires the Coan dress itself to have a negative valuation if the line is to have any real force; against this see below and notes 13 and 14.

and syntactical deviancies. The interpretation remains possible, but it leaves the line an unsatisfactory one.

However, there is another way to take the line which avoids all these difficulties, and poetically is immensely superior. 'Coa veste movere', to move (something) with a Coan dress, can readily act as the kernel of line (like 'ornato procedere capillo' in the previous one) with 'tenuis' preparing for an object to follow 'movere'. 'Sinus', carefully delayed till the end, then precipitates a sentence with devastating multiple ambiguities. The word strictly refers to the folds of the toga over the upper body, but it had two common meaning by transference: the emotions, since they reside in the breast, and a purse, since money was kept in these folds. Propertius was fond of puns on these two secondary meanings.[9] 'Movere' establishes the first of these as the main meaning here. This word had a common meaning in a rhetorical context of "arouse, stir up".[10] 'Sinus' would be an unusual but not difficult substitution for 'mentes' (or something of that kind). These 'sinus' would of course belong to Propertius's rivals, not to Cynthia.

This makes Cynthia's art of adornment a kind of sartorial rhetoric, a highly significant connection in a culture in which rhetoric played so dominant a role.[11] Rhetoric of itself was not unequivocally either good or bad for a Roman. Here Propertius's pun on 'sinus' indicates his attitude to Cynthis's "rhetoric", which is aimed at purses rather than minds. Conversely, the attraction of these rivals is reduced to the power of their wallets. 'Tenuis' compounds the insult. Qualifying 'sinus' as emotions it suggests shallowness, lack of force: with purses it suggests meagreness.[12] The proximity of 'tenuis' to 'Coa veste' probably brings out the primary concrete meaning of 'sinus' as well. As in the traditional reading of the line, 'tenuis' could easily be used of materials like Coan silk. The effect of this would be to make the object her persuasion works on the same kind of thing as the means she employs – a notion that certainly underlies line 4. Both means and end are equally external things: she is engaged in nothing more elevated than a trade in cloths.

(9) Cp. e.g. I viii 37–8 'avara sinus', II xvi 12 'semper amatorum ponderat una sinus'.

(10) See e.g. Cic. Brut. 185; 'Tria sunt enim . . . quae sint efficienda dicendo; ut doceatur is apud quem dicetur, ut delectetur, ut moveatur vehementius'. Cp. also Quint. VI ii 1 and VI i vii.

(11) The ornaments of rhetoric are fairly commonly compared in metaphor to the clothes of thought; cp. e.g. Cic. Brut. 274, 'De Oratore' I xxxi 142 etc. Propertius is merely reversing this common form.

(12) The range of appropriate meanings is represented by e.g. 'tenuissimum patrimonium' (Cic.) 'ad Her.' IV xxxviii 50, 'servus sit an liber, pecuniosus an tenuis' Cic. Inv. I 25; and 'tenuis atque infirmus animum' Caes. B.C. I 32, 'ingenium tenue' (opposed to 'forte') Quint. X ii 19.

On this interpretation words are doing an unusual amount of work, but they do this by exploiting their usual meanings. With remarkable economy Propertius has introduced the two main themes of the poem. The connection between Cynthia's extravagance and rhetoric, the art of language, gives a serious context to the Nature-Art opposition, but he has also expressed his more urgent personal worries on Cynthia's behalf. In other places Propertius shows no animus towards Coan silk: he always mentions it with approval.[13] Moreover, Coan silk was especially famous in the ancient world for its transparent quality.[14] According to the aesthetic of nudity presented in line 8 Propertius ought to have approved of this. However, even at this stage of the poem Propertius is concerned that Cynthia should have her proper lover as well as her proper lack of clothes.

There is an oscillatory movement between the first and second lines which is continued in the next couplet. 'Aut quid' marks a break with the preceding couplet. The hexameter that follows is again concerned with hair, and the pentameter again sees her action in mercenary terms. The criticism now is sharper, however. Line 3 is still more complimentary than line 4, but there is a critical note compared to line 1. The adjective 'Orontea' perhaps suggests the effeteness of the East:[15] 'perfundere' intensifies the more neutral 'fundere' to hint at excessive amounts.

The striking word in the next line is 'vendere'. Commentators often uneasily suggest that the force of this word should be muted to something like "set off as though for sale", but 'vendere' itself naturally means to sell. Propertius is accusing her of actually selling herself. The accusation is harsh, but the pun on 'sinus' has prepared for it.[16] The nature of the transaction is brought out by the ablative 'muneribus', where a more neutral word like 'ornamentis' might have been expected. 'Munera' in elegy comes to have almost a technical meaning, referring to the gifts lovers use to win access to their mistresses.[17] The implication is that all Cynthia's finery must have

(13) E.G. II i 5–6 and IV v 23.

(14) Cp. Hor. Satires I ii 101 'Cois tibi paene videre est ut nudam' and see also Enk on this passage.

(15) Perhaps: Propertius seems to be the first Latin poet to use the river name Orontes (the adjective here, of course) and he does so also at II xxiii 21 – 'et quas Euphrates et quas mihi misit Qrontes' – where there is a strong suggestion of the second rate.

(16) The commentators on the whole rather weakmindedly do not want Propertius to Propertius to really criticise Cynthia, and obviously the traditional reading of line 2 makes 'vendere' much harder to take. But the word simply means 'sell' and the blatancy of this makes the purse-pun on 'sinus' much more likely. 'Munera' has to be similarly softened on the traditional reading; e.g. Camps 'this can hardly mean "gifts" ...'.

(17) This word is used twenty one times in Propertius, fifteen/sixteen times as a lover's gifts.

come from wealthy admirers; the word here becomes almost a euphemism for fees. (If 'muneribus' is an ablative of price as well as means the implication is strengthened.) Cynthia is selling herself with ornaments that are the proceeds of an earlier sale. 'Peregrinis', foreign or alien, defines the true quality of these gifts, geographically foreign, from places like Cos and Orontes, and extrinsic, foreign to her essential character.

The third couplet gives the terms of the underlying opposition, 'naturae decus', the grace of nature, opposed to 'cultus mercatus', bought culture. But the opposition is neither simple nor total. 'Decus' always implies a good kind of ornament, including some rather vague kinds (Cicero used the word for what a knowledge of letters is to a man's old age),[18] but its normal associations are with civilisation rather than with nature. So the genitive is slightly surprising, preparing for the paradoxes of the next section. 'Cultus' also normally, though not so necessarily, had good associations, so its epithet 'mercatus' would be surprising and carries most of the pejorative force of the contrast.[19] A 'cultus' that can be bought in the shops is a singularly extrinsic (cp. 'peregrinis') and trivial kind of cultivation, one which would not normally be dignified with that word. So Propertius is not necessarily suggesting that Cynthia should abandon art, but that she should respect her material and not add trifling ornament to it.

The third couplet differs in a number of important ways from the pattern established by the two previous ones. First, it inverts the content of the hexameter and pentameter: now it is the hexameter which points out the terms of her bargain, while the pentameter tells how she really ought to be adorning herself, thus preparing for the transition to the next section. The pentameter itself introduces two significant variations into the prevailing syntax of these first six lines. One is that this line has two infinitives instead of one as in the rest. In the others Cynthia was the active subject of the only verb, here she is the subject of 'sinere', 'to allow'. This verb describes an action which is the cessation of activity, or at most one whose effect is to transfer the action away from what the girl is consciously trying to do, thus allowing the wisdom of her body (or of whoever gave her that body) to do its own work, 'to shine', ('nitere'). As well as the two infinitives, this line has the preposition 'in' governing its ablative. The profusion of loosely attached instrumental or quasi-instrumental ablatives was the syntax of instrumental goods, goods that are merely functional and remain extrinsic to essential beauty. In line 6, describing the proper kind of ornament, both the preposition and the word 'propriis' emphasise the same point, that true ornaments

(18) Cic. 'de Or.' I 45 99 'decus ornamentumque senectutis'.

(19) On 'cultus' see O.L.D. 6 and possibly 9; Pliny and Petronius give the word a straight forward trivial concrete meaning 'ornaments, clothes', but earlier meanings in this range are more generalised. 'Cultus' is used once before Prop. with a derogatory sense ('over-refinement of living'), Sall. Catullus 13 3.

should be intrinsic, proper to oneself. But the commercial values he used to mark the absurdity of her dressing up still act through 'bonis'. This could also mean 'goods' in the mercantile sense, but this time the word does not undercut the value of her activity. In contrast to the poor bargain she has made in the previous lines, he implies, she would do better to realise what are her true assets.

The poem so far has been among other things a finely rhetorical declamation against Cynthia's use of the rhetoric of appearances. 'Crede mihi', 'believe me', continues this paradox. It is a colloquial version of the verbal gesture an orator would use to introduce material which is surprising but — he insists — true.[20] However, the statement that follows is too obscure to be obviously either true or false. Even the text is the subject of dispute. The main tradition gives 'tua est', your medicine is worthless, but one Ms. has 'tuae est', the medicine of your 'figurae' is worthless.[21] This second has become the more popular, but its sense is less satisfactory. Propertius purports to be arguing a general case, as line 8 makes clear. With 'tuae' qualifying 'figurae' the proposition would be too specific to Cynthia: others may doctor themselves, but in Cynthia's case it would be pointless — a double-edged disclaimer, incidentally. 'Tua medicina' will mean "doctoring the body, as you are doing". 'Tua' serves to make the generalisation apply to Cynthia, while the pentameter gives the general rule, a common relationship between hexameter and pentameter for Propertius.

The striking word in this line, and the key to its interpretation, is 'medicina'.[22] This connects her activity to another art, that of medicine. The comparison between rhetoric and medicine occurs early in the formalisation of the art.[23] Used of the cosmetic art, the image is more vivid and disgusting: her perfumes, powders and silks are seen as ointments and bandages. Cosmetics are designed to enhance beauty: medicines are to cure disease. Cynthia's attention to her appearance suggests sickness, Propertius implies.

Line 8 repudiates the perverse practice in the name of Love. The tone is witty. 'Amor non amat', Love does not love, is a light paradox, and the argument from iconography in 'nudus Amor' is amusingly erotic. But the line

(20) On the colloquial nature of 'crede mihi' see Enk.

(21) NAFP 'tua est' Vo. V 'tu(a)e est; Pasoli argues that these MS readings simply represent different divisions of an original 'tuaest'. He is probably right, and so the tradition is neutral between the two. The decision must be made on grounds of sense.

(22) 'Medicina' (as opposed to 'medicamina', which could be more easily transferred to cosmetics, and in fact was) is a strong metaphor.

(23) Cp. e.g. Eur. Phoen. 471

ends with 'artificem', Cynthia as doctor, as she was in the previous line.[24]

Two words remain puzzling here, 'figurae' and 'formae'. 'Forma' and its cognates are to be prominent in the rest of the poem as one of Propertius's major categories, but throughout he seems to use it in an idiosyncratic way. The word normally meant either form or beauty, the two alternatives of course obviously connected. In line 8 the word must refer only to beauty of the surface, a curious limitation in its range of meanings. 'Figurae' in line 7 is strange for the same reason. It was normally used of an outline or contour: here it seems to mean a quality of the surface.[25] Perhaps this strange use of the two words is meant to reflect Cynthia's perversity: she mistakes a superficial appeal for beauty, so Propertius redefines the word accordingly.

The poem continues with another rhetorical gesture by the poet, 'aspice!' 'Look!' This of course does not guarantee that the poet is actually looking at the scene he describes. Lines 9–12 are syntactically parallel, as were lines 1–6, and again there is an alternating movement between hexameter and pentameter. In line 9 the soil is described as 'formosa' and is covered with colours, whereas ivy grows 'sua sponte', where it will: in line 11 the arbutus (or wild strawberry tree) is 'formosius' in the wild, and was probably a colourful tree,[26] while the water in line 12 is untaught ('indocilis') again suggesting spontaneity of form. So Nature is not simply contrasted with Art. The hexameter celebrates beauty of surface, the pentameter a more wayward beauty of form. Nature has both surface and form, art and spontaneity. Assisted by the context, 'formosa' and 'formosius' continue the unusual bias given to 'forma' in line 8. The obvious patterning of the lines here is another way of reinforcing the idea that Nature has its art.

Line 9 is probably an imitation of Lucretius I. Line 7 'tibi suavis daedala tellus/summittit flores'. The changes Propertius has made are illuminating for what he is doing here. 'Humus', the ground or the soil, is a less dignified word than 'Tellus' who was a goddess with a temple in Rome.[27] The word suggests something inherently shapeless, so it is surprising to find it half-personified and described as 'formosa'. 'Formosa' replaces 'daedala', cunning, artful, but the new context helps to retain something of that meaning still. 'Colores' instead of 'flores' emphasises one aspect of the flowers, their decorative appearance. The line as a whole describes an activity deriving from what

(24) 'Artifex' does not always mean doctor, but 'medicina' makes that meaning inevitable here; cp. also Propertius's later echo of this line at II i 58 where 'artificem' can only mean 'doctor'.

(25) Cp. Ovid's imitation of this passage at 'Amores'. I x 13–14, where 'figura' also refers to outer beauty as opposed to inner truth – 'donec simplex eras, animum cum corpore amavi; / nunc mentis vitio laesa figura tua est.'

(26) Cp. Ovid; Metamorphoses X 101 'pomo onerata rubenti arbutus'.

(27) See Cic. 'ad Q. Fr.' III i 4 14.

is internal ('summittat' sends up from inside itself) which produces an effect that is ornamental and full of 'formositas'. The source of this beauty is the lowly 'humus'.

Line 11 is the least clear of these lines. The main difficulty lies with the phrase 'in solis antris'. 'Antris' is usually interpreted loosely here, as glen or even grove, but there is no need or justification for this.[28] The point of the line is presumably the dramatic effect of the bright red arbutus against the rocky hollows amongst which it grows. Both "grove" and "glen" would lose this point. 'Solis' makes isolation an important part of the effect, which keeps the secondary theme alive. Cynthia like the arbutus would look more impressive if set off against a suitably lonely background: she would certainly be more safe.

In these four lines in praise of Nature there is an increase in both energy and purposiveness. The earth "sends up" relatively passively, the ivy "comes", the tree "rises", and the water finally has an almost human combination of intellectual and physical activity ('sciat', 'currere'). This progression leads into the final couplet of this section, syntactically independent, but a natural culmination; line 13 praises the rhetoric of nature, line 14 the more wayward beauty of song.

The key word of line 13 is 'persuadent', but no editors have noticed the kind of progression involved, or the poem's concern with rhetoric, so the word has seemed impossible, and it is usually emended or obelized.[29] The word has the same relation to 'canunt' as 'formosa humus' has to the ivy, and the arbutus to the stream. It is more formal, more of the surface. To reinforce the connection, 'picta' refers to colour (like 'colores' of line 9). In this context 'picta lapillis' must recall not the art of mosaic as is sometimes suggested, but the use of 'color' and the related 'pingo' as almost technical terms in rhetoric.[30] The connection with Cynthia's arts of adornment comes through 'picta', which could be used of cosmetics, and 'lapillis', the jewels which she ought to eschew, like Hippodamia in line 21. The epithets 'nativis' and 'picta' set up a Nature-Art paradox, continuing that concern.

(28) The loose use of 'antrum' is usually supported by I i 11, where the meaning 'cave' or perhaps 'rocky hollow' is perfectly appropriate, and by Manilius V 311, which by itself is not sufficient evidence or support for this meaning.

(29) The difficulty is mistakenly seen to be a lexical one, and editors search vainly for a parallel to show that 'persuadent' can mean 'entice'. If the oddity springs out of the boldness of the metaphor, however, it is not surprising that no parallels are found. The successive emendations offered have seemed implausible to everyone except their begetters. Camps, who obelises, probably represents modern orthodoxy.

(30) See. e.g. Quintilian IV ii 88 where 'color' means a tone or emotive colouring given to a false statement in order to lend it an air of verisimilitude, and Cic. Brut. 44 162 'quidam sine fuco veritatis color' (here, of course, 'color' has the favourable sense which follows from the Ciceronian view of rhetoric). For 'pingo', See e.g. Cic. Brut. 37, 141 and 'ad Att'. II xxi 4, etc.

'Picta' implies the use of art: 'nativis' emphasises the naturalness of these stones to this shore.

The language at this point is supremely artful. The line is formally nearly perfect, symmetrically deployed around the verb in a kind of "golden line".[31] Musically too it is highly effective. The pattern of p's and l's echoes the sound of water lapping on the shore. This is consummate and self-conscious artistry devoted to praise of the artifice of Nature. The opposition between Nature and Art could not be more totally resolved. 'Persuadent' is the key-stone in this structure, not an embarrassment as other commentators have found it, but a daring and brilliant metaphor that locks the multifarious themes into place with effortless virtuosity.

A new section now begins, as Propertius turns for support to the world of myth. The three stories that follow are ostensibly meant to describe girls who used no art to win their lovers. However, this fact is indicated only in an off-hand way, through the vague 'non sic' of line 15, 'cultu non' of line 16, 'non', line 17, and 'nec falso candore' of line 19. An absence of adornment played no significant part in any of these myths, and was certainly not an obvious moral to draw from them. But Propertius is not indulging here in 6 lines of irrelevant amplification. He is working typically allusively, relying on the readers' knowledge and intelligence to supply the well-known plots and the latent moral. The women played a passive role in these myths. The stores all involve a violent abduction, and the suitors show an increasing amount of duplicity. So Propertius gestures in passing at the moral that a girl should avoid unnatural adornment, but then draws the surprising conclusion that the beauty of these girls derived from their discretion and fidelity. Behind this curious shift lies the motive that has been latent from the beginning, the fear that far from detracting from her natural beauty, Cynthia may be making herself dangerously attractive, that she is indicating her availability to all who have the money to pay.

Lines 17—18 refer to the story in which Castor and Pollus fought Idas and Lynceus for the daughters of Leucippus.[32] In the fight Lynceus was killed. The violence here is hinted at through 'succendit', which could be a kindling to rage as well as to love. Lines 19—22 hint more strongly at the violence of the story being told. The myth here is that Evenus, king of Aetolia, had a beautiful daughter called Marpessa. He challenged all prospective suitors to a

(31) A 'golden line' is strictly of the form epithet a epithet b, verb, noun a noun b, but this codification is late. Propertius's line has an intertwined form Na Eb (V) Ea Nb which is arguably more artful than the so-called golden line itself. The prosody of 'persuadent' increases the sense of art: a molossus word (3 longs) at this point in the line was used by Vergil to achieve a particularly sonorous effect. See P Wilkinson, pp. 129 and 215.

(32) The two surviving sources for the story are Theoc. Idyll XXII 137 ff. and Pind. Nemean X 60. In both these Idas dies. This would make it impossible for him to reappear two lines later chasing Marpessa. However, Ovid 'Fasti' V 700 ff. suggests a version in which Idas does not die; Propertius may be following this.

chariot race. Idas, however, abducted her while she was dancing in a temple. Evenus was unable to catch them, and threw himself into a river which subsequently took his name. Idas still had to contend with Phoebus, who also wanted Marpessa. This second quarrel was settled by Zeus, who allowed Marpessa to choose. She preferred Idas, because the god might desert her in her old age.[33] The violence that is part of this story comes most obviously through 'discordia', referring to Apollo's opposition, but more strongly if indirectly through 'patriis litoribus'. This seems like an innocuous reference to her native shores, but in the light of the story it becomes a macabre kind of pun, "the banks of the river where her father died".

In the first part of the this story at least, Idas has a morally somewhat equivocal role. The next 'exemplum' shows an even more morally ambiguous male. Hippodamia may have avoided falsity but her suitor did not. In the well-known story, he bribed the charioteer of Hippodamia's father to draw the linchpins from the chariot wheels, and so won the race for the girl at the cost of his father-in-law's death. (This race had been instituted for all suitors by the girl's father, with the girl as prize and death for failure.) When the charioteer came to claim his bribe, Pelops threw him over a cliff.[34] The story parallels that of Idas in the incident of the chariot race, but there is a much greater amount of violence by treachery involved. This is not explicitly stated by the poet, but there are several pointers to the character of Pelops. Firstly 'Phrygium', not a necessary ethnic adjective for the man, suggests the effeminacy and untrustworthiness of the east.[35] Perhaps the immediate juxtaposition of 'falso' also colours the tone of 'Phrygium'. More important is 'externis' in the next line, which means "foreign" and sums up a quality akin to 'peregrinis' in line 4 and opposed to 'propriis' (line 6) and 'nativis' (line 13).[36] Pelops is decadent, treacherous, and foreign. The women of the 'exempla' are said to avoid art, but their suitors are progressively more involved in treacherous manipulations.

The poem now moves towards its conclusion. Inevitably the language is opaque, since Propertius's motives are mixed and his position involves a contradiction, but what he says is self-consciously and ingeniously confusing, not simply confused. The sequence of thoughts can be followed with entire certainty, so long as the implied argument is appreciated as an important factor.

(33) The fullest version of this myth is in the scholion to Iliad IX 557.

(34) Cp. Apollodorous Epitome II 3–9, Soph. Electra 504 ff., Pind. Olympian I 67–90.

(35) Cp. e.g. II xxii 16. Virgil revalued the term, applying it to Aeneas, but even this revaluation was not complete: the Italians can use the word as an insult against the Trojans, e.g. 'semiuir Phryx' of Aeneas in Aeneid XII 99.

(36) Cp. Ovid's reworking of this line, where 'externis rotis' is normalised to 'peregrinis rotis', Her. VIII 70.

Lines 21—22 are a straightforward summary of the overt moral of the myths, that beauty is independent of art. But the comparison with Apelles prevents any simple opposition between Nature and Art, for it makes the painter's skill the measure against which the success of Natural beauty is judged. 'Obnoxia' in line 21 recalls the criticisms of lines 2 and 4. The word means both "indebted to" and "addicted to", nearly always with perjorative implications.

'Illis' at the beginning of line 23 refers to the mythic heroines, but this couplet needs to be taken closely with the next if Propertius's purpose here is to be understood. Otherwise line 25 is scarcely comprehensible: not surprisingly it has caused considerable difficulties for commentators.[37] Formally 'non illis' . . . 'non ego' . . . binds the two couplets, but the content of the pentameters is a more important link. 'Forma' and 'cultus' have been keywords, the first in the section on Nature, the second as used of the heroines of myth. Propertius proceeds to redefine them both, but in a most unusual sense, which does not follow at all from the ostensible point of the myths.

'Non . . . studium' at the beginning of line 23 makes an initial reference to the ostensible theme, asserting that these girls did not work hard at being beautiful, but with 'vulgo amantes' his other concern takes over, his hostility to the owners of the hearts/purses Cynthia seemed to be aiming at in line 2. 'Forma' is then equated with 'pudicitia', a word which signified a modest and chaste demeanour in the unmarried, and the appearance of strict devotion towards the husband in a wife. It was paradoxical to equate the two: Ovid's cynical view, 'lis est cum forma magna pudicitiae' ('Beauty and virtue are at loggerheads') was closer to the normal view.[38] In Propertius's terms, 'pudicitia' can be 'forma' because both are discreetly ordered and of the surface.

'Nunc' in line 25 brings the action back from the mythic past to Propertius and Cynthia in the present. 'Istis' refers to rivals like the collection of suitors whom these heroines rejected.[39] 'Cilior', 'cheaper', 'more base than', recalls the quasi-commercial terms of the opening, and offers himself as a better bargain than these shallow-purses. 'Non vereor' pretends a confidence that seems uneasily over-assertive, but he proceeds to justify the claim in what follows.

Line 26 then gives a very strange definition of 'culta puella'. The phrase will naturally be taken to mean either a well-groomed girl or an accomplished

(37) V. e.g. Camps "The thought seems to be . . . . ". Shackleton Bailey's long note on the line points to the difficulties experienced by various editors here. .

(38) Heroides XI 288, quoted by Otto as proverbial, p.141.

(39) The line makes much better sense if 'istis' is taken to mean "rivals" rather than "these mythological characters"; the second meaning would also seem to be barred by the fact that 'iste' often implies contempt; Cp. L & S II B.

one.[40] What precedes would predispose towards the first, what follows to the second. But to please a single man has no natural connection with either of these meanings, for a Roman or anyone else. The point of contact is through a pun on one meaning of 'colo', to pay court to someone.[41] The past participle here must mean "to be the object of assiduous attention and respect" for the sentence to be initially plausible. Heavy weight is thrown on the initial 'uni' in this definition: if she is pleasing to one then she is sufficiently 'culta', has admirers enough. However 'culta puella' retains its more usual sense as well. The result is a proof by pun: the paradoxical equation can be made because the past participle of 'colo' can have these different meanings.

A serious point underlies this connection, which he will expand in what follows. A girl only wants to be 'culta' (well-dressed or refined) in order to be 'culta' (treated with high regard by her man). A virtuous girl will want this only from the man whom she loves in the quasi-marital relationship that is the elegists' ideal. The pun unites the two strands of the poem to this point, that she should not be over-dressed, and that she should be faithful to Propertius. But such seriousness would not be sufficient to redeem so outrageous and contrived a pun. If Propertius had stopped there he would have failed, because in a poem of this kind he could be illogical but not inept.

So in the next two couplets he attempts a sophistic justification. The poem might seem to contradict itself here, because 'cultus' was admirably lacking from the exemplary heroines, yet now Cynthia appears to possess admirable skills and attainments. "He apologises for his criticisms", Butler and Barber conclude lamely. But this is not a retraction. The poem up to 22 had given 'cultus' its most trivial range of meanings, mere ornaments and grooming. It could, however, refer equally well to more admirable arts, such as skill at poetry and conversational ability. A woman should seek to be 'culta' in this second sense, and not in the first. This is a distinction, not a retraction. Propertius's opposition to art was never total.

The form of words used to describe these accomplishments of Cynthia's then allows the third meaning of 'culta' to work, and justifies his paradox. Instead of saying that she writes fine poetry, he says that Phoebus gives her his songs. Here 'donet', "gives", is a vivid present, not the expected perfect, and the possessive 'sua', "his", makes it less easy to take the whole as a vague periphrasis for "the gift of poetry".

Phoebus gives actual, personal gifts to her, 'donet' recalling the 'munera' of line 4. So the paradox begins to be justified. To be 'culta' by these gods is to be 'culta', a person of accomplishments. The kind of attention implied by 'culta' is not of course specifically erotic. That would become a grotesque

(40) Cp. O.L.D. 3 and 4.

(41) O.L.D. 'colo' 7; "to cultivate the friendship of"; the past participle occurs in this sense, e.g. Livy XXXVIII li 2, though it is uncommon.

thing to say of the female Calliope. A god or great person could be 'cultus' by persons of both sexes.

'Carmina', poems, then gain a new role. They become the 'munera' appropriate to a girl like Cynthia, gifts to outdo Coan silk. This notion is of course a commonplace for impecunious poets. Propertius alludes to it more directly in a later poem, even to the point of mentioning Coan garments.[42] In the present case he leaves the connection with himself implicit, but the connection cries out to be made. He is the one 'uni' referred to in line 26 who makes Cynthia 'culta'; and he is of course a poet. Phoebus and Calliope are the two deities he normally invokes as the source of his own inspiration. In II i 3, perhaps in an echo of these lines, he names them both, but attributes his poetry to Cynthia instead. In the present poem a similar kind of shift of responsibilities seems to be taking place but of a more complex kind. The form of words could equally mean that she, inspired by the two gods, writes poetry; or, that Propertius is inspired by them to write poetry, which he gives her from them. The poems that he writes make her 'culta' in one sense, and they are hers as much as the ones that she herself wirtes. 'Ipsa puella facit' as he will claim in the later, more public poem. This is an inclusive ambiguity: both halves of it are true. She is 'culta' because of her poems and his own: both enhance her beauty more than Coan silk could do, though the process is ultimately the same, silks for fine purses, poems for poems.

Lines 29—30 praise other delights of their relationship. Again these are connected with deities: Cynthia is 'culta' by Venus and Minerva too, making four deities plus a poet who pay tribute to her. The polarities of the earlier part of the poem remain, but are combined in Cynthia. Lines 27—28 referred to more artificial accomplishments, poetry and music. This second couplet praises the less formal pleasures of conversation. Within these two couplets a similar contrast is lightly made. 'Libens' of line 28 seems to suggest a greater freedom to Calliope's lyre, as the birds' song was less trammelled than the rhetoric of the stream. Venus and Minerva, who rule in her conversation, are goddesses of Love and Wisdom, and perhaps by extension represent Nature and Art. But if such oppositions are intended at this point they are only just touched on. The emphasis now is on harmonious reconciliation.

These lines celebrate a genuine positive. 'Nec desit', is not lacking, suggests an abundance to which nothing could be added. 'Unica', made prominent by its position in the line, derives of course from 'unus', but also suggests 'rare', 'excellent'; excellent because single, a point that reinforces line 26.[43] This

(42) IV v 57 'qui versus dederit, Coae nec munera vestes'. This line is preceded by the first couplet of I ii. If this is a deliberate self quotation, as it could be, it would seem that I ii was Propertius's paradigmatic statement of 'carmina' = 'munera'.

(43) 'Unicus' often has the meaning "of unparalleled excellence", Cp. e.g. Livy VII xii 13 'eximius imperator, unicus dux', XXIV xxxiv 2 'unicus spectator caeli siderumque', etc.
A personification of 'gratia' here, which is what Enk seems to suggest, is probably inappropriate, but if there is one it is an addition to the number of divine beings who cultivate Cynthia.

84

'unica gratia' becomes 'omnia . . omnia . .' in the pentameter, one becoming all.[44] 'Gratia' refers to a quality that wins approval. 'Iucundis verbis' are words that both give and express delight. The couplet as a whole evokes a richly satisfying reciprocal relationship with the utmost economy.

The final couplet then contrasts the two kinds of adornment, natural and meretricious. This is done through a series of antitheses, between 'his (sc. gratiis)' and 'luxuriae', 'gratissima' and 'taedia', 'nostrae vitae' and 'tibi'. 'His tu', "with these things you", the ablative next to the pronoun, suggests the close relationship between the person and such attributes. 'Nostrae vitae', "to our life", is not a mere periphrasis for 'mihi'.[45] 'Nostrae' makes the phrase less egotistical than 'mihi' would be, and 'tibi' in the next line is' 'Vitae' recalls 'vita' of the first line: here it has acquired a much fuller significance. 'Gratissima' is a strong word, Propertius's only use of this superlative form. In all this there can be no distinction made between Cynthia and her adornment. She herself along with her attainments ('his tu') are a supreme source of pleasure and honour ('gratissima') to a life in which she too participates.

The alternative is dismissively referred to through the paradoxical 'miserae luxuriae'. Strictly 'misera' ought to mean cheap, wretched, worthless. 'Luxuria' may be vulgar but it would not usually be regarded as 'misera'. But this conjunction has been prepared for from the very first words of the poem, 'quid iuuat'. Yet despite the triumphant conclusion the poem ends on a slightly sour note. The confident 'semper' is undercut by 'dum', "as long as", in the pentameter. "For ever", it seems, may not last very long. 'Taedia sint tibi' is not the same as "you are indifferent to". 'Taedium' refers to a kind of disgust, the revulsion that could naturally follow excessive over-indulgence ('miserae luxuriae'). Perhaps Cynthia will be able to remain simple in dress and faithful to Propertius only in the lucid intervals brought on by satiety. The poem offers no certainty that Cynthia will change her ways, in spite of all that Propertius can say to persuade her. The hexameter promises a delightful union of self and adornment, beauty and fidelity, Propertius and Cynthia, but it is followed by a pentameter in which all the elements of the hexameter reappear inverted, and ordered by a different syntax.

The poem is a splendid but highly unstable achievement. The game with the Nature-Art oppositions is intricate enough, but Propertius manages to combine this with an appeal for fidelity as well. The feat is brought off by an incredible display of virtuosity, coruscating in multiple ambiguities and moving deftly between levels of meaning, but the strain shows. The near-failure of the 'cultus'-pun, for instance, is poetically right, like a tight-rope walker just managing to recover his balance. Even the audacious triple-pun on 'sinus' has a bitter edge. So the performance is not for its own sake, not a

(44) Propertius is rather fond of this paradox, versions of which appear at I v 12, xiii 10, 30, 36.

(45) Camps takes it as simply = 'mihi'; Rothstein and Enk have a view closer to ours.

mere game, nor "intellectual" in any limiting sense.

However, while the personal dimension should not be ignored, it should not be allowed to overwhelm the poem either. The depths are real, but so is the surface. The patterns generated are themselves richly satisfying, the witty and sensuous overt theme playing against the harsher more urgent tones of the latent theme to create new and complex harmonies. Propertius delights in the 'forma' of the poem: it is written with the combination of love and art, spontaneity and craft that it celebrates.

POEM III

Everyone must find this a delightful poem. The reasons may seem obvious, yet its combination of qualities is a rare one. The narrative is strong and clear, so that the situation can be imagined in vivid physical detail, but Propertius's mood is also evoked powerfully through rich images and stately diction. There is a potential disparity here. Propertius's imagination sees Cynthia as a splendid creature from the realms of myth, but his vision is compounded of love and wine. He has drunk too much, and is not in complete control of his physical self. Cynthia when she wakes is also all too human, petulant and self-concerned. The sense of a gap between illusion and reality could have been painful or ridiculous. Some critics have seen the structure of the poem in such terms, contrasting Propertius's tender romanticism with the harsh reality of Cynthia's reply,[1] but the poem is more subtle and generous than this. She may be shrewish, but he is drunk. A potentially subversive reality has been present from the beginning. Throughout the poem Propertius modulates between myth and reality, subjectivity and objectivity, evocation and exact observation. This kind of movement is embodied in a major characteristic of the poem's style, the constant juxtapositions of literal and metaphoric language. But the magnificent descriptions are not turned into burlesque by a sense of an intractable physical reality outside the dream. The experience is powerful enough to accommodate any such reality. Propertius's state of mind is dreamlike, but the experience itself is real, particular, conveyed with utter fidelity. The poem celebrates a relationship, not simply a fragile dream that had to shatter when Propertius or Cynthia woke.

The first 10 lines form a single sentence that encapsulates the diverse qualities of the whole poem. The initial three couplets described three heroines of myth. The diction is elevated, the syntax highly wrought, the movement supremely leisurely, three couplets making up a suspended structure that waits till 'talis visa' at the beginning of line 7 to complete the comparison. The fourth couplet, describing Cynthia, is coloured by the previous exotic images but describes her physical position in precise detail. The fifth couplet then turns to Propertius, beginning with the jarringly prosaic 'ebria', drunk. But Propertius's unfortunate condition is also described in more elevated terms, 'cum multo Baccho' instead of 'cum multo uino'. The apparently redundant phrase is obviously different in status to the descriptions of the heroines, but its effect is not quite burlesque. It gives Propertius a curious but real dignity. The two descriptions of his state correspond to two ways of seeing it, both of which are valid.

The three heroines are not chosen solely for being beautifully asleep. The first couplet concerns Ariadne, but the person alluded to in the first line is Theseus, her lover, described in the act of deserting her. The language here is exotic: 'Thesea' is probably a coinage, 'carina' is literally a keel, its trans-

(1) Especially Allen in his brief but very suggestive account of the poem (pp. 132–4) followed by R.O.A.M. Lyne.

87

ferred meaning of "ship" being elevated in diction,[2] and the construction with 'cedente' is remote from normal usage. The image of the "Thesean keel" withdrawing also has an erotic suggestiveness that 'Theseos nave' for instance would not have.[3] The erotic quality is reinforced in the next line by 'languida' used of Ariadne: the word suggests a post-coital lassitude.[4]

Ariadne is beautiful, and asleep, pathetically abandoned by her lover. The male in this myth is a cruel betrayer – like Propertius, according to Cynthia's accusation when she wakes. She even used the same word, 'languidus', of him as he uses of Ariadne. But Ariadne might not be entirely pathetic here. 'Languida' could imply the same accusation against Cynthia, since she ought not to be capable of being compared to someone who is 'languida'. 'Gnosia' perhaps connects her with the legendary sexual greed of females from Gnossus.[5] The couplet casts one or both of them in a glamorous but immoral erotic role.

The male is not mentioned specifically in the next episode, but 'accubuit' alludes to his presence. The word normally has a sexual significance for Propertius.[6]. The usual form of the myth concerned has Perseus transport Andromeda straight back to her father, leaving her no time for either sleep or love.[7] Propertius follows or wittily invents an alternative version, which allows her a brief sexual interlude on the crag. There is a slight uncertainty about 'duris cotibus' in this line. Some take it closely with 'libera', "freed from the harsh crag", which is grammatically possible and of course describes what happened. However, the other two couplets in this section give the place where the heroine is lying, and it is more satisfactory to read this phrase as a locative ablative.[8] A whole set of contrasts can then work between the two myths. Andromeda lies on a hard rocky bed, not on a soft shore like Ariadne, but Perseus is kind and faithful, and was to be a loyal husband. 'Libera iam'

(2) Cp. Ennius Annals. 478 'Labitur uncta carina' and Verg. Aeneid. V 115 etc.

(3) 'Carina' is sometimes used with 'sulco' – "plough" (Cp. e.g. Verg. Aeneid. V 158) ploughing is a common metaphor of sexual activity; e.g. ('arare) fundum alienum' Plaut. As. 874, Truc. 150. The connection is remote, but activated here by an obviously erotic context. 'Navis' is not used with 'aro' or 'sulco' before Ovid.

(4) So L.C. Curran resisted by Lyne p. 67, but only because his overall scheme for the poem does not accommodate it.

(5) Apart from Ariadne, there is her sister Phaedra and her mother Pasiphae; cp. Eur. Phaedra 337 and Barrett's note on the passage.

(6) See II iii 30, xx 36, xxxii 36, III xv 12: only IV iv 68 is not unequivocally erotic. Outside Propertius, the word does not have so clearly an erotic meaning.

(7) There is no indication of time span in Apollod. II iv 2, but Ovid's account (Met. IV 663–739) certainly allows no time at this point in the story.

(8) So Rothstein and Pasoli: Enk and B & B take the phrase with 'libera'.

on this reading refers to both physical and emotional release, the first due to the breaking of the chains that bound her to the rock, the second to Perseus's tender and faithful love.

The third couplet introduces an elegant variation into the prevailing structure, delaying 'qualis' till the pentameter. A more significant change concerns the heroine, who is a Bacchante not a lover. However, as the poem progresses Bacchus and Amor will emerge as collaborators. In line 14 Bacchus is to be referred to as 'Liber', which perhaps retroactively gives 'libera' in line 4 a similar implication. This Bacchante is tired from her revels, where the other two heroines were tired from their labours in love. At first the parallel seems incomplete, since there is no obvious lover to be seen. However, this is implicitly supplied through the pentameter. 'In herboso Apidano' is the relevant phrase. This has troubled many commentators, since it seems to put her actually in the river, so they kindly transport her to safety, and read the phrase as "by the banks of the Apidanus".[9] However, this would be a most unusual sense for 'in'. Two accounts are possible if the word has its normal sense. She may have dropped in a shallow, reedy ('herboso') river, and not noticed the fact, or she may have fallen in the dry, grassy watercourse which becomes the river when the rains come. The second is a more common image, and is not nearly as grotesque and implausible as the first one is.[10] The "grassy bed" connects better with the kind of place Ariadne, Andromeda and later Cynthia lie on.

The couplet as a whole then has ominous implications for both male and female. Bacchantes were notoriously vicious when woken, liable to tear the offender to pieces. This Bacchante, however, has fallen in the path of a river/god, who are commonly associated with tumultuous sexual passion.[11] This couplet is less elevated than the two previous ones — the Bacchante is anonymous — and closer to the reality which is to follow. Propertius will at least contemplate descending on her in a torrent of passion, and she will wake and rend him.

These implications of course are not consistent, and not fully serious. The poet is casting himself and Cynthia in a series of incompatible roles, through a succession of pleasantly whimsical fantasies. 'Visa', she seemed, immediately signals Propertius's self-consciousness, his capacity to distinguish the real Cynthia from these fancies.[12] The ostensible point of the comparison is her

(9) So Enk & Rothstein: Camps agrees, but points out in a suggestive note that a river would suggest to an Italian not only 'water' but the dry watercourse.

(10) Ovid seems to recall this passage twice. In Amores I xiv 21–22, the girl drops onto green grass: in I x 5, she wanders in 'dry fields': these two passages taken together suggest that Ovid interpreted the Propertian image as "in the (temporarily) dry but grassy river-bed".

(11) Cp. e.g. Soph. Trach. 9 ff., and Ovid Amores III vi 23 ff.

(12) Ovid's imitation of this (Am. I x 1–8) has the expected 'erat'.

'mollem quietem', but the verb 'spirare' contributes a slight tension to the description. The three preceding couplets all had a static, posed quality, even though the last especially described a potentially dangerous stillness. 'Spirare' does not itself refer to a violent action, but it is commonly used of strong emotions, like rage.[13] It is slightly odd to find it governing 'quietem': the verb suggests a vehemence of response that ought to be incompatible with true peaceableness. The pentameter then perceives Cynthia precisely and kinaesthetically, as she rests on unsteady hands, liable to jerk awake. This awareness that she might move and wake at any moment will remain with the poet for the rest of the poem, till the fear is fulfilled.

The next line brilliantly conveys the sensations of drunkenness.[14] 'Traherem vestigia' conveys a drunken kind of double-vision. 'Traho' usually describes action applied to something other than the agent. This makes his feet seem not quite part of himself. 'Ebria' is mimetically separated from 'vestigia' as though the drunkenness itself was distinct from his feet as his feet were from himself. 'Vestigia' instead of 'pedes' contributes to the sense of dissociation, as though he is looking at the trail he has left and inferring drunkenness. The sensations are recreated vividly, but the state of mind is too interesting and complex to be simply absurd. The phrase 'cum multo Baccho', substituting 'Baccho' for the physical cause, 'uino', implicitly claims that he is divinely inspired, a claim which has been made at least tenable.

Literal and metaphoric language, physical and divine interpretations coexist more unobtrusively in the next line. The couplet literally refers to slave-boys lighting the drunken poet home, fanning their torch to keep it alight. That fact would hardly be worth mentioning except for the metaphoric possibilities.[15] A torch is a common elegiac image for passion.[16] 'Quatere' has a common transferred meaning of excite, agitate. There are several boys but 'facem' is singular. There may of course have been only one torch between them, but this detail makes it easier to take the single torch as the flame of passion in the poet. So these 'pueri' have a double existence: as slave-boys (who disappear immediately from the poem), and as Love's representatives. In a later poem, II xxix, which seems to be a reworking of the present one, the 'pueri' are explicitly and solely a band of cupids. Their appearance here is more intriguingly ambiguous. However, the line in its metaphoric sense is wittily erotic: the reality it refers to has nothing to do with slave-boys.

13) See L. & S. II B3, where most of the examples are of strong passions: See also Lyne p. 68.

14) Edwards p. 132, sees a "transient ambiguity" in 'ebria', which for three words could be taken with Cynthia, seeming to accuse her of drunkenness. This could grow out of the implications of 'Edonis' and 'non certis manibus' — as though attributing his drunkenness as well as his lust to her.

15) Pointed out by Lyne p.63.

16) For 'fax' cp. I xiii 26 and I xvi 8, with our discussion of these passages.

A new section now begins, describing his attempts on Cynthia. Line 11 is wittily self-mocking, repeating, explicitly now, the claim that wine had not entirely dampened his sexual appetite. The word-order is again mimetic. 'Hanc ego' juxtaposes the poet with Cynthia, the object of his desires, but the verb is delayed until the next line. This turns out to be 'conor', emphasising the difficulty of the attempt rather than the successful attainment of his end. The protestation that intervenes between subject and attempted action betrays him by its over-insistence. 'Etiam' would not normally be required with 'nondum', and 'omnes' coming right at the end of the phrase tacitly admits that he may have lost some of his faculties though not all. The phrase as a whole may be an ironic echo of Catullus LI 5–6 'omnis sensus eripit mihi'. If so, Propertius would be claiming to be far more in control than Catullus, who was rendered incapable by the mere sight of his beloved. Propertius is a better lover for being partly drunk, or so the echo might claim.

Propertius completes the analogy with the heroines of myth by mentioning the couch on which Cynthia lies. The image is highly sensuous, justifying his claim in the hexameter that his senses were not wholly destroyed. 'Molliter' is the determining word. Its first function is to direct attention back to Cynthia after the prolix self-concern of the parenthesis. Grammatically it goes with 'impresso', defining a quality of both Cynthia and the couch.[17] Something into which Cynthia sinks is obviously soft like Ariadne's beach and the Bacchante's grassy bed. 'Molliter' transfers the quality to Cynthia and her way of sinking into this couch – 'impresso' otherwise could indicate something hard imprinting something soft, like a seal-ring marking wax. The image as a whole works kinaesthetically, through an awareness of her soft body pressing gently into the yielding couch. It is odd for a locatival ablative to be so far from the word it qualifies: 'hanc' is separated from 'impresso' by 7 words. But the main interruption comes from

(17) 'Molliter' presents a genuine difficulty here. Lyne p. 70 takes it with 'adire' ("he approaches 'softly' "), Butler with 'impresso', but understands that it is Propertius 'lightly pressing' on the couch (so Rothstein and Enk). However the commentators do not offer any explanation for their decision on this question: on the majority view, 'molliter impresso toro' will have to be a kind of instrumental ablative going with 'conor adire'. But 'impresso' is a past participle and so strictly ought to have occurred before 'adire' – and this would force 'adire' into a specifically erotic sense. The point of all this would be primarily stylistic, a play on the literal and metaphorical meanings of 'adire'. But the interpretation implied by Allen's translation "so soft a burden for her couch" which we follow, gives a much stronger image and is also more relevant to the poem's concerns.
Lyne's view implies that he takes 'impresso toro' as Propertius's action, though he is significantly silent on the point, since he would avoid an erotic meaning for 'adire' as he suggests that as yet Propertius only wants "to sit beside her without waking her".
This note may seem to crush a butterfly on a wheel: but the point is that there is in general a curious failure to argue for interpretations adopted even when these interpretations obviously need defense, both in the more traditional commentaries and even in many intelligent modern analyses of Latin poetry.

the parenthesis, which is meant to convey the disjointed syntax of the drunken raconteur. 'Molliter' recalls Cynthia's presence sufficiently for the original construction to be resumed as though no break had occurred.

The next 6 lines need to be taken as a whole, or the precise sequence and the status of the various actions will be missed. The tense of the verbs in particular is crucial. The past participle, 'correptum', in line 13, describes the powerful effect these two gods had on him before they issued their pernicious command. However, 'quamvis' along with the subjunctive form of 'iuberent' have signalled from the beginning that this command will not be obyed. The command is then presented, in lines 15—16, but is conveyed so vividly that it almost seems to have happened. Line 17 then insists again that it did not happen, and that Propertius would not have dared to waken her. The effect of the pluperfect 'ausus eram' here is to make this emotion a thing of the past, prior to the commands of Love and Wine. Line 18 then goes further back into the past, to the experience of her fury ('expertae saevitiae') which is behind his present fear ('metuens'). At the centre of this complex temporal structure is the couplet, lines 15—16, which has an unreal existence between the impulse and the fear, just as the poem's tenderness is poised between the 'experta saevitia' of the past and the 'saevitia' that is to come in line 35.

The action recommended by Amor and Liber is tenderly excessive. 'Temptare' in line 15 implies an act of assault, of an undetermined kind. The word-order is mimetic of the embrace it describes: 'positam', referring to Cynthia, is exactly in the middle, with 'subiecto . . . lacerto' on either end. 'Lacerto' is used in its strict sense here, the upper part of the arm, which is the part that would actually be under her if Propertius was lying as close to her as he would want. The role of 'leviter' is uncertain. It is usually taken with 'temptare', which is the main verb in the line, but it could equally well go with 'positam'. He is tempted precisely because she lies so lightly, offering the possibility of his sliding his arm underneath her. This action, of course, would have to be performed lightly, impossibly so.[18] The uncertainty with 'leviter' may be intentional, diffusing the force of the word through the line as tended to happen with the related adverb 'molliter' in line 10. The two lines are closely connected. Line 15 is an inflamed version of line 10. 'Temptare' is more aggressive than 'adire', while 'positam' conceives of her as more passive than 'impresso', and therefore more easily available. 'Leviter' is less sensuous than 'molliter' but is more appropriate for an effortless seduction: used of his actions it indicates greater dexterity, applied to her it suggests lack of resistance to his designs.

The pentameter (line 16) is more obviously strange: some have even wished to emend it.[19] The difficulty arises with the syllepsis on 'sumere', which some have felt is too bold. The word is used literally with 'oscula' but

(18) See Lyne p. 70.

(19) See Shackleton Bailey on this passage. Barber's Oxford Text obelises.

metaphorically with 'arma'. But this kind of sharp shift between literal and metaphoric is characteristic of this poem: the present image is only a particularly intricate and erotic example of it. The shift is not confined to the zeugma on 'sumere' either. 'Sumere arma', to take up arms, is metaphorical, but 'admota manu', by movements of the hand, is not only literal, it is probably crudely physical.[20] From line 19 a new movement begins, signalled by a sequence of imperfects.[21] What follows actually happened, unlike the hypothetical assault of lines 15—16. The tense conveys the peculiar quality of the experience. The imperfect is a continuous tense, which does not mark the beginning and end of an action. But the lines themselves are self-contained, and the actions described follow a kind of sequence, as Propertius grows increasingly careless. So the actions merge imperceptibly into one another, but time also passes. Propertius has managed to convey both a subjective and objective sense of the progression of time.

Following lines 17—18 he at first insists on how still he was. Line 19 emphasises his rigidity three times over, through 'intentis', 'haerebam' and 'fixus', but the repetition is only mock-serious. The choice of Argus in the comparison of line 20 is also witty. Argus had the intentness of a guardian, not a lover. Yet the choice is not entirely inappropriate. Propertius is preventing himself from molesting her. In terms of the myth he is both Jupiter and Argus, lover and guardian. He is of course really restrained by fear of her 'saevitia', represented here by Io's horns. 'Ignotis', unknown, as often in Propertius suggests something frightening.[22] The dangers this sleeper could present are never entirely forgotten.

Predictably he does not stay motionless long, but proceeds to offer her gifts. In line 22 the scene has become so real that he addresses Cynthia directly, 'tuis, Cynthia, temporibus'. Distinctions of time and place have been blurred. All his erotic feeling has been sublimated into a wish to adorn her. The verbs convey the quality of his feeling, delight ('gaudebam') and generosity ('dabam', 'largibar'). The apples he gives in line 24 have both literal and metaphoric import. They are both symbols of his love[23] and actual apples taken from the feast. 'Furtiva' recalls this literal source, but not obtrusively.[24] Propertius gives these gifts from cupped hands ('cavis

(20) See Lyne's discussion p.63.

(21) A heavy stop after 'saevitiae' is therefore preferable to the semi-colon of the Oxford text.

(22) Cp. e.g. I xvii 17, xx 15, xxvi 40, etc.

(23) For apples as love gifts, cp. Theoc. V 88 and Gow's note on the passage; 'The apple is a love token . . . . and to throw it at anyone is to make an overture'.

(24) Enk takes this reductively as = 'furtim': the apples are not exactly stolen, but he has taken them from the feast; cp. Cat. XII.

manibus').[25] The realistic detail conveys the quality of his love. The shape of his hands is both protective and designed to contain as much as possible, a natural symbol for his generosity and tender concern.

Lines 25–26 again refer to his generosity, but it is less sensuous, more consciously hyperbolic. 'Omnia (munera)' is juxtaposed with 'ingrato (somno)', his generosity with her ingratitude, though he tactfully blames this on Sleep, not her. 'Munera' is repeated in the pentameter, but the gifts are now perceived objectively, as physical objects over which Propertius has limtied control, not as expressions of his love. This line significantly departs from the pattern established in the previous five lines, since it has no imperfect verb with Propertius as subject. The apples roll out from his toga in spite of his intentions.[26] 'Voluta' is a past participle, which tends to imply that this action occurred before that of the main verb 'largibar'. The grand munificence was, it seems, partly involuntary. The image gives an impression of super-abundance which is not fully distinguished from drunken loss of control. The action is seen as ludicrous as well as tender.

This renewed self-awareness is increased sharply in the new section which begins with line 27. The change in his mode of awareness is signalled by a change in person and tense of the verbs. The perfects 'duxit' and 'obstupui' have a sharpness of temporal focus that had been lacking in the previous imperfects, as he is jolted out of his lingering mood by sudden anxiety. 'Duxit' is third person: the scene has become remote again, and he no longer imagines that he is almost directly talking to Cynthia.[27] 'Suspiria' recalls 'spirare' of line 7, and his sense of the instability of her sleep. 'Obstupui' reverts to his Argus-like immobility: he is now Argus as guardian, wary lest a phantom lover should seduce her in her dreams.[28]

The next couplet (lines 29–30) describes what he fears. The syntax here, however, is irregular. There is no verb of fearing to introduce the construction formally. Between them, 'obstupui credulus' and 'vano auspicio' communicate

(25) Lyne (p. 64) takes this as dative supposing that Propertius had forgotten what he wrote in v.8 — this in a poem so rich with internal echoes (of which Lyne shows himself well aware) and so precise about physical detail.

(26) The majority of commentators assume that the 'sinus' belongs to her (so Rothstein, Enk, Camps). Lyne argues (following Butler in the Loeb translation) cogently that it is the poet's (p. 65). The sheer absurdity of the usual interpretation seems not to have been realised by its proponents. The light sleeper who will wake to a moonbeam is apparently able to sleep through a pile of fruit rolling about her bosom!

(27) 'Duxit' is normally emended to 'duxti', an unjustified departure from the tradition. The impulse behind this emendation is a desire for consistency, but Propertius is not trying for such consistency in this poem; certainly he switches back to the third person for Cynthia in line 34. So for the sake of a spurious and uninteresting tidiness, editors have eliminated Propertius's skilful manipulation of persons.

(28) This is Allen's interesting suggestion.

the required emotion, and the emotion itself stands for the necessary verb, 'timeo'.[29] The effect is to give the fancies generated by his fears, indicating the fact that these fears are unreal, but leaving the whole process curiously disembodied, unattached to a specific and stated act of fearing.

The poem moves swiftly now towards the moment when Cynthia wakes, roused by the moon. The description again blends literal and metaphoric meanings. The moon's action is described accurately, but the moon is also wittily personified. The personification is clearest in line 32, where 'sedula' and 'moraturis' are juxtaposed, 'sedula' describing a bustling officiousness, 'moraturis', "disposed to linger", indicating a contrary inclination, as though the moon has been deflected from its customary diligence by Cynthia's beauty.

Line 31, however, has occasioned some difficulty to commentators, especially focussed on 'diversas'. This has usually been taken as either "opposite" (to the bed) or "open".[30] But both meanings are lexically nearly impossible. Both also affect 'praecurrens', which must therefore be given a weakened sense. Both are thematically irrelevant. The difficulty is resolved, however, when the same process of personification is seen to be acting in this line as in the next one. 'Praecurrens' is the key word, corresponding to 'sedula' in line 22. The moon is envisaged as hurrying past these other windows. 'Diversas' then has a common enough significance "of different kinds", referring to the immense variety of windows that the moon has passed over in its haste to see Cynthia.[31] The joke is a tender compliment, that works by projecting his own motives onto the moon, assimilating subjective wish to the objective fact.

Line 34 then contrasts harshly with the mellifluous flow and gentle imagery of the previous line. The opening 'sic ait' has a brutal brevity. This is immediately followed by 'molli', referring to the softness of the couch and recalling 'molliter' of line 12, but the effect is one of contrast. 'Fixa' similarly contrasts with his own devoted rigidity in line 19.

Cynthia then speaks directly. Her accusations are unjust, her tone self-pitying, entirely dissonant with what has gone before, though not unexpected. Allen and Lyne see this speech as the reality that shatters his dream, but there

(29) The commentators on the whole do not notice any grammatical anomaly here, but the couple is anomalous, and our account attempts to describe the agrammatical way the words are working. Lyne, pp. 73–4, has a slightly different and more elaborate account of the anomalous processes involved.

(30) B & B take it as = 'opposite' the bed (so Enk); Camps is judiciously unconvinced by either explanation. Shackleton Bailey following Postgage takes it to mean 'open' (so Rothstein), but fails to explain the consequent contradiction between 'praecurrens' and 'moraturis'.

(31) For this meaning of 'diversus' cp. e.g. Cic. Philippic. II 37 'sunt ea innumerabilia quae a diversis emebantur'; 'de Imp. Pomp'. 'varia et diversa genera et bellorum et hostium'; Ov. Met. I 40 '(flumina) diversa locis', – etc.

is more to the juxtaposition than this. Hostility is only one element in Cynthia's response. Her stance throughout is one of aggressive fidelity. The fidelity of course is used as a weapon, but it is her constant theme.

Cynthia's opening accusation, however, has proved obscure, partly because she exploits the same abrupt shifts between metaphoric and literal meanings as did Propertius earlier. 'Iniuria' seems to be abstract when it occurs in line 35, but becomes the subject of a vigorous physical verb in line 36. Line 35 is usually interpreted as "another's rejection of you has brought you back to our/my bed", but this is linguistically nearly impossible. 'Iniuria' otherwise always includes the notion of wrongful damage: Cynthia could not seriously mean that Propertius has been wrongfully rejected.[32] Nor is it clear how a "rejection" can expel ('expulit') someone: most translations in effect eliminate 'iniuria', replacing it by a sense derived from the verb. But 'iniuria' can be taken in its usual sense, as an offence, the nature of the offence being given by 'nostro . . . lecto', against our bed. Exactly the same phrase occurs later in Propertius, at IV viii 27. The plural 'nostro' here makes this their common bed, a proper symbol of their relationship.

The hexameter on this reading describes Propertius's unfaithfulness accurately if abstractly, as an offence against their bed. 'Referens' seems at first to offer a respectable reason for his return, his sense of having offended. But the pentameter by giving the abstract noun a physical and personal verb translates Propertius's supposed excuse into an unflattering concrete. The girl who threw him out is contemptuously reduced to "an offence against our bed", but Propertius is seen in an even less dignified light by this twist. Cynthia's accusation has also cleverly pre-empted one obvious line of defence. Propertius can no longer use the fact that he has returned as proof of his fidelity.

'Namque ubi', "for where else" is a slight retraction, indicating the hypothetical nature of her accusation. She is unable to imagine any other explanation, but he is given the opportunity of satisfying her. 'Meae noctis' asserts her absolute claim to his time at night (with 'meae' revealing a more one-sided concept of the relationship than did 'nostro lecto'). 'Languidus' of line 38 implicitly accuses him of being exhausted by his sexual activities, like Ariadne in line 2. 'Exactus sideribus' is a difficult phrase which probably has similar implications, with roots in the image of the torch in line 10. There the evening is far gone, and the torch (his passion) needs to be fanned. Here the stars, · the lights of evening, are used by a trope for night (the phrase is equivalent to 'exacta nocte').[33] The passing of night thus becomes an image for burnt-out sexual energies. The echo of line 10 has the effect, however, of

(32) Lyne argues for the only tenable interpretation which accepts the normal account of these words and particularly 'iniuria': he takes the word as an example of Cynthia's sarcasm, p. 75 of his article.

(33) See Enk and Rothstein on this passage.

denying her accusations. His "torch" was able to flare into flame: he is not 'languidus' and so has not been unfaithful.

The next couplet (lines 39—40) stresses how dutifully she has obeyed his demands — and how unfair those demands are. As Lyne perceptively observes, it is the complaint of a dutiful wife to an erring husband.[34] The next couplet continues in that vein. The image of weaving in line 41 recalls the most famous wife of antiquity, faithful Penelope, who delayed the importunate suitors by weaving and unweaving a cloth. Cynthia too goes to myth for images of herself. In the image Sleep is cast as her suitor.[35] The only departure from the austere morality of the myth comes through 'purpureo', an exotic and costly colour that gives a luxurious quality to her otherwise pious self-image.

In line 42 she calls herself 'fessa', recalling the same word used of the Bacchante in line 5. This time her image for herself comes close to Propertius's. Her reference to her "Orphean lyre" reinforces the connection between her and the Bacchante, for Orpheus was torn to pieces by maenads. Cynthia does not, of course, see herself as a Bacchante. Her words here are given this implication by recalling words she had not heard, thought by the poet over her sleeping body.

In lines 41—42 she briefly participates in myth, Penelope to his Odysseus, Orpheus to Sleep/Death, but in her the process is less explicit, elaborate, witty and controlled. The two couplets, lines 41—44, are organised around two imperfects, a shorter version of Propertius's own rich sequence from lines 19—25. The effect of the comparison is rather ungracious: Cynthia's version of the common experience is inferior by contrast, wilful and confused.

The poem closes with her dropping off to sleep at last. The image she uses has puzzled some commentators.[36] 'Lapsam' seems so close in meaning to 'sopor impulit' that it is hard to assign it a clear place in the sequence of events. Again the difficulty comes from a juxtaposition of literal and metaphoric meanings. In line 9 he was both drunk and full of Bacchus: now she literally falls and is metaphorically pushed by the wings of Sleep. The two alternative kinds of account coexist, with the fall first (indicated by the past participle) but the metaphoric in the ascendant. Her image of herself as 'lapsam', fallen, probably connects with Propertius's two images for her, in 'impresso' and 'positam'.

(34) P. 75 of his article

(35) Similarly 'ingrato sonmo' at line 25 is used for Propertius's beloved. somno' certainly and 'somno' perhaps should be capitalised to indicate the personification going on.

(36) Most comment on it: the more perceptive notice the real difficulties, e.g. Camps, who offers no resolution, and Lyne (p. 65) who sees it as involving a logical confusion which passes unnoticed by the poet because of the beauty of the line.

The metaphor used for sleep is attractively sensuous but is not simply decorative or conventional. Sleep performs his action 'iucundis alis', 'with delightful wings'; the image suggests a feathery softness, and 'iucundis' carries erotic overtones. But 'impulit', delayed till nearly the end of the line, is an unexpectedly strong word, describing a forceful action, certainly not the quiet approach one would have expected of Sleep. Cynthia wants to insist that she was overpowered by a superior force, raped rather than seduced.

This picks up an argument that has been implicit earlier, at lines 41–42, where she made wakefulness the sign of her fidelity, with Sleep the importunate suitor she held at bay. This line of argument lies behind 'cura' in the last line, which has been found awkward. 'Illa' naturally refers this 'cura' to the previous line, but it has not seemed clear why sleep should cause her worry. However, when Sleep is conceived erotically, as a kind of rival, her "fall" is something for Cynthia to feel guilty about. She immediately mitigates any criticism, of course. The irresistible force that Sleep exerted ('impulit') is part of her defence. 'Lacrimis meis' also pre-empts criticism: she wept for her fault at the moment of committing it (just as he had protested his dissociation from the lascivious promptings of Love and Wine at line 17). And obviously her 'lapsus', into sleep's arms, is as nothing compared to what she imputes to him. Her "confession" is really a way of implying her own much more rigorous standards of fidelity.

So although the woken Cynthia is not as tenderly loving as Propertius was to her, her anger and self-pity come from love. She does not reject Propertius. On the contrary the point of her complaint is how totally she is his. She offers this aggressively, but such aggression is not incompatible with passionate love. 'Dulcis ad hesternas fuerat mihi rixa lucernas' wrote Propertius in a later poem in praise of the sweet quarrels of love, 'nam sine amore gravi femina nulla dolet' ("for no woman is vexed unless she is deeply in love", III.viii. 1–2). Cynthia's reaction is not necessarily a douche of cold water to her lover as some critics have supposed. It is a complaint, but an erotic complaint, a devious but unmistakeable invitation to a sophisticated lover. Propertius could answer the main charge in the most delightful way possible, proving that he was not 'languidus' and that his fires still burnt. Perhaps, as Allen writes, "Cynthia returns in the reader's consciousness, to a realm of timeless being and permanent reality" (p.133): but perhaps Propertius returned to bed.

But the poem is open-ended, without the gnomic conclusion Propertius often favoured. He allows juxtapositions to do the work, not a simple juxtaposition of illusion and reality but a more interesting juxtaposition, of two consciousnesses. His own state of feeling is conveyed with a fullness and precision that would make a fine poem on its own. Hers is communicated indirectly but dramatically, through the words she speaks. The intricate web of echoes binds her statements to his thoughts, and by implication her to him, though not in an easy harmony. The poem presents his relationship with

Cynthia more directly than any other poem in the book, registering the sources of pain and tension which loom larger in other poems, but celebrating the satisfactions which are inseparable from the tension and make the pain worth enduring. It is witty, wry, tender, honest, distorting nothing, holding in suspension all the apparent contradictions of a complex mood and relationship: a great poem.

POEM IV

Cynthia of course provides the subject of this poem, but Bassus as addressee determines the tone and character. Essentially the poem is a defence of Propertius's love for Cynthia against Bassus's well-meaning incomprehension. Bassus's attitude as implied by the opening line seems akin to Gallus's in poems V and XIII, but Propertius engages much more closely with Gallus. In the present poem, vv. 11–16 praise and describe Cynthia and their relationship, but before and after this Propertius writes as though Bassus will not understand the central experience, as though it can't quite be talked about to him or in his terms.

So we need to know something about Bassus. He was almost certainly an iambic poet in Propertius's immediate circle. Ovid mentions him in the same line as the epic poet Ponticus, the addressee of poems vii and ix.[1] Ponticus's role as an epic poet is important to both those poems, so it is reasonable to suppose that Bassus's role as an iambic poet has some relevance for poem iv, and that Bassus's inability to comprehend the elegist's subject matter relates to the nature of iambic poetry.

Unfortunately we have no iambic poetry surviving by Bassus.[2] None of Ponticus's epic output has survived either, but we can guess more easily what his epics would have been like. We have much less to go on with Latin iambic verse. Greek iambics were scurrilous lampoons: Latin iambics may have in general been different in many ways, but it is safe to suppose that the form was still lower in subject and diction than both epic and elegy. Those of Horace's epodes which seem to owe most to the violence of Archilochus and the scurrility of Hipponax are pretty unedifying and combine moral and physical abuse in an unpleasant mixture.[3] Elegy would certainly be somewhere intermediate between epic and iambic poetry, and could define itself against both. Propertius found it easy to mock the representative of epic, by insisting on the reality and power of Love, in spite of the greater dignity of epic. An iambic poet would be harder to write against, too irreverent to be easily mocked or to be answered seriously. So against Bassus, Propertius wants to insist on the value and dignity of a love like his, yet cannot lapse into portentousness. This may account for the level the poem works at, and point to the kind of virtues that can be looked for in it: adroit management of a difficult case, sure control of tone and diction, and an unpretentious integrity and conviction.

The language of the opening is unadorned, and the 'multas puellas',

(1) Ovid Tristia IV x 47–8. See also our discussion of vii and ix below.

(2) Bardon, vol. II p. 52, throws up his hands in despair on Bassus – "nous n'avons aucune indication sur ses iambes".

(3) Cp. esp. Epodes VIII and XII; and see Fraenkel's comments on these poems, p. 58 f. in his book on Horace.

especially in view of their champion, are likely to be more notable for numbers and availability than for rare beauty and attainments 'light beauties', as he will put it at line 9. But the second line presents the apparent freedom Bassus is arguing as only another kind of constraint. 'Cogis' is the operative word. It implies not simply pressure, but a restrictive force.[4] To exchange one Cynthia for many light beauties is not freedom but a more constraining servitude. The idea is developed in the second couplet, where Propertius appeals to be left alone to his accustomed servitude. The implication is that his choice is not between freedom and slavery, but between kinds of slavery.[5] At this stage he seems to be making no claims for the relationship. He tacitly admits all that Bassus could urge against it, and claims only that nothing can be done about it.

'Tu licet' at the beginning of line 5 contrasts with Propertius's servitude. Bassus may praise these heroines: Propertius cannot. Line 8 gives the reason in an ironically ambiguous form. Either Cynthia is so beautiful that by contrast the fame of these heroines is diminished – or she forbids the mention of any potential rivals. 'Sinat', delayed till the end of the line and sentence, gives the sentence a twist in the direction of the second. Propertius can write only what Cynthia permits. He appears abject from this, and Cynthia seems arbitrary and vain.

It would be interesting to know what the tone of an iambic allusion to such heroines would be. This couplet (lines 5–6)[6] sounds surprisingly elevated in diction and intent, though 'quascumque' in line 7 is perhaps dismissive, with a similar force to 'tam multas' of line 1. Lines 9–10 sound more as if they refer to what one would expect from an iambic poet, and the effect of 'nedum' is perhaps something like "much less the kind of comparison you prefer to make, with common street-girls, not heroines from antiquity". What follows is a parody of the judgement of Paris. As in line 8, Cynthia's victory is not presented straightforwardly. The judge who would decide is described as harsh, not unjust. 'Inferior' gives the possible verdict, and 'turpis' the result. This is a strong word, indicating humiliation and disgrace, the ugly scene that Cynthia would make if she lost. Lines 21–26 will give a graphic description

(4) Cp. I i 8 and our note; v 19, 29; xviii 8, 30 etc.

(5) One may compare the similar notion in I i 31–2 and 35–6.

(6) Antiope had two consorts – Lycus, who rejected her in favour of Dirce (v. Prop. III xv, Hyg. Fab. 7) and Zeus (Apollod. III 42). Hermione also had two husbands, Neoptolemus and Orestes (Hyg. CXIII) the former of whom usurped Orestes' rights over her and was killed by him. It may be that Propertius expresses by the use of these two mythical heroines a kind of sympathy for an Antiope figure supplanted by a rival (this is what Bassus is trying to persuade him to do towards Cynthia) and simultaneously a fear of himself being supplanted, as in the story of Hermione. We suggest this rather tentatively, but as a rule, the myths in Propertius seems to have a close connection with their context – see our comments on V 15–20 and VIII 35–36.

of Cynthia's bad sportsmanship, and make explicit what is hinted here. Cynthia would win the prize because the judge (if he was Propertius) could not be so harsh as to award it against her, if she did not win it outright. Again Propertius has pre-empted any jibe Bassus might make, by presenting both Cynthia and himself in a ludicrous light.

With line 10 Propertius becomes more direct and serious. The beauty that would win or lose such a competition (all the beauty that a Bassus is capable of appreciating) is superficial compared to the source of Propertius's infatuation. 'Extrema' here, as elsewhere in Propertius, signifies an outside edge:[7] the word promises that Propertius's feeling will be much deeper, and be a response to more intrinsic qualities. Lines 13—14 then give the satisfactions that would be well worth dying for. 'Ingenuus' and 'decus' attribute the virtues of nature and art to her. 'Ingenuus color' indicates a natural beauty of complexion, the mark of good breeding. 'Decus' indicates not vulgar ornamentation, but the graces accruing from her many accomplishments. The line reads like a compressed reminiscence of the argument of I ii.[8]

Line 14 is difficult. Some commentators have preferred 'ducere', the reading of the inferior manuscripts, in place of 'dicere'. 'Veste' will then be the sheets that tell no tales, 'gaudia' the joys of the bed. The paradosis, however, yields a more difficult yet finally more subtle and satisfactory sense. The centre of the line is the juxtaposition of opposites, 'tacita dicere', her clothes which are silent, her poet who speaks. 'Gaudia' can by a natural metonymy be the sources of joy, and refer to those deeper causes of his 'furor' he has undertaken to reveal. Her clothes are "silent", concealing what arouses his passion, but the poet expresses what they conceal. The line begins with the sexual joy implied by 'gaudia', and finishes with the quieter pleasure of 'libet (dicere)', the intense pleasures of their love, and the milder satisfactions of the kind of poetry that can express it. Part of the achievement . of the couplet is Propertius's ability to be erotically suggestive without any trace of the kind of coarseness an iambic poet might import to such a description.

'Bassus' is also unaware of the real nature of the relationship, as lines 15—16 go on to insist. He tries to unloose ('solvere') a relationship that is intricate to a degree he cannot comprehend. 'Fallit' in line 16 does not simply mean to fail or be defeated.[9] The word indicates an error or delusion:

(7) Cp. XX 29, 50 and our notes. The construction with 'pars' seems reminiscent of the even more difficult construction in XXI 4. From the two it appears that for Propertius a statement of the form 'y+esse+pars+spatial adjective+genitive' expressed a causal or quasi-causal relationship between 'y' and the noun in the genitive with the spatial adjective indicating the strength of the relationship.

(8) See our discussion of this poem.

(9) As Camps and B & B gloss it in their notes.

the more Bassus tries to part this pair, the greater his mistake, the deeper his incomprehension. The whole phrase 'accepta uterque fide' emphasises the utter mutuality of the relationship, in contrast to the onesidedness implied by the early part of the poem.

The tone of the poem then lightens to a more bantering vein. He warns Bassus of the likely consequences of his mistake. First, of course, Cynthia will abuse him. Line 18 seems a curious periphrasis. 'Non tacitis' seems redundant, since 'voces' are of their nature not silent. But 'hostis' may perhaps be a pun on 'Hostia', which is usually accepted as Cynthia's real name.[10] 'Tacitis vocibus' might possibly then refer to the prudent suppression of real names that iambic poets may well have had recourse to on occasion, as elegiac poets certainly did, including Propertius in this very line. This would make it a nice joke against himself. It also presents Cynthia as outdoing Bassus at his own game, the art of invective. Her abuse is peculiarly powerful, since it would make him unwelcome at any girl's door.

But the next two couplets (lines 23–26) surprisingly describe her reactions if Propertius were to reject her. The extravagance of her response moves into burlesque. No altar would be too humble for her tears, he says in line 23, which could be serious hyperbole, but line 24 goes beyond that possibility, with its scatter of words designed to include every conceivable recipient of this indiscriminate weeper's tears. 'Quicumque' makes both 'qualis' and 'ubique' redundant, except to make trebly sure that no possible stone has been left dry.

Lines 25–6 are more serious, describing the real distress Cynthia would feel at the loss of her lover. The thought behind these lines is that of line 16: the relationship is mutual to a degree that Bassus can hardly realise. Though Cynthia might appear a harsh and tyrannical mistress she would be genuinely grieved if she lost Propertius. Propertius by implication could not endure her distress, since he immediately goes on to pray that their relationship may endure.

The general sense of line 26 is clear enough, but the precise construction is obscure. 'Deus' causes the difficulty, since 'rapto amore' seems to make the phrase 'cessat deus' (= Amor) redundant.[11] But 'rapto' juxtaposed with 'cessat', violent activity with cessation of activity, can help us to see how to distinguish between 'amore' and 'deus'. It is a lover (Propertius) who is in danger of being snatched off (with Bassus as intermediary). The narrative sequence is her losing one lover, and Amor then standing by idly, not providing another. Cynthia's grief is one reason for Propertius not to want to leave her: her keenness to replace him should he go is another. Again he is as disparaging about Cynthia as Bassus could be, yet derives reasons for fidelity from this.

(10) See Introduction. pp 5–15

(11) 'Deus' is usually emended to 'decus', and the apparent redundancy of 'deus' is essentially the objection that B & B urge against the MSS reading.

Line 27 is usually punctuated with a period after 'nostri'. 'Nostri' i;
then taken with 'amore', as = "my love (for her)". Formally this is awkwar(
and ugly, leaving 'praecipue nostri' attached loosely and obscurely to th(
previous line. Linguistically it involves some strain, since 'amor nostri' woul(
more usually mean "love of me".[12] The sense it yields is also unsatis
factory, "especially *my* love", a gratuitous arrogance whose complacency i;
out of keeping with the rest of the poem. If 'amore' = a lover, there is no wa}
of saving this line of interpretation. But the line can easily be taken as a syn
tactic unit, as most Propertian lines are, with only a light pointing afte
'maneat'. The prayer then is that Cynthia remain "ours", 'nostri' as usuall}
in Propertius suggesting mutuality. The last line then expresses total satis
faction with Cynthia, by way of warding off the possibility of its opposite
So a poem that begins with Bassus urging Propertius to leave Cynthi:
finishes with Propertius hoping that Cynthia will not leave him. It is ar
unobtrusively total criticism of Bassus's values and understanding of th(
situation. Yet the poem makes Cynthia appear more consistently ridiculou;
than any other poem in this book. It is as though Propertius wanted to show
Bassus that even if Cynthia were as ridiculous as the iambic poet could pain!
her, that would be irrelevant to their love. Shakespeare's Cleopatra, according
to Enobarbus, did

> Hop forty paces through the public street,
> And having lost her breath, she spoke, and panted,
> That she did make defect perfection. (A. & C. II.ii. 237)

Cynthia has a similar power to transcend apparent deficiencies. Obviously it is
not as rich or powerful a poem as those addressed to Cynthia or even Gallus,
but it has a quiet strength and integrity that commands respect.

(12) Cp. Camps. Modern editors have not considered any other punctuation of this line.

POEM V

This poem was probably among the last composed by Book I.[1] The relationship with Cynthia has apparently deteriorated. His distress and sense of deprivation as something that must be lived with is an essential feature of the background to the poem. The dramatic situation emerges quickly and clearly. Gallus has shown an interest in Cynthia, who is now completely estranged from Propertius. The poem goes through the process by which Propertius comes to terms with this threat. His response is never the expected resentment, and as the poem progresses he arrives at a kind of compassion or fellow-feeling, which is partly a ploy but goes deeper than that.

Gallus is the addressee of four poems in Book I. No one apart from Cynthia has more. The relationship seems much closer in all of these poems than with any of his other friends. There have been speculations that this Gallus might be the poet Gallus, but the tone rules out this possibility. The present Gallus is given a vividly recognisable and consistent character. He seems an intimate friend, gay, promiscuous (xiii.5), homosexual (xx. 5–6) and of noble birth (v. 23–4). But this nobility is not an oppressive difference in status, as is the case for instance with Tullus. Gallus was probably a kinsman, which would make for a closer bond, so that Gallus's status would confirm Propertius's and be available for raillery. It is important to the poem's success that it communicates a sense of the reality of the relationship. The continuous interaction with Gallus gives life to the details of the argument, and validates the curious generosity of the conclusion.

The opening exclamation, 'invide', already indicates a surprising reaction to Gallus's attempt on Cynthia. It ought to be Propertius who is 'invidiosus', full of envy and hostility. The word used of Gallus already implies that it is Propertius who is in control. 'Compesce' indicates control of things that otherwise may run wild, like horses or emotions. 'Molestas' could mean annoying (to Propertius) but in this context it stresses that these words ('uoces') are dangerous to Gallus. There is a total contrast between Propertius's position and his tone. He is watching his friend move in on his estranged mistress, but talks like a wise and disinterested friend.

The second line mostly implies that his relationship with Cynthia is stable and happy. 'Nos' is used without further explanation for Propertius and Cynthia, taking that partnership for granted. 'Pares' normally indicates a harmonious match.[2] As the poem progresses this comes to seem untrue, but Propertius still claims a special relationship with Cynthia (see lines 9

(1) The percentage of polysyllabic pentameter endings is 12.5; see Introduction pp 5–15

(2) L.A. Moritz argues that 'pares' in line 2 means Propertius and Gallus. But the fact that 'pariter' refers to them both in line 29 cannot alter the natural meaning here, and a different explanation of the relationship between the two words may be offered; see our account below.

and 31 especially), in spite of all appearances to the contrary. 'Cursu quo sumus', however, is more equivocal, though it still indicates that Propertius and Cynthia are on this course together.

Lines 3—4 pretend an even greater amazement at Gallus's folly, and fear for his safety. 'Quid tibi vis' is energetically colloquial.[3] 'Insane' intensifies 'invide'. With 'infelix' in the next line the story of his downfall has been told through the vocatives: first envy at Propertius's "happy" state, then the mad attempt, finally the inevitable woe. The tone is one of urgent warning, not resentment or fear.

Line 4 begins to make Gallus's folly evident. 'Ultima' as often in Propertius refers to death.[4] 'Nosse', to know, introduces the concern with kinds of knowledge that is to be important in the rest of the poem. He would not have hurried if he had known what he would find. He is being urged on by a blind desire for fatal knowledge.

'Mala' is the last word in line 4, evils revealed only at the end. A similar pattern of knowledge and ignorance is played out in the next line. The fires of love, true love, are unknown to him ('ignotos'), in spite of his imagined expertise (cp. line 7 in this poem, and xiii. 5). But 'ignotos' is followed immediately by 'vestigia', "footprints". 'Ferre pedes' would be the expected phrase for directing one's feet. The substitution of 'vestigia' for 'pedes' here draws attention to the traces left by this journey, a journey that Propertius has undergone without Gallus being any the wiser.[5] The footprints all go one way, like the footprints into the lion's den in the fable, but Gallus has not understood. The knowledge of a lover is incommunicable, or almost so, as Gallus will find if he foolishly perseveres.

Propertius then goes on to point out the irrelevance of Gallus's previous experience of women, from line 7. She is nothing like these others. 'Vagis' indicates one point in which she is different. They are shallow, unstable, changeable, like Gallus himself: she isn't. 'Collata' seems pleonastic after 'similis', but its effect is paradoxically to neutralise the comparison. Its force is something like a parenthetic "if we were to compare her at all", which implies that we would be foolish to do so.[6]

Another difference is her anger. Line 8 works with deceptive mildness

(3) Enk's parallels for the use of this phrase imply a conversational or colloquial tone.

(4) Cp. e.g. I xvii 20, II x 34, III vii 56, etc.

(5) 'Ferre vestigia' is a slightly unusual locution for 'ferre pedes'; see O.L.D. 'ferre' 3: the meaning of the latter phrase is "direct one's feet". It is not necesssary or rewarding to try and read this line in any literal sense (one may compare the difficulties that such a reading involves in e.g. Camps). The ordinary metaphor contained in 'ignes' carries all the force necessary for an understanding of the line.

(6) Commentators have felt this 'collata' to be superfluous, but Shackleton Bailey cites a somewhat similar case from Varro L.L. IX 28 'non bos ad bovem collatus similis et qui extis progenerantur inter se vituli?'

towards a sting in the tail, which is achieved at the cost of some syntactic strain. It begins with 'molliter', softly, but this is followed by 'irasci non solet', which immediately inverts it. 'Solet illa' then seems to promise a general statement describing her unusual behaviour. We would expect to have some vague generic dative following this, or perhaps 'mihi', but instead we get the startlingly specific 'tibi', the particular Gallus suddenly placed in the firing line as the object of Cynthia's habitual fury. The trick, which is what it essentially is, has puzzled commentators. Some have suggested that 'tibi' is an ethic dative, loosely attached to the sentence as a whole, but this is made unlikely both by its emphatic position, and the presence in the same line of 'irasci'.[7] Others have accepted the inferior Mss' 'sciet' for 'solet', but this would be mere padding, a suspicious quality in an emendation of Propertius. But the only word Propertius has used unusually in the line is 'solet', where he has put the present predictively, for its shock effect, as though Gallus is already the object of her rage, instead of Propertius.

The paradosis gives even odder sense at line 9, so the early emendation of N2 is usually accepted, 'tuis' for 'ruis', and 'votis' for 'nostris'.[8] 'Votis', vows or prayers, would make Cynthia here the deity invoked, as well as the object to be gained. This would normally be difficult, but would be plausible here, since Cynthia is going to be represented as a kind of goddess. But the paradosis is not as implausible as is usually supposed. 'Si forte ruis' makes good sense, picking up and intensifying 'properas'. The difficulty concerns the next clause, 'non est contraria nostris'. However, it is not hard to see what this must mean. It seems an extraordinary thing to say, but then, Propertius's attitude in this poem is deliberately strange and paradoxical. The present tense 'est' has her in a state of permanent readiness for Propertius's friends, ominously easy to approach. The thought is similar to that of the conclusion: she is dangerously likely to respond to his advances. 'Nostris' is "to our friends", Propertius's and therefore Cynthia's. This seems to make friendship with Propertius a sure way in to Cynthia's favours, a bitterly ironic reference to his present influence over her. This is not at all an impossible sentiment for Propertius to have written, so emendation isn't justified.[9]

The brief calm of her welcome is followed by a multitude of cares. Line 11, his introduction to the state of bondage, still seems pleasant. He will lose sleep, but that isn't so bad for a lover. His eyes will be held in bondage by her beauty, but the diminutive 'ocellos' suggests the eyes of a favoured lover. Line 12 then begins' to build up Cynthia as a supernatural force. 'Feros'

(7) Enk, e.g., considers 'tibi' to be ethic; Camps argues against this, but considers it the only possible construction with 'solet' and so adopts the reading 'sciet'.

(8) By e.g. Rothstein, Enk, Camps.

(9) On the conventional reading of lines 9–10, 'at' is somewhat difficult to translate since it does not oppose a clause of the same syntactical order. On the Ms reading, it opposes simply and obviously the equally main clause 'non est contraria nostris'.

initially could be a noun, wild beasts, giving the image of a goddess taming savage nature, but 'viros' at the end makes these savage captives men. 'Una' makes this power seem even more supernatural. They are masculine and many, she is only one, yet tames them. Since they are wild she seems a beneficent force, but 'alligat', binds, indicates irresistable force, not mild persuasion. 'Una' can also suggest excellence, which would be appropriate here.[10] 'Animis' probably goes with 'feros', fierce willed, indicating the level her power works at, on hearts or minds not bodies.

But in the next couplet, lines 13—14, Propertius predicts the inevitable rejection, with Gallus coming to him for advice. 'Informem notam' in line 16 focusses on some of the contradictions in his new condition. 'Notam' recalls 'vestigia' of line 5: he cannot speak, but his appearance is eloquent, for those who understand. These marks are ugly, obscure, ('informem'), but paradoxically the previous line, which describes these disfiguring griefs, is beautifully formed, nearly a "golden line", perfectly shaped, and accomplished: 'formosa'. Its effect is to make a work of art out of Gallus's distress. The line is perfectly expressed though Gallus is unable to say a word, and is himself 'informis'. But the content of the work of art that the lover becomes is grief beautifully disposed and its form is the image of a prison, with one pair of words, epithet plus noun, enclosing another pair, with the verb enclosed by both.

A new phase of Gallus's existence begins with 'tum' in line 19, as he accommodates himself to his new condition. 'Nostrae' now is Propertius and Gallus, united in their common subjection. Lines 21—2 contain a mild jibe against Gallus: Propertius now will at least be spared Gallus's going on so endlessly ('totiens') about his pallor and generally emaciated state.

Lines 23—6 mock another source of Gallus's confidence, his noble birth. It will no longer be of any help to him, and will even add to his disgrace. Lines 25—26 are difficult. 'Parva' could mean either "too small", as at xviii. 17, or "even a small". The first is less likely, since both 'vestigia' and 'culpa' would have to be interpreted in a strained sense merely to accommodate it. 'Culpae' could refer to either the crime of his being in love with Cynthia, or the crime of straying from her. The first is unlikely here. Propertius has been insisting on the dangers, not the disgrace of this affair. Cynthia was probably not the prostitute she is usually supposed to be[11] but even if she was, a man with Gallus's reputation as a womaniser would have had little to lose from the liaison. In any case, this interpretation makes nonsense of 'parva'. Gallus is choked with sobs, unable to speak, doesn't know who he is or where he is. What "small traces of guilty passion" are there left to reveal? So 'culpae' must mean the crime of straying, or more exactly Gallus's well-

<hr>
10) Cp. e.g. Cic. Verrine II iv 13 'quae tibi una in amore atque deliciis fui' and Verg. Aeneid V 704 'Nautes unum Tritonia Pallas quem docuit'.

11) See Introduction pp 5—15

known tendencies in that direction.[12]

Having imagined Gallus in his own situation, Propertius can now admit his present distress and powerlessness. 'Tum' in line 27 might refer to what immediately precedes. The sense then would be "after such an indiscretion I could not console you". This might hint that this was his fault, too. Otherwise 'tum' would pick up 'tum' from line 19, and the couplet would refer to his general inability to help.

Lines 29–30 describe the only comfort left to them. 'Pariter' picks up 'pares' from line 2. But the yoke-mates, the "we", are Propertius and Gallus now, 'miseri' indicating the nature of the bond that unites them, their common grief. Strangely there is real comfort in this. 'Socio amore' is a shared, companionable love. Each makes their love this for the other. The underlying thought is not unlike I.ix, 34: 'dicere quo pereas saepe in amore levat'. The picture in line 30 is faintly ludicrous, with its erotic overtones. Gallus's desire to clasp Cynthia to his breast will lead to his embracing Propertius instead. The image is meant to be ridiculous, since Propertius wants to dissuade Gallus, but at another level the attraction of it is real for Propertius. One of the aims of the poem has been to create a Gallus who will understand Propertius's state. This is more clearly the drive of poem XIII as well. There, Propertius wants to believe that Gallus is in love in the same way as he is himself. He wants Gallus's companionship in his love. There is a curious strand in Propertius feelings towards Gallus – one should compare also the oddities of poem X.[13]

This has prepared for a neat conclusion. The final couplet warns Gallus off not because Cynthia won't listen to him but in case she might, a fate no man would wish on his friend. But the impressive quality about this ending is its total lack of self-pity or resentment. Cynthia has become 'mea Cynthia' again, the certainty of the relationship re-affirmed. In these two lines she seems more than ever a kind of divinity, the effect already prepared for by lines 7–12. 'Non impune' is an almost amused under-statement, like the earlier 'molliter irasci non solet'. The final emphasis is not on the pain he suffers, but the divine status of the inflicter of the pain. The note the poem ends on is not resentment at all, but a kind of worship.

(12) Cp. O.L.D. x 3 b, where the examples show 'culpa' as sexual misconduct in straying from one's established partner or from an established virginity.
   The meaning of the word here gives commentators considerable difficulties. Camps sets out the three alternatives with admirable clarity. Our view agrees with B & B and implies a reaction on the part of Cynthia similar to that described in poem IV 19–22.

(13) The test of the pentameter endings gives no indication as to the relative dates of composition of the three poems v, x, xiii. For reasons discussed below we consider that xiii must be earlier than x. Poem v seems to represent Gallus as more of an adept in Propertian love than he is in xiii and his plight seems in general more desperate, so it seems likely that it comes later than xiii also; there is a play on 'una' in both poems (v 12, xiii 30) which is more explicit in xiii, and this should point to an earlier date of composition for that poem. The almost divine character of the mistress in xiii (29 'proxima Ledae') is also much more explicit than in v. But v could be seen as composed either before or after x without involving any tonal contradictions.

POEM VI

Tullus was clearly the most influential man in Propertius's early acquaintance.[1] He seems to have been a friend, perhaps from the same neighbourhood, kindly disposed and in a position to help. Propertius wrote two poems to him to refuse invitations – two out of the four poems to him in Book I do this, a proportion that suggests some tensions in the relationship. Of these two, XIV is the more assured and successful. It is an early work, rich in imagery and formal structure, seemingly untroubled by the attraction of Tullus's greater wealth. VI in contrast is more troubled, even confused, yet it is also strangely opaque. There is no hostility towards Tullus, but there seems a veil between the two men, as if Propertius cannot be entirely frank. There was a veil between them in XIV too, but it was so richly embroidered, so satisfactory an object, that the non-relationship didn't matter. The obvious contrast is with the poems to Gallus. These are much more direct and almost colloquial. The antagonisms are more overt, but Propertius can engage in debate at the deepest, most intimate level. In VI it seems that Propertius doesn't believe that Tullus could understand his experience of love, the force that made him decide to stay with Cynthia. But there is also a sense that Propertius finds it hard to admit to himself or Tullus that he found this invitation distressingly difficult to refuse.

Before the poem opens, Tullus has evidently asked Propertius to accompany him on a trip abroad. This must have been rather tempting. It could have been the start to a respectable public career for Propertius. The form of the poem is not exactly a refusal of this invitation, as is usually supposed. Details make it clear that Propertius originally accepted, and is now withdrawing. That makes the decision evidently a closer, more difficult one for him to make. The debate with Cynthia was obviously the crucial exchange, but that is outside the poem. Propertius announces his decision to stay, but hasn't dramatised it, as though unwilling to display the real tensions.

'Non ego nunc vereor' indicates that he has changed his mind,[2] but defends his decision from one possible interpretation. He isn't suddenly afraid. The language of this first couplet is more direct than the opening of XIV, and seems to describe the journey Tullus has in mind. His destination was probably the Roman province of Asia, so he would go through the Adriatic and the Aegean. In line 1, 'noscere' is used for sailing, the first of

(1) His uncle was probably L. Volcacius Tullus, who was one of seven consular colleagues of Augustus in 33 B.C. This man was a 'nobilis', the son of a consul, and was appointed proconsul of Asia in 30/29 B.C., an appointment which is alluded to in line 19 of this poem. The family was from Perugia in northern Italy; for Propertius's birthplace, see our discussion of poem XXII. (For L. Volcacius Tullus, see Syme, pp. 242 and 466.)

(2) Cp. I ii 25 and xix 1 and our accounts of these passages.

many words for knowing in the poem. This sees the journey as an experience, rather than as an achievement, which was probably the attraction it had for Propertius.

Line 2 is much more elaborate in diction, but still describes part of the real journey. Lines 3 and 4, however, describe scenery that Tullus would hardly have visited. The Rhipaean mountains were far north, in Scythia. Ethiopia ('domos Memnonias') was far south, a hot desert region. This is an elaborate way of saying that Propertius would go to the ends of the earth with his friend. The unusual comparative, 'ulterius', usually normalised to 'ultra' by commentators, has a similar point: he would go beyond these and even further than beyond.

The next four couplets describe the scene with Cynthia. Line 5 is mimetically tangled. 'Me' is the object of two verbs, 'complexae' and 'remorantur': she clasps him tight, and her words restrain him. This is a kind of double determinism. But 'complexae' is closer in the line, the more urgent and physical reason. Tullus doesn't have arguments like that. The next line is less witty, but the way it works is not entirely clear. 'Preces' at the end seems to be the pivot, with all the other words in the line defining these prayers. They are vehement ('graves') and frequent ('saepe' going better with 'preces' than 'mutato').[3] Again there is a physical dimension which Tullus's arguments lack. She changes colour, a sign of intense passion. Strangely, it will be this that will make it so hard to leave her, her passion not simply his.

Her line of argument in lines 7–10 does not sound especially winning. 'Argutat' in line 7 is a key word. It indicates a shrill, harsh, incessant voice. Cynthia is not made to seem attractive here, and something of Propertius's resentment comes through in this hostile description. 'Totis noctibus' is a comic exaggeration of this effect, a device similar to the coinage of 'ulterius'. 'Totis' indicates that the harangue lasted the whole night, the ablative changing the duration into a point of time which is completely filled by her voice.[4] We then find in line 11 that he capitulated after less than an hour. Line 7 has made it seem to last without a break for nights on end, because that is what it felt like.

But 'ignis' at the end of the line 7 gives a different impression. This is the fire of intense feeling. It is not an exact synonym for 'amores': Propertius uses it more to describe a passion, where that is seen as all-consuming.[5] The use of the word here acknowledges the strong and painful feelings which lie behind her harangue. It is a strange object for the verb 'argutat', since it is so far from anything that could seem like indirect speech. 'Argutare' is related to 'arguere', to make plain, and perhaps has something of that meaning here. She is unpleasantly shrill, but makes the real intensity of her feeling plain.

(3) This is essentially Rothstein's interpretation and disagrees with Enk and Camps.

(4) Cp. 'toto anno' in line 7 poem I and our comments.

(5) Cp. e.g. I ix 17, III vi 39, etc.

111

Again it is what she is and does and feels that is more important than what she says.

'Queritur' in line 8 introduces a clause in indirect speech. The form is as careless of logic as she is. She might claim that if she were deserted, then the gods are proven not to exist. But 'relicta' is a past participle, seeing herself as already abandoned even though Propertius is at that moment in front of her. Line 9 then gives her strongest line of attack. 'Denegat' is a strong word, deny vehemently, but this is ambiguously either a threat or a complaint: she is no longer his mistress, she has withdrawn all her allegiance, or, she is no longer his, he no longer cares for her. The pathos is as powerful as the threat, though they work together.

The pentameter here has one word so unexpected that many have wanted to emend it, 'irato'.[6] But there is nothing unacceptable about it except that it is surprising. It implies that if she was aggrieved, he was actively angry. The debate was more two-sided than he has so far indicated, though his tone has conveyed his considerable resentment. It is strange that otherwise he didn't want to tell Tullus how hard he argued. The single word 'irato' implies a whole poem, which he didn't choose to show to Tullus.

Lines 13–14 then describe the satisfactions he sacrifices for Cynthia's sake. The two infinitives indicate two different kinds of cognitive act. 'Cognoscere' is a more intellectual act, the proper response to "learned Athens". 'Cernere' indicates close attention, a discriminating response to the rich and ancient monuments of Asia. They pick up 'noscere' from line 1. All three words indicate the kind of appeal the trip would have had for him. They point to the experience and knowledge he would have gained, not to any hopes he might have had of advancement.

But that hypothetical satisfaction is outweighed by the distress he knows he would feel at seeing Cynthia on the wharf as he left. 'Convicia' is a derogatory word: he still does not pretend that her rage is pleasant or graceful. The participle 'deducta' probably indicates that the boat is launched and on its way, so that the cheeks she tears at with maddened fingers must be hers.[7] As with 'ignes' in line 7, it is the destructive fury of her passion that finally destroys his resistance. She is neither beautiful nor frightening in her rage, just affectingly, intensely hurt.

Lines 17–18 give the reason that finally proves sufficient. These are her accusations that his own love was not genuine. An intricate little narrative is often invoked to explain line 17: the ship ready to sail, but held back by a contrary wind, Propertius trying to kiss her, and Cynthia saying he is

(6) So Enk, Barber, Camps, etc. all print 'ingrato', the reading of the 'deteriores'.

(7) Most commentators, if they notice the passage at all, think that it is Propertius's cheeks that will suffer (see Camps) but such an action would be more likely to encourage him to go than persuade him to stay – not that Cynthia would have been incapable of it, but Propertius would have re-acted differently.

only doing it to kill time.[8] She would probably have been right. But this speech is hypothetical, meant to be a general accusation, not a particular little mini-narrative. It is much easier to suppose that the ship is now under way, as 'deducta' has implied, and that 'debita' refers more widely to all his attempts to prove his love to her, in the days or weeks preceding departure. A hostile wind springing up just as they were about to depart would be fortuitous, but departures were normally planned well ahead to catch the best seasons (see e.g. VIII 9–12).

The poem now changes direction sharply, and turns to Tullus and his prospective trip. Tullus's uncle, C. Volcacius Tullus, went to Asia as proconsul in 30–29 B.C.[9] Actium had been won only in 31 B.C., so there was an important job to be done in restoring harmony to the region. Line 20 refers to this task as a worthy one. The phrasing unobtrusively but strongly endorses Tullus's task as wholly right and beneficent. 'Vetera' claims venerable origins for the regime. Repeating 'veteres' in line 14, it seems to suggest that the ancient wealth of Asia belongs to Rome by rights equally ancient. 'Oblitis' juxtaposed to 'vetera' suggests that anyone who supposes that this regime is new has simply forgotten: the opponents of the regime were the innovators.[10]. 'Sociis' is the establishment euphemism for a kind of subject people[11] (like Russia's "allies", Hungary or Czechoslovakia). The deft expertise with Augustan propaganda suggests how mentally prepared Propertius was for the expedition. In this poem he endorses imperialist conceptions more than amatory ones, though his decision has gone the other way. This suggests how much of him wanted to go with Tullus, though he does not dramatise the conflict directly.

Line 19 is flatteringly optimistic about Tullus's political prospects. He must aim to go beyond his uncle. 'Meritas' insists that the uncle has deserved his high office, so that to out-do him Tullus must reach an even greater eminence by merit too. Some commentators have interpreted this line literally, as advising Tullus to take the head of the procession, in front of the

(8) Compare the strain of Camps's description, an unnatural 'reductio ad absurdum' of this account.

(9) Enk and B & B cite in support of the proconsulate Dittenberger 'Inscr. Gr.' 458 38 ff.

(10) What precisely 'vetera iura' means is difficult to say, and it may be essentially a propagandist phrase. Pompey had originally organised the administration of the province of Asia and established constitutions for the cities. Perhaps the deposition of petty tyrants is sufficient to justify 'vetera iura', though the strategic changes brought about by Antony were left unaltered. See Syme pp. 300 ff.

(11) The euphemistic deterioration in meaning had started however well before the time of Augustus; Cp. Cic Verrine II 1 15 'rogatu sociorum atque amicorum populi Romani', at a time when Sicily was a long established province. The word is perhaps more debased in its application to Asia, since this was notoriously one of the provinces from which Rome and Romans drew a large amount of wealth.

113

axes of his uncle's office, as though Tullus did not know the proper place for him in the procession, or would do himself some good by slipping out in front.[12] With lines 21—30 the sense of conflict goes out of the poem. Propertius contrasts the two modes of life, Tullus's and his own, in general terms, as though there was never the possibility of their ways coinciding, so that there was never a decision to be made after all. The contrast is elegantly managed, and some mild mockery of Tullus now becomes possible. In lines 21—2 there is a hint that Tullus's imperviousness to love is unnatural. 'Aetas' was the prime of life, when love is normal and natural to man.[13] Tullus, it seems, was too busy. 'Cura' in line 22 gives rise to a slightly ludicrous image. Normally the word could refer straightforwardly to the cares of office, but the implicit comparison with a lover brings out its specific meaning in elegy, the cares of a lover. The object of this love is his 'patria', which 'armata' personifies, and conceives as an armour-plated maiden, a much inferior object of erotic attention than a lover's silk-clad mistress.

Propertius's description of himself in lines 25—30 is fairly conventional, displaying his feeble condition in a self-gratulatory way. 'Animam reddere' in line 26 normally means to give up one's life, but 'longinquo periere' suggests a very protracted dying, one which many people find desirable. The image continues the implicit contrast between the two kinds of life, in favour of the lover's. The soldier fears death, the lover enjoys his "dying". Line 30 closes the comparison by seeing love as a kind of warfare. The metaphor allows him to see himself as having gone on a campaign, an alternative one to Tullus's. 'Fata', like 'fortuna' in line 25, ascribes the decision to a force outside himself, which came into existence long ago.

Lines 19—30 are symmetrically arranged, three couplets to Tullus, three to Propertius, with the two kinds of life linked by common imagery. It is formally organised in Propertius's early style, something of a reversion here to the manner of a poem like XIV. Lines 31—2 seem reminiscent of XIV in content, too. XIV has an imaginary Pactolus running through Propertius's bedroom. Tullus is to have it in reality. This seems like a complimentary allusion to his previous poem to Tullus.

'Mollis Ionia', soft Ionia, sounds surprisingly effete for Tullus the brisk career officer, a suspiciously soft substitute for his 'Patria armata'. But these lines are the myth of 'Pax Augusta', offered to Tullus but clearly very attractive to the poet too. 'Arata' suggests how the myth of the golden river is

(12) So Camps, whose reason against the other interpretation is that Tullus would be too young to have such an ambition. But this is an exhortation, not a statement of fact: Tullus might not have shown Camps's admirable humility and realism. Enk and Rothstein offer a different solution of the difficulty, and have supposed that Propertius could not possibly have had the bad taste to make such an exhortation if the elder Tullus was actually to be in Asia at the same time as the younger. So they suggest that it is the past eminence of the uncle that is being referred to: but this is again taking the poet's words much too seriously in the wrong sort of way.

(13) Cp. Cic. Pro Caelio 27 ff., and esp. 28 'Datur enim concessu omnium huic aliqui ludus aetati, et ipsa natura profundit adulescentiae cupiditates'.

114

made true by Roman rule: the legendary river of gold runs through a land actually made golden by the industry that Roman rule allows. The periphrasis with 'carpere' in line 33 suggests motion which is also at the same time the assertion of possession. Whatever part of the land or sea he passes over will become Roman by the act. Line 34 makes the idea of an easily accepted rule explicit. The phrase implies that nothing will have to be done to assert this power. Roman rule is already welcomed. No-one has to be threatened, imprisoned or bribed: Tullus only has to be there.

This imperialist fantasy of effortless power is offered to Tullus, but it shows how attractive the idea of the expedition was to Propertius himself. The last couplet indicates genuine regret. The hard state he lives under recalls 'fortuna' in line 25, and 'fata' in line 30, but the descriptions there implied his acquiescence in his fate. In this last line the tone is closer to resentment. A hard star in Propertius would usually be one that made his mistress scorn him. (cp. 'adversos deos' in I. 8). But in this poem it is clear that Cynthia is not at all hostile; that is what is hard about his fate. This poem is the closest Propertius gets in Book I to regretting that he is a lover and elegiac poet, rather than a man of affairs or imperial ideologue.

POEM VII

Ponticus seems to have been the epic poet in Propertius's circle, at least during the period of Book 1.[1] Both the poems Propertius addressed to him seem motivated by professional rivalry, designed to score points on behalf of elegy against epic, its more prestigious rival. Poem VII is probably the earlier of the two.[2] It is an ingenious and intelligent defence of Propertius's commitment to elegy, and though it is a performance rather than a manifesto, it does indirectly reveal something of Propertius's conceptions of his art.

The main argument is a version of the immortality argument.[3] The elegiac poet will live on because successive generations of young Romans will be lovers, and so will recognise their experience in his, and value his poetic mastery of it. Epic poetry for all its grandeur is irrelevant to real human concerns, as Ponticus will find. (History has crushingly endorsed Propertius in this exchange, for Ponticus hardly exists outside Propertius's two poems.) This is not a commonplace account of the function of poetry. Poetry in this view does not teach by delighting, nor clothe universal truths in telling images, as in standard classical accounts of the role of poetry.[4] It is highly personal and self-involved, giving such pleasure as it gives by its insight into the lover's pain. Experience correspondingly is incommunicable unless shared. The experience creates the original poetry, and the poetry to survive must be created afresh out of the experience of new readers. The conception of poetry underlying this is surprisingly "modern" in its tacit denial of universals, and its acute sense of the autonomy of individual experience.

The first eight lines form a carefully organised unit in which the two poets, with the kinds of poetry, are significantly opposed. Even the syntax makes some implicit contrasts. When we come to line 5 we will find the poet in the nominative case, the subject of a series of verbs, and immersed in activity which will generate poetry almost as a by-product The only verb in the first couplet is 'dicuntur', the passive vehicle of Ponticus's grand theme. The highly-wrought periphrasis in the second line implies grandly heroic activity, of course, but does it entirely through nouns and adjectives. Ponticus does act in the next couplet, as subject of 'contendis'. This is the major activity of the epic mode, as love is of elegy, but Ponticus does not do battle physically, with heroic foes, only metaphorically, with dead Homer's reputation.

The words 'primo contendis Homero' initially seem high if conventional praise. "Homer" virtually meant "Prince of poets". But the praise is

(1) See I iv 1 and our note 1 on this poem.

(2) The percentage of polysyllabic pentameter endings in vii is 30.7 and in ix 5.9. Independently of this, ix reads as a natural successor to vii. See Introduction

(3) For other versions of this popular theme cp. e.g. Hor. Odes III xxx, Ovid Amores. I xv, etc.

(4) This is the general implication of Hor. Art of Poetry 343 'omne tulit punctum qui miscuit utile dulci', etc.

pitched so high that the final effect is equivocal. 'Primo' is usually understood as referring to quality rather than time,[5] but that would be almost redundant of Homer. The natural meaning of 'primo' as "first" also makes better poetic sense. The Homer who wrote the Iliad is the first Homer, Ponticus by implication already the second.[6] This is all prefaced by the formulaic phrase 'ita sim felix', a form which seems to have been used to reinforce superlatives. But reinforcing phrases of this kind are liable to suggest exactly contrary motives: "methinks the lady doth protest too much".[7]

The next line (line 4) hints at the danger that threatens Ponticus's ambitions, and introduces the immortality theme. 'Sint modo fata' sounds like the beginning of a wish for long life, since the Fates controlled life and death, not poetic inspiration. The object of this wish, however, is Ponticus's poetry. Behind this lies the recognition that though poetry may confer a kind of immortality, not all poems are immortal. Some can die, as Ponticus's were in fact to do. Propertius offers to ward off this possibility from his friend, but does so in terms that for the first time suggest the strengths of the elegiac mode. 'Mollia' comes from the world of elegy, where hard-hearted mistresses must be softened by soft verse (cp. 'mollem versum' at line 19 and also the later IX 12). If the Fates are like mistresses, to be persuaded not impressed, then the techniques of an elegiac poet are the relevant means of achieving poetic immortality.

In line 5 Propertius turns to himself. Initially he seems self-depreciatory. 'Consuemus' makes his activity seem unremarkable, hardly worth mentioning alongside Ponticus's epic battle with Homer. The poetry that comes out of his troubles is described with dismissive vagueness, 'aliquid', "something", seen purely functionally, as a means to win over his mistress.[8]

But the humility is only apparent, and tactical.[9] The claim of artless sincerity contained in the opposition between 'ingenium' and 'dolor' of line 7 has affinities with the standard topos in rhetoric, where a speaker claims to

(5) By e.g. Enk and also apparently by Rothstein.

(6) Shackleton Bailey quotes in his Appendix a similar sort of word play involving a comparison between Vergil and Homer:—
Anth. Lat. 740   De numero vatum si quis seponat Homerum,
                            proximus a primo tunc Maro primus erit.
                    at si post primum Maro seponatur Homerum,
                            longe erit a primo quisque secundus erit.
Cp. also the comparison between the Iliad and Aeneid made in Prop. II xxxiv 65–6.

(7) Camps suggests that it has "an affectionately ironic tone".

(8) Camps's comparison with Tibullus II iv 15 is apposite.

(9) Cp. Cat. I which is addressed rather ironically to Nepos who he pretends is a much more important writer than himself.

be an artless man speaking unpremeditated words from the heart.[10] This was a 'captatio benevolentiae', meant to win a sympathetic hearing for the speech that would follow. Propertius is laying the foundations for his claim to be valued more highly than Ponticus, offering himself as spokesman for all who have felt love's pains.

'Aetatis tempora dura' contains a key premise in the argument. 'Aetas' here must stand for a particular stage in the life of a man, obviously early manhood, when love is a common condition.[11] The naturalness of this stage, as a normal stage in a man's development, is what will guarantee Propertius the successive generations of readers that will assure his immortality. The opening word of line 5 had begun this generalising process. 'Nos' instead of 'ego', as in the English editorial "we", gives Propertius's experience a representative status. As lover he is 'nos', though as poet he will be 'ego', as in lines 11, 13 and 21–22, a supremely successful individual talent, In retrospect, 'consuemus' can also be seen to be pointing to his source of strength, his fidelity to the habitual and usual.

With lines 9–10 Propertius makes the transition from his present painful condition ('conteritur') to his joyful commitment to it, and his hopes of poetic fame from it. Lines 11–14 then explain how this will happen. The two couplets have a clearly marked parallelism of structure, 'me laudent . . . me legat', pointing to the two classes of reader who guarantee his fame, and their different reasons. 'Doctae puellae', fair readers of poetry, will praise him for having been able to please his mistress (Cynthia is the indirect object understood of 'placuisse'), and will approve of his stoic endurance of her unjust threats. This will then give immense value to his poetry ('post haec' indicates consequentiality) for unsuccessful lovers, who will turn to it avidly. 'Nostra' in line 14 again insists that the experience is common, after 'me solum' of line 11 has claimed that the success is unique. 'Cognita' then gives the special quality and function of Propertius's poetry. The lover's suffering has been entirely understood by the poet, and is recognised immediately by the 'neglectus amator', whose condition is helped ('prosint illi') by this insight.

At line 11, 'doctae puellae' is usually taken as dative after 'placuisse'. But this is formally most unsatisfactory. It makes the apparent parallelism between the two couplets awkwardly irrelevant, and 'laudent' has to be taken as impersonal, a rare use at best, and especially unsatisfactory here, since Propertius in this poem is specific about who will value his poetry. His admirers will be those who are acquainted with love, not everyone. The sequence implied by 'post haec' would also become nonsense. People in general may finally come to respect his verse (cp. line 22), but only after he

(10) Cp. ad Her. II – 'Exordienda causa servandum est . . . ut non apparata videatur oratio esse'. For interesting contrasts between 'ingenium' and 'dolor' in modes of persuasion, see Shackleton Bailey on this passage.

(11) Cp. 'aetas' I iv 21 and our note. Others interpret it differently. Camps, evidently with great strain, glosses 'the trials I endure day in day out', where 'aetas' = 'vita'.

has been championed by lovers.

The poem then begins a new, less serious argument 'ad hominem', suggesting that Ponticus himself may fall in love. There would be some basis for the thought in the previous argument. Since Propertius, the lover, can show himself to be as ambitious for fame as the epic poet, Ponticus may corrrespondingly fall in love. But the suggestion really works through its disrespectful implausibility. In line 16 Propertius pretends to hope that such a terrible thing will not happen to his good friend. The line concerned is possibly corrupt and has been variously emended.[12] The paradosis 'eviolasse' would have to be a coinage, with 'e' redundantly intensifying an already very strong word. The point would be the totally destructive power of love, with the absurd coinage consistent with the mocking tone. It would be a parody of a heightened epic strain, a linguistic sledgehammer to smash a nut. That would explain why it is unparalleled.

Lines 17–18 are certainly a brilliant deflation of epic. Seven whole armies turn out to be useless to him, simply do not hear him when he has need. They have an impotent kind of immortality ('in aeterno surda iacere situ') waiting for their poet to give them existence. But their poet is otherwise engaged. Lines 19–20 then cheekily predict that Ponticus will not be able to adapt poetically to the new kind of poetry he will want to write. He will be too old.

So the poem pretends to include Ponticus among Propertius's future admirers. The second last couplet envisages his future fame. 'Iuvenes', people at the time of life when love holds sway, will be unable to refrain from saluting the master of love-poets. Physical death is acknowledged, in 'sepulcro' and 'iaces', but is transcended by the admiration of a new generation who fell the same passions ('ardoris nostri').

The final couplet switches from this self-gratulatory fantasy to a more modest appeal, that Ponticus should at least not despise the verses of lovers. He then returns to the attack with a light-hearted warning that recalls the argument of lines 15–20. Middle age will be no safe-guard from Love's power. On the contrary, Love is a debt, on which the interest piles up. 'Faenus' in this context is faintly ludicrous, an unpoetically mercantile image serving a pseudo-argument, whose malicious point is to contrast Ponticus's middle age with the youth of Propertius's admirers.

Propertius deliberately ends the poem on this personal note. to avoid any suggestion of portentousness. But the apparently extravagent claims for his art have served as a witty vehicle for unpretentious but interesting reflections on poetry. The result is a pleasant and successful poem of its kind, the enjoyable product of what must have been a valuable professional association for the young Propertius.

(12) None of the emendations offered has met with general currency since none is at all persuasive in its own right. The lack of real consensus here suggests that there is no justification for departing from the paradosis. On the Mss reading 'quod' will be an internal accusative of 'eviolasse'.

POEM VIII

This poem regrettably requires a rather lengthy preamble. Before we can even begin to discuss it, we have to decide whether we are discussing one poem or two. The Mss are unanimous in offering us a single poem, but Lipsius in the sixteenth century made a second poem start at line 27. All subsequent commentators have accepted this division, whether they describe the last 20 lines as a pendant or a coda or as a separate companion poem.

Initially, the two main reasons for dividing the poem at this point appear strong:

1. Cynthia is addressed as 'tu' during "viii (a)", but referred to in the third person throughout "viii (b)".

2. The first part reads like an attempt to persuade her to remain in Rome, but in the second part the poet talks as though she has decided to stay. In lines 27 and 28 'hic iurata manet' and 'vicimus' seem unequivocal on this point.

Poetically speaking, however, "viii (b)" is left in a most unhappy position by this arrangement. Its first line is an implausible start for a Propertian poem, even when its first words 'hic erat' are altered to the reading of inferior authority, 'hic erit', as is often done.[1] The poem that follows is a distressingly bathetic corollary of "viii (a)" — 20 lines of unrelieved self-congratulation, a mere expansion of the sentiment contained in 'vicimus'. To point out this sad consequence of Lipsius's decision is not of course a proof that he was wrong, but combined with respect for the paradosis, it provides a motive for looking again at the reasons for the Lipsius line.

These reasons turn out to be far less conclusive than they have appeared. Cynthia in fact is referred to in the third person in the last three lines of "viii (a)" as well as throughout "viii (b)". This should be a reason for dividing at line 24 or 25 if at all, not at line 27. Moreover, the Mss are no guide to punctuation. The decision to open inverted commas before 'licet' in line 25 is indicated by the text, but the decision to close them after line 26 is an editorial one for which no reason is usually given. Obviously, if the poem ends there, the speech will have to end as well: but if the speech does not end, nor can the poem.

If "viii (b)" is not direct statement but a (hypothetical) speech introduced by 'dicam', the status of 'hic iurata manet' changes. Cynthia could not be simultaneously present but preparing to go, and absent but resolved to stay. However, Propertius himself could say, or say that he will say, a variety

---

(1) 'Hic erat' is very difficult if there is a division here. It must mean either "she was here all the time" (B & B) — as though she had been hiding and Propertius had not noticed her (and immediately forgot her again, since he continues as though she was not present): or "she was here (ten minutes ago)" which is a pointless remark to begin a poem with. 'Hic erit' "she'll be here in a minute" is only slightly less gratuitous.

of things about her and to her that are not strictly true or compatible with each other. He does so even during the course of "viii (a)". Distressed lovers and poets are not as bound by logic and fact as classical scholars must be. So Lipsius's division turns out to be not only not necessary but actively misleading. It is usually taken as a response to a clear break in the sense, but there is no obvious break at this point until the division has created one. In fact it is only a strategy for dealing with the strangeness of 'hic iurata manet' and what follows; and it is not the only solution possible. Unfortunately it seems to have imposed itself on subsequent scholars as an independent fact, which generates another problem of its own, the problem of the relation of the two parts created by the division. After four centuries, it is time to return to the real problem again and try out an alternative solution.

If we read the whole poem after 'dicam' in line 25 as a single dramatic utterance, there are no consequent linguistic difficulties. The poem that results is manifestly a single poem, daringly innovatory in technique, but with clear roots elsewhere in Propertius. It falls naturally into two parts, but the division occurs after line 16 not line 26. In the first part he supposes that she can be persuaded from going: in the second he tries to come to terms with the fact of her imminent departure. An emotional logic underlies the two parts and makes a natural progression from one to the other. At first Propertius pretends incredulity that she should go and pictures the dangers of the voyage and the harshness of the destination. Then the possibility becomes more real to him and he first invokes a storm to prevent her sailing, then imagines himself deserted on the shore. The second part reverses the mood but continues on the imagined journey, giving blessings instead of curses, following the proposed voyage with propitious images. Then he turns to himself, offering now an image of total trust, so naively total that it communicates the exact opposite, the acute doubts he was unable to control. He casts himself in a stock role, that of the simple-minded faithful lover lamenting on his mistress's threshold, meaning to defend her honour, but in the process providing all the evidence for a hostile judgement.

Technically a close analogue for this poem and a probable ancestor, is I xvi, where another naive lover persists for 28 lines of lament in believing that only the mistress's door is keeping him out: the mistress herself surely could not be responsible! The present poem also sets counterfactual direct speech in a framing narrative, but marks an immense advance in the use of the technique. The speaker in lines 25—46 is apparently naive and trusting, but is also self-consciously defending the indefensible. The whole speech is a virtuoso piece of double-meaning, justifying the paradox of Cynthia being present while absent, and therefore faithful while (possibly) betraying him. The difficult phrases that caused Lipsius to mark a break across the poem itself can be seen to have an entirely different significance, marking a deep division within the poet himself that continues throughout the poem.

Another way of understanding how Propertius arrived at the form of this poem is through seeing its relation to the propemptikon form, a rhetorical form appropriate to a departure.[2] This form, as described by the fourth century rhetorician Menander, consists of two parts. First, the speaker tries to dissuade the traveller from going by emphasising the dangers of the journey. Then he accepts the fact that the person is departing and wishes him well. A propemptikon allowed formal expression to the conflicting emotions of the one left behind, and this probably drew Propertius to the form. This does not mean that the poem must be merely 'rhetorical' and fictitious, as some have supposed.[3] On the contrary, some of the details make it essential to assume a specific occasion for the poem. The organising presence of a form like the propemptikon does not of itself deny the reality of the occasion: it only guarantees a degree of objectivity and self-consciousness in ordering and presenting the material.

The abrupt opening, "Are you mad, then?" plunges us dramatically into the latter part of a debate. Propertius skilfully implies the gist of the earlier argument and the relationship out of which it grew. The important qualities to note are the surprising confidence of the tone and the insecure foundation on which this rests. The tension between these two elements is to provide the dynamic of the rest of the poem. Just before the poem opens, she has obviously repeated her decision to go, and his first reaction is closer to incredulity than despair. The next question "does not my concern concern for you hold you back?" implies that if she were not mad, it would. This is the question of a confident lover: the rejected one knows that his 'cura' constitutes no hold on a girl.[4]

The tone of the second line seems equally confident, but introduces a new element even more disturbing than her departure; the rival. Propertius seems to be wittily pretending that Cynthia's choice is between a man (Propertius) and a country, and not between Propertius and the man she is evidently going to accompany there: but the wit is also a way of not yet admitting that the man exists. However, his existence is perhaps hinted at through 'gelida', a word which was commonly used of the coldness of old

(2) Cp. Enk on this who also quotes the relevant passage from Menander (Spengel, Rhet. Gr. III p. 397 12). There is not much evidence for the form prior to this poem of Propertius, though the fact that the poem does comply more or less with Menander's formulation suggests that the propemptikon was already established as a type by the time of the poet. R.O.A.M. Lyne on this poem suggests that the poem of Gallus referred to in Verg. Bucolics X may have been a propemptikon.

(3) Cp. Lyne. Lyne and others suggest that Gallus's supposed propemptikon may have provided the idea and some images for Propertius.

(4) 'Mea cura' is probably best taken as 'my love for you' as is the implication of the pun in I vi 22; 'cura' in this context obviously includes anxiety for her safety. If the phrase means 'your love for me' (as Rothstein and Enk think) it implies even more strongly that their relationship is a good one.

age.[5] The rival's sexual prowess would thereby have been discounted before he has even appeared in human form.

When he is mentioned directly in the next line, he is of course dismissed peremptorily. 'Tanti', does he seem so important to you?, is immediately answered by 'iste', a distancing, usually contemptuous pronoun, and 'videtur': he could only "seem" not actually be of any great worth. 'Quicumque est' is usually taken as dismissive too, but more probably acknowledges his rank, before going on immediately to disregard that as sufficient reason for undertaking such a dangerous journey, especially without Propertius.[6]

The startling thing about this rival is that he then totally disappears from the poem until line 37. An accidental oversight by the poet?[7] That would be an incredibly gross error, especially in view of his subsequent reappearance. If the silence is significant and deliberate on the poet's part, it must signal either a total confidence in Cynthia, or more probably a willed blindness arising out of either his need to believe in her or his reluctance to admit the rival's existence. The tactic is similar to that in XVI, where the lover acknowledges the existence of a successful rival for only a couplet (lines 33–4), otherwise maintaining the fiction that the door alone has been unkind.

So the rival is a potent if silent presence in the poem. What can we know about him and his relationship to Cynthia? The questions may seem to lead outside the poem, but some kind of an answer to them becomes part of the meaning of this poem. If Cynthia was a courtesan, as is usually supposed, he would be a rich rival. But this is very hard to reconcile with the poem's tone. Propertius is less confident than he pretends, but still talks as Cynthia's accepted lover. How could he do so if she was about to depart with another man for an indefinite period, far from Rome and Propertius? Only one possible rival could conceivably possess her so long and so exclusively without arousing intolerable jealousy and resentment: her husband.[8]

The next four lines (5–8) are a standard feature of a propemptikon, a warning of the dangers of the journey, but the two couplets also grow naturally out of the images and mood of the preceding couplet. So 'vento quolibet', any wind that comes, is intensified into the unpleasant weather he predicts for her. But these gloomy forecasts are not presented simple-

(5) On 'gelidus' see O.L.D. 2.d.

(6) The question of the implications of 'quicumque' is a question of tone and citation of parallels is really no help in determining it. The earnestness of Propertius's question is increased if one considers the word to be equal here to 'However important a man he may be': this fits in much better with 'tanti'.

(7) Lyne, who was the first to draw attention to this curious feature of the poem, regarded it as proof that the incident was imaginary.

(8) See also below p.   and introduction pp 5–15 for a discussion of Williams' hypothesis concerning Cynthia's status.

mindedly. 'Vesani murmura ponti' is reverberantly epic:[9] here there is a hint of the mock-heroic in the sudden elevation of tone. This contrasts markedly with the prosaic factuality of the pentameter, with its mention of the hard decks that the soft Cynthia will have to lie on.

The next couplet arrives in imagination at her destination, made to appear unattractive and unsuited to a girl of her delicate upbringing. Again the hexameter is highly wrought compared to the pentameter, and the image in 'positas fulcire pruinas' is so strained that it has given difficulty to commentators. The image expected is of Cynthia treading on hoar frost, but 'fulcire' ought to mean action in the opposite direction, to support. Most commentators have despaired of making sense out of the image if 'fulcire' has anything like its usual meaning, but efforts to parallel 'fulcire' – to press down are unconvincing.[10] However, an image is indeed possible if the word means 'support': this would be of Cynthia's delicate feet covered with the oppressive weight of layers of frost, like a sentry who has stood all night, frozen to the spot. This image is of course grotesque and ridiculous, but the poet is not aiming to flatter Cynthia here.

With line 9 the tone changes, becoming more urgent as the thought of her departure becomes more real. So the bad weather that would make Illyria unpleasant is invoked closer to home, to prevent her departure more directly. But again the tone is not simple-minded or self-indulgent. The image of 'double' ('duplicentur') is imitated in the language itself, by having two words for winter, 'hibernae' and 'brumae', and the whole periphrasis 'hibernae tempora brumae' takes even longer. This is witty virtuosity, not portentous afflatus: he can mock the extravagance of his own reactions.

Each successive appeal, from lines 9–16, tacitly acknowledges the failure of the previous one, as his imagination follows the remorseless sequence of her departure, or step by step comes to admit its inevitability. So lines 9–10 attempt to hold back the seasons; lines 11–12 then refer to the moment of departure. The sailors are aboard, and Propertius invokes the sands as a last desperate resort. His awareness of the futility of this appeal is part of its effect. It is signalled in line 11 by the jingling assonance of 'Tyrrhena' – 'harena', virtually an internal rhyme, unusual for classical Latin verse.

The choice of 'Tyrrhena', indicating a port near Rome, perhaps Puteoli, has puzzled commentators, since someone sailing for Illyria would normally leave from Brindisi. One can only say that we do not know her reasons for leaving from Puteoli. But the choice is given a poetic function by the image

(9) See Enk on this passage.

(10) The only parallel from Augustan Latin is Verg. Bucolics VI 53 'Ille latus niveum molli fultus hyacintho': but an examination of the context here shows that Vergil is indulging in some fairly innovatory 'cacozelia' (see Donatus 'Life' 185) and so the lexical oddities displayed here cannot reasonably be used to support interpretations of passages where there is no obvious imitation.

associated with it. The appeal to the sands to grip the cable magically has some rationale for Tyrrhenian sands, since the Tyrrhenian coast was Rome's coast, especially subject to Rome's influence. In lines 31—2 the connection between Propertius and Rome is made explicit. It may be epic to go to Illyria, but a good Roman girl should stay at home with her Roman lover out of sheer patriotism. The sands near Rome can be hopefully invoked to procure that end.

Lines 13—16 are the culmination of the first part and of its complex underlying logic. Both couplets have been variously misunderstood and emended, but no emendation is required.[11] Again the progression is made through a common image which changes its emotional value. Line 12 attempted to ward off a hostile breeze that would have both dispersed his prayers and at the same time carried her away. This breeze now becomes 'tales ventos', the plural form adding to the impression of the increased force that 'ventus' has in itself compared to 'aura'. 'Tales' makes these winds that proved hostile to him potentially hostile to her.

This development is entirely uncharacteristic for a propemptikon. It sounds ominously like the beginnings of a curse, although he might still be wishing only for a strong following breeze to speed her journey out and back. That would be a common wish in the propemptikon form. Editors have reacted uneasily to this ambiguous but potentially outrageous sentiment and have altered the paradosis accordingly, to make Propertius more polite and amiable towards Cynthia (the most popular changes are of 'non' to 'tum' with Heinsius, which exactly reverses Propertius's sense, or of 'talis subsidere' to 'tali sub sidere', a much less violent emendation, though perhaps a slightly odd expression).

But Propertius of course knows that his resentment is highly improper and even dangerous in terms of the propemptikon form whose basic principle was a magical belief that wishes have power over the elements. So the next couplet (15—16) reverts to himself and asks for permission ('patiatur') to express the resentment he cannot contain ('libertas quae velit ira loqui' as he puts it in I i 28). 'Et' of the Mss is correct, but heavy punctuation is necessary after 'ratis' to make it clear that 'patiatur' is parallel to 'videam' rather than dependent on it.[12]

'Sed' at the beginning of line 17 marks the crucial switch from resistance to resignation required by the propemptikon form. In Propertius it also marks his return to the form, a return to his rhetorical responsibilities which he had been in danger of forgetting. However, he prefaces this return with an ungracious reminder that he knows what Cynthia is really like ('periura').

(11) Cp. Lyne who used similar reasoning in defending the paradosis here, but chooses the reading of the 'deteriores' in line 15, 'patietur'.

(12) One might prefer 'sed' or 'at' rather than 'et' in line 15, but 'et' is possible with a somewhat adversative force especially after a negative in the previous clause: see O.L.D. 14.

Yet as so often in this poem, even an explicit statement can imply its opposite. The rudeness he can allow himself argues paradoxically the strength of their relationship. The confidence and trust of the opening was not all pretended, and Propertius was not wholly committed to gloomy weather forecasts. There were always reserves of love and even trust that could motivate the benedictions that follow.

Galatea, the nymph he calls on first, is a slightly surprising choice. Neptune, or a whole troupe of Nereids might have been expected.[13] One reason for the choice might be biographical. If Cynthia really was leaving from Puteoli, her ship would go through the straits of Messina. Galatea, as a Sicilian deity, would thus be an especially relevant guardian. But the form of words suggests another function served by Galatea here. 'Via', like the English 'way', can refer either to a physical journey or to a way of life. So 'tuae non aliena viae' could suggest that she should be an exemplar as well as a guardian deity (the two notions of course not being entirely exclusive anyway). The Galatea myth involved Acis, a youth, and Polyphemus. In both Theocritus and Ovid, Polyphemus pleads his wealth and tries to minimise his proverbial ugliness.[14] Galatea rejects his advances and is therefore a suitable model for Cynthia. The allusion casts the rich and powerful 'iste' of line 3 in a nicely ridiculous role.

In the next couplet (19–20), Propertius imagines her sailing safely past the dangerous promontory of Acroceraunia, which formed the entrance to the bay where Oricos was situated. The geography of all this is still accurate and consistent, suggesting that a real voyage is being envisaged.

The text here is difficult, the better attested reading being 'ut te'. 'Utere' has inferior support and moreover involves an awkward and ugly construction: it ought not, therefore, be considered, since 'ut te' of itself is felicitous and yields good sense. 'Ut' introduces the benevolent wish; 'te' which follows immediately is mimetically separated from the verb 'accipiat' in the next line by the dangerous journey past Acroceraunia. The problem arises with 'praevecta Ceraunia'. Löfstedt suggested reading this as a vocative, but the participle makes that intolerably strained.[15] But it is also possible to read it as an adverbial accusative on the Greek model, after 'felici', "an oar happy in respect to Ceraunia having glided past". The construction is almost equally anomalous perhaps, but poetically far more satisfactory and more likely because better motivated. 'Praevecta' here attributes movement to Ceraunia rather than to the ship, recreating the illusion that a moving vessel is still, while the land moves. If this is how the line works, even a Roman reader would have found the construction strained and odd, but the adroit navigation past the syntactic difficulty would have a

(13) Cp. Stat. Silvae III ii 5 ff. esp. line 13.

(14) See Theoc. Idyll VI and XI and Ov Met. XIII 778 ff.

(15) See Shackleton Bailey's comment on Löfstedt on this passage.

mimetic force, and would give a pleasing highly-wrought quality to the hexameter.

With line 21 Propertius switches to Rome, where the poem will remain to the end. The opening word 'nam', "for", is puzzling. It implies a sequential argument, yet line 21 does not obviously follow on from the preceding couplet. To make sense of it, we have to supply an argument that is obliquely implied by the two previous couplets, to this effect: "You are unfaithful ('periura') and deserve the same from me ('mereris'); but I can only wish you well (lines 17–20), for I cannot want anyone else (line 21)'. So 'nam' is the last explicit indication that his intelligence continues to function, that he knows the grounds on which his faith rests, and knows also that he must still be true to her.

The text of lines 21–2 requires minor attention. Line 21 is usually broken with a comma after 'corrumpere'. This attaches the final 'de te' to the following line, where it specifies 'verba querar', vaguely and inexactly however, since a lover's 'querelae' would concern his faithfulness and love and general unhappiness as much as the mistress. Formally, too, such an enjambment would be graceless and uncharacteristic of Propertius. However, 'corrumpere' can be followed by 'ex', so 'de' should be a possible construction.[16] The resultant sense is implicit even without the 'de te', since 'corrumpere' refers to breaking faith with Cynthia. If line 21 is composed as a syntactical unit, the structures of the two lines are significantly contrasted: in line 21, Propertius and Cynthia are far apart, separated by the hypothetical 'other women', whereas in line 22, 'ego' is juxtaposed with 'vita', Cynthia as his life.

In line 22 'verba querar' is often emended, since 'verba' seems redundant. However, this is insufficient reason for emendation, for Propertius often uses 'verba' apparently almost pleonastically.[17] Here it perhaps promises articulate complaints, the lengthy address that is to follow. 'Vera', which has met with favour, is ironically inappropriate, since what follows is to be far from true.

The key word for determining the tone of what follows is 'limine' in line 22. This is the conventional place for a lover to lament, and it is the cue for Propertius's transformation of himself into the stock lover of I xvi. The absurdity of the stance is quickly indicated. 'Nec me deficiet' (line 23) is an elaborate and unusual phrase 'Nor shall I miss any occasion to', but the rest of the line plunges into bathos. 'Rogitare' is a prosaic word,[18] and 'citatos', "hurrying", tacked on to the end of the line, completes a ludicrous picture of Propertius clutching at passing sailors who hurry on their busy way.

(16) 'Corrumpere' can take 'ex' meaning 'to corrupt from a into b' and with 'de' the meaning of the preposition would be as in Cic. Sest. 44 'senatum . . . totum de civitate delerunt'; see O.L.D. 'corrumpo' 4 and 'de' 3.

(17) See e.g. I xv 25.

(18) See Axelson p. 28.

His question when it comes in line 24 is pathetically naive. He identifies Cynthia only as 'mea puella', as though that would be identification enough, and as though she was still essentially his. But although to be in port is safety for a ship, it is far from safety for a girl.

'Citatos' has already implied the reaction of these sailors, practical men who would be out of sympathy with poetry of the elegiac convention. Propertius does not give their answer directly (that would be out of character for the naive lover), but it is still implied sufficiently by what he says he will then reply. 'Licet Atraciis . . . licet Hylaeis' refers to two ports in the general area but a long way apart.[19] The two names stand for the many no doubt ribald suggestions of these hurrying sailors. Through the concessive 'licet' the naive lover admits the apparently damaging physical side of their case, the implication that she has been wandering promiscuously from port to port. Against this he can only assert his continued faith in her. 'Mea est' is picked up from line 24 and echoes it like a refrain, made especially prominent by position. In line 24 it was a naive projection of his past rights over Cynthia onto a hostile present. Now it seems something stronger, a strange assurance of his future possesion in spite of what the sailors might say. But this assurance is simply juxtaposed with concessions that ought to make it possible.

It would have been very unsatisfactory if Propertius had stopped there as Lipsius thought. The paradox has only just been broached: Propertius could hardly have left it undeveloped. Moreover "viii (b)" treated as a sequel negates the achievement of the poem and destroys its character as a propemptikon. The first part of this form was not really meant to dissuade the traveller from going: the purpose of the propemptikon was to express a proper regret, and finally to arrive at the resignation of the second part with its wishes for a safe and speedy journey. Propertius had tacitly stopped supposing Cynthia might cancel her journey by line 12 and had gone a long way towards accepting the fact of her departure. For her then to have stayed would have been a personally satisfying outcome, no doubt, but poetically a disaster he ought to have kept to himself.

So it is fortunate that we do not need to end the poem there. The repeated 'hic' grows naturally out of the setting already established, pointing to the 'limen' he will never desert, contrasting it with the remote ports the sailors referred to. 'Considat' and 'futura est' have prepared for the tricks with time and place that 'erat' and 'manet' will continue. 'Considat' admitted her physical absence, but the form of 'futura mea est', echoing 'mea est' of line 24, made the claim that she will be his seem like a statement that somehow she is his now, by virtue of his faith that she will be his. 'Hic erat' like 'considat' is a statement of physical fact, reality in the sailors terms. It admits her absence now, while insisting that she once was here.

(19) The text is corrupt here, but the effect is the same whatever two ports are mentioned. The geographical vagueness here is especially significant in contrast to the precision of reference outside the speech.

But Propertius's emphasis is on 'hic', the threshold as guarantor. He moves from this to his vulnerable paradox through a strained pun on 'manet'. The word seems to indicate her physical presence, but, especially in conjunction with 'iurata', it could also refer to her constancy in abiding by her oath, her pledged faith. Even Cicero could pun familiarly on this double sense of 'maneo'.[20] Of course, Propertius does not positively know that she remains, even in the metaphoric sense: in line 17 he called her 'periura' and the Cynthia implied by the sailors seems not to have remained faithful at all. Propertius (or the naive lover he pretends he has become) relies solely on his absolute faith that she will have strictly kept to her vows.

The argument is tenuous in the extreme: Propertius could not conceivably have offered it seriously. But the point is its very tenuousness: by implication, this is the best a faithful lover could do on Cynthia's behalf, so the reasoning must be felt as specious. This then gives a dramatic function to 'rumpantur iniqui'. These 'iniqui' who are required to burst with frustrated envy and malice, have an obvious referent, the sailors who apparently did not receive his earlier remarks with due reverence. Dramatically the aside comes at an appropriate point, responding to the guffaws that would greet his most outrageous claim.

'Vicimus' of line 28 is his triumph over these 'iniqui' – or the triumph of his will to believe over all that they can say. Now he has launched himself into this argument, he never explicitly admits that it is all fallacious, but this couplet (27–8) is the highest point of his pretended certainty. As the speech progresses,the ambiguities sustain the fiction less convincingly, till the last four lines virtually give the game away.

This process has already begun with 'assiduas non tulit illa preces'. There is a different kind of ambiguity involved here. The two meanings revolve around 'tulit': either "She has not withstood my prayers" i.e. she has been persuaded to stay; or "She has not tolerated my prayers" (a sense of 'ferre' closer to his own use of the word at line 8), i.e. she has found my constant suit objectionable (and has gone).[21] The important difference with this ambiguity is that the other meaning, the meaning that makes the statement sayable, is the unpleasant truth that the sailors think. He can only oppose them by agreeing with them in a form of words that also means the opposite. This is no longer naivety, but sophistry. But Propertius could not pretend to be naive for very long and does not need to. He sets out to show the cost to truth of any defence of Cynthia's fidelity, making bitter criticism under this ostensible celebration, but also offering the whole endeavour as an equivocal proof of his real devotion.

(20) 'Gaudere ais te mansisse me et scribis in sententia te manere' Ad Att. IX ii 1; see also Cic. Sest xxvii 58 and Verg. Aeneid XI 160.

(21) See O.L.D. s.v. 'fero' 20, esp Verg. Aeneid IX 622 'talia iactantem dictis . . . non tulit Ascanius'.

The renewed abuse of the 'iniqui' in line 29 is already more temperate and less naive. 'Cupidus livor' implies sexual jealousy as the motive for their cynicism, something the naif of lines 23—27 would never have thought of. But the pun that makes line 30 true is similar to the 'manet' pun. 'Via' as in line 18, can be either a physical journey or customs, way of life, especially when qualified by 'novas', as here. The second is true, or so he maintains, and this allows him to seem to claim the first.

In the next couplet (31—2) the statement of how dear Propertius is to her and how much dearer Rome is for his sake, is then undercut by 'dicitur' at the beginning of the pentameter. 'Sine me dulcia regna negat' in 32 seems at first to imply that she has not gone, but in fact it describes only her attitude, not where she is. Either "She says that kingdoms would not be sweet without me" (so she did not go), or though she has gone "She says that kingdoms are not sweet without me". 'Negat' in this elliptical construction allows both versions; and the second is perhaps the more natural interpretation of the sentence. 'Sine me' at its head echoes ominously the same phrase at line 5 like a fulfilment of that disastrous possibility.

Lines 33—4 work similarly: they say that she has preferred life with him, not that she acted on that preference. The metaphor that follows (35—6) is interesting for other reasons. The wealth she is said to reject is the kingdom that was Hippodamia's dowry, plus the wealth the horses of Elis won: i.e. the wealth appropriated from her defeated suitors. The language seems too involuted for this to be a mere periphrasis for "great wealth". The point of the details in line 36 is unsurprising: the source of the wealth she rejects is Propertius's rivals. But line 35 strangely insists on the fact of the kingdom being Hippodamia's dowry. If the details have any point, they can only suggest that Cynthia rejects (or would want to reject) her dowry as well as love-offerings from others: her legitimate husband as well as all her other admirers. This implication, however, is carefully coded, for Cynthia's ears only, not for the hypothetical sailors nor for the general public.

The 'rival' having been covertly alluded to in this couplet at last reappears openly in the poem at line 37. This line has an obvious symmetry marked by the repeated 'quamvis', with a wittily mimetic increase of syllables in the second half, as the even better future gifts pile up. The pentameter that follows (38) exploits a favoured pun on 'sinus'.[22] Following 'fugit' it will naturally signify Propertius's loving breast, but 'avara' immediately juxtaposed, and following on from the allusion to gifts in the previous line, activates its secondary meaning 'purse'. Her greed is satisfied by the riches of Propertius's love, the pun suggests.

But there is another, much harsher ambiguity in this line centred on 'non'. The statement concerns flight, but 'avara' is also an important element in the meaning. So there are two things to deny in Cynthia, avarice and flight, with a single negative. So 'non' might negate either of these separately or

(22) See I ii 2 and note 9.

both, by a natural ellipsis. Either "She is avaricious but did not flee": or "She was not avaricious and did not flee": or "She did not flee through avarice (but went for some other reason)". The second, the negation of both, is the usual interpretation, but the other two lurk subversively as possibilities with their derogatory implications about Cynthia. It is clear that the ambiguities are moving away from the apparent certainties of line 27.

In lines 39—42 he reveals the wealth that, he claims, has prevailed: predictably, it is poetry. The sense of lines 41—42, however, is not entirely clear 'Sunt igitur Musae' is usually explained as a self contained sentence "The Muses exist". But not only does this involve linguistic oddity, it makes implausible sense. What Roman poet ever doubted that the Muses exist?[23] It is much more satisfactory to take this clause with 'quis ego fretus', with '-que' attaching Apollo to the Muses and 'ne-' negating 'tardus': 'The Muses and not-slow-to-help-lovers Apollo are those on whom I depend'.[24]

The couplet 41—2 ends with the powerful exclamation 'Cynthia rar mea est!' where 'mea est' sets up a strong resonance with lines 24 and 26. But 'mea est' has changed its value significantly as the poem has progressed. In line 24 it marked a foolish faith. In line 26 it is asserted as a deliberately paradoxical and apparently unsupportable act of faith. The rest of the speech then "proves" the claim that she is his faithful mistress and constant companion, even though she is not. The repetition in 42 acts as a triumphant restatement of the thing to be proved and participates in an incantatory refrain of apparently confident possession.

But of course, the whole argument is meant to be seen as fallacious, as Propertius indicates subtly but unmistakeably in the penultimate couplet. The oddity of the image in line 43 is the clearest give-away. To touch the stars with the soles of the feet, not the head, is manifestly ludicrous. Enk points out that such an image is used elsewhere of drunkenness:[25] it naturrally indicates a drunken euphoria, not a justified delight, and is especially suitable for the persistent inversion of truth Propertius has engaged in.

The next line (44) is also stranger than is usually recognised. The difficulty concerns the tenses. Following the future 'venerit' in the protasis, we would expect a future tense in the apodosis. The whole sentence would then refer to a definite time in the future —presumably when she has returned, but not now. 'Mea est', however, is general, not limited in its application to any particular time. The effect of this unusual conjunction of tenses in apodosis and protasis is to set up a disjunction between the modes of existence of the

(23) No parallels have been offered to suggest that 'sunt' may mean 'have a potent existence'.

(24) That 'neque' can negative a word other than the verb following is obvious enough from the dictionaries. The difficulty here arises from the fact that the verb 'sunt', comes first; but that is a relatively minor difficulty.

(25) See Enk. It is obvious that the Lipsian interpretation can offer no account of the oddity of this image.

131

two statements. The implication is not that she will be his equally by day and by night, but that the sequence of day and night (the subject of the protasis) is irrelevant to his mode of possessing her, which therefore occurs outside normal time. This is the real if bitter truth that underlies all the previous paradoxes. The final statement of 'mea est' gives the conditions under which the claim is true.

He does not entirely abandon his mask in the last couplet, but the double meanings are directed more towards Cynthia than the almost forgotten sailors now. If 'certos amores' stands for Cynthia, line 45 says that no rival has carried her off, where 'subducit' would have a mainly physical sense. However, 'amores', especially in the plural, can also refer to his feelings. They are 'certos', fixed, even if she is not. The basic sentiment repeats that of line 21: he cannot help but love her, and he at least will be faithful. He can guarantee that, even if he cannot be sufficiently certain of her. So 'gloria' in the last line contains the subsuming ambiguity: it is either the empty vaunt of the previous speech, or the fame that his faithfulness justly merits.

It is only when the underlying situation is not perceived that the formal complexities and ambiguity of feeling of the poem become confusing and impenetrable and make editorial surgery seem essential. The poem is elaborately structured and tightly disciplined, yet enigmatic and intensely private. Something of the basic situation must be grasped in order to distinguish fact from fiction, or to locate the centre round which the fictions twist to weave the intricate fabric of the poem. Cynthia is going. That is the intractable fact that generates the otherwise bewildering variety of the poem's fictions. She loves the poet but is leaving with her husband. A lover cannot be jealous of a husband, yet Propertius cannot fully trust her either, or not feel betrayed by her decision. His doubts and fears and resentment are unworthy and cannot be expressed too directly in the poem, but they lie below what is most puzzling in its form and language.

Yet this is a poetic strategy, not a failure of insight or retreat from emotion. There is no lack of self-honesty or self-awarenss: the poet's control of language and feeling never lapses. So in spite of the difficulties its obliquity causes, it is an achieved poem, a work of art, not an autobiographical fragment.

POEM IX

This is the second of the two poems Propertius addressed to Ponticus. It is clearly a later work, designed as a sequel, and probably one of the last poems composed for this book.[1] As such it is immensely more accomplished, but Propertius deploys his poetic expertise almost self-indulgently. Ponticus was an inadequate object or stimulus for his talents. In VII Ponticus's status as epic poet motivated some interesting reflections on poetry, but poem IX does not carry this thinking any further. Propertius merely scores easy points off the fact that Ponticus writes epics. His present concern is with a kind of love. The theme briefly rouses Propertius to some powerful images, worthy of a better poem, but the whole remains unsatisfactory.

The poem begins by apparently gloating over the fulfilment of VII's prophecy, that Ponticus would fall in love. Most commentators take this claim at its face value, and suppose it describes Ponticus's situation for this poem. But as the poem goes on to show, this is only true in a limited sense. The second couplet gives the situation more precisely. Ponticus has not fallen in love with a Cynthia. He has simply acknowledged sex, and is satisfying himself with common prostitutes. Propertius's main point is not how ridiculous this makes him, but how dangerous even this could be. Such casual liaisons can lead insidiously to the real thing.

But the tone of the poem is bantering, and the accusations are not consistent. 'Irrisor' in the first line announces this tone: Propertius applies the word to Ponticus, but it also obviously describes himself. 'Venturos amores' picks up 'venit Amor' from the last line of VII, a triumphant "I told you so". In the light of what follows, the plural form 'amores' is probably significant, referring to generalised feelings of passion rather than a specific love.[2]

The second couplet is crucial for understanding the situation of the poem. Because commentators suppose that Ponticus must be in love with a single girl, they have twisted the couplet to make it say so, reading 'quaevis' in line 4 as "some unknown girl" (Butler's translation).[3] But 'quaevis' normally means "any girl at all". The other meaning is very hard to support,[4] and even harder to justify in the present poem, since Propertius goes on to

(1) 5.9% polysyllabic pentameter endings as compared to 30.8% for VII; but see introduction pp.

(2) Ovid Amores I ii makes a similar distinction between erotic feelings and an erotic object.

(3) Enk emends here, B & B following Rothstein translate 'a mere nobody', Camps 'some girl': all twist the natural meaning.

(4) The parallels advanced are all unsatisfactory. Camps cites Prop. II xiii 44 'quaevis de tribus una soror'; but though 'de tribus' limits the scope of 'quaevis', the word itself has its usual sense.

use the word in its normal sense a little later, at line 14. Moreoever, there is no need for such linguistic contortions, for the words make easy if savage sense if they have their normal values. 'Quaevis empta modo' is any prostitute just hired off the streets. 'Imperat' juxtaposed with 'empta' points the absurdity. He buys her services, yet she is the one who exercises total authority. 'Modo' rubs it in: this inversion of statuses does not slowly evolve, it is almost instantaneous, happening almost as soon as they enter the bed-room. So 'iura puellae' in the previous line, a slightly obscure phrase, must refer generally to the dominion of woman, a state where all women exercise power.[5]

The first two couplets describe Ponticus, while the second two concern Propertius, perhaps mirroring the opening of VII. 'Ecce iaces' doubly insists on the abjectness of Ponticus's present position, while lines 5–8 seem to claim eminence for Propertius, though this claim is heavily ironic. The language in line 5 is elevated. 'Vincant' (for 'sint meliores.) implies an actual conquest, though doves are not exactly formidable opponents. But the content of the claim so grandly introduced is trivial and gossipy, and is expressed in more prosaic language. The sentiment of lines 7–8 is also fairly stock: he laments the cost of his expertise in love. But the language here is strained, for no apparent reason. He means that he is rightly regarded as an expert ('merito dicar') but would like to become a novice again ('fecere'). However, he has exchanged the verbs, sacrificing clarity apparently only to conceal the banality of the thought.

The next 6 lines proclaim the superiority of elegy over epic for a lover. 'Tibi misero' in line 9 gives the basic emotional state of the lover, for whom the 'grave carmen' of epic is serious in the wrong way. Line 10 compresses two ideas. Ponticus is engaged in writing a Thebaid, hence the reference to Amphion's lyre, but Ponticus the unhappy lover can only weep. The two ideas are fused together through the substitution of 'flere', to weep, for a word like 'canere'. Ponticus wants to sing about Thebes, but can only weep. Even that is no help to his condition. 'Flere' here may recall 'flebis' from VII 18, where it described what Ponticus would do instead of composing his epic.

The singular 'versus' in line 11 is probably significant: a single line from Mimnermus outweighs the whole of Homer, for a lover.[6] Love requires a smooth style.[7] From this follows the advice in lines 13–14 that Ponticus should try his hand at elegy. Line 13 in this sequence is unclear. 'Tristis istos'

(5) The parallel is with phrases like 'ius domini', where the rights are legal or semi-legal and the genitive is subjective. See O.L.D. 13, and cp. also Enk's citation of other examples of this or similar phrases in amatory poetry in his notes on this passage.

(6) Cp. Postgate on this passage.

(7) The Mss tradition divides between 'lenia' and 'levia' here. The difference between the two in the context is negligible, so the better attested 'levia' should be kept, though most edd. print 'lenia'.

is usually understood as Ponticus's gloomy epics.[8] 'Compone' must then mean "put aside". But that is not a common meaning, and there is a strong tendency for the word in this context, especially when governing 'libellows', to mean "compose".[9] 'Tristis' refers more naturally to elegy than epic in this poem, since elegy expresses the pains of love. (cp. 'misero' in line 9). 'Flere' in line 10 may have misled some, but that does not refer to the normal mood of the epic poet. So 'istos' is best read as referring to elegies. It is distancing and contemptuous in tone, flinging Ponticus's words back in his face: "those books you used to despise".

But Ponticus might not be able to compose such poetry. The objection has special force since in poem VII Properrtius had unkindly predicted that he would be too old (lines 19–20). So lines 15–16 tacitly retract this, asking the question on Ponticus's behalf, then answering it. 'Copia' in line 15 is often interpreted as "access', but Pasoli has cogently argued that it means "supply of poetic material".[10] "Access" would be irrelevant both to the preceding argument, and the following image. It makes the question too sensible to be greeted by 'insanus', and the image of a "river of accesses" is barely comprehensible. But the complaint that he might lack 'copia', abundance of material, is a pertinent doubt, which Propertius tries to dispose of in lines 17–18. A lover's condition is a rich source of material, and in spite of what he might suppose, Ponticus has hardly experienced the condition as yet.

Propertius then gives Ponticus a demonstration of how to write love poetry. The images in lines 19–23 are fairly stock, though the hellish experience mentioned in line 20 is maliciously apposite to Ponticus's case, since Ixion's crime was to copulate with a cloud, an apt image for Ponticus's unfocussed eroticism.

Lines 23–4, however, are difficult. The basic point is Love's double aspect, giving joy and pain, a sense of freedom alternating with a realisation of restraint. But it is not easy to arrive at a single consistent image for the whole couplet. Line 23 on its own is comprehensible enough: Love provides wings, which are called "easy" to describe the flight that results. The action described in 'presserit' also yields a clear image, whose significance recalls Love's action in 1.i.4. The difficulty centres on 'alterna manu'. The regular meaning of the phrase would be "with the other hand, working in turns". This would entail supplying another hand to perform the action in line 23. If this is what Propertius meant, 'manu' could only be understood figuratively in line 23, but is conceived physically in line 24. 'Alterna manu' would be a

(8) So Camps, Enk, Rothstein, etc.

(9) Cp. VII 19; even when the word does mean an action of disposing, as in Livy 26 29 8, ('ad componenda armamenta'), the emphasis is on the orderly nature of the stowing away and such an emphasis would be out of place here.

(10) See Pasoli p. 60.

vivid concrete for 'alterno', the difficulty being a consequence of Propertius striving too hard for effect.[11]

The main point, however, is clear, and is continued in the next couplet (lines 25—6). Ponticus must not be misled by the apparent ease of his present progress. 'Parata' in line 25 could mean simply "ready", but could also be a more polite way of saying 'empta'.[12] The paradox of line 4, 'imperat empta' is then developed. As soon as she is yours ('tua') you become hers to command.

The three lines that follow build up to a fine climax in line 29, in the course of which Propertius powerfully imagines Ponticus's trivial womanising transforming into a profound and disturbing experience of real love. The transformation begins with 'liceat' in line 27, the impersonal form detaching the petty prohibition from any individual girl. This word initially seems to govern both 'seducere' and 'vigilare', till 'cedat Amor' appears at the end of line 28. 'Cedat' does not usually take an infinitive, so it remains a strain for it to govern 'vigilare'. The effect is as though both 'liceat' and 'cedat' act on 'vigilare', the impersonal force she has become now personified as the god.

'Cedat Amor' is only insecurely attached to this line, and the sense flows over the boundary of the couplet, a significant departure from Propertius's prosodic norms. The image in line 29 has been prepared for by the more conventional image of love as an archer, in line 21, and is perhaps also affected by the image of line 24. Strictly, of course, it should be the arrow that penetrates to the bone, while the hand shoots it. This particular compression of the process, however, is an image in its own right. The sensation of a hand suddenly arriving at and touching the bone is a strange one, curiously powerful and internal, and no less disturbing for its being physically impossible.

This sequence is almost enough to justify the poem, but Propertius immediately lapses into banality, which lasts till the end of the poem. The image is too good for Ponticus alone, so it is addressed more generally ('quisquis es'). But the advice is only to flee.[13] Flint and oak, standard images for hardness, are then invoked in line 31. Since even these are possibly not proof against Love, Ponticus's chances of resisting are very small. The final couplet, however, is much cooler in tone. Propertius suggests only that Ponticus should confess his error, and speak about his condition. The suggestion seems tacitly to acknowledge that Propertius knows far less about Ponticus's affairs than he has pretended. The poem has been generated out of almost nothing, and returns there, finishing on the note of friendly badinage from which it started.

(11) Certainly all attempts to derive a consistent picture for this couplet have been implausible and linguistically strained; cp. Postgate, Camps, B & B.

(12) Cp. L & S under 'parare' II B.

(13) The text is possibly corrupt here. 'Aufuge', the reading of the Mss, ought to take an ablative, so it is usually emended to 'a! fuge'. Exclamations are usually suspicious emendations, since they neutralise meaning into a vague expression of emotion. Here however, Propertius may not have been writing with his usual poetic scrupulousness.

POEM X

The situation we are thrust into by the opening of this poem is very odd. But after 10 lines from a voyeur whose frankness is outstanding in Roman literature,[1] we suddenly have the poet in a surprising version of the 'praeceptor amoris' stance. It is natural to wonder what unites the two parts, and whether Propertius is entirely in control of the poem's tone.[2]

A prime source of uncertainty is the obliqueness with which the basic situation is presented. The opening is sensationally particular: the second part seems at the other extreme, entirely general. An intermediate level of generality is missing, which would give direct answers to questions we will inevitably ask about the relationship which lies behind the particularity of the opening. Such questions do not come from an irrelevant biographical interest, but are essential in understanding the poem.

To gain a context, it is helpful to start outside the poem. Poem XIII in this book is also addressed to Gallus and refers to what must be the same incident. Metric evidence indicates that it was probably composed at nearly the same time.[3] This poem is explicit exactly where X is most opaque. Moreoever, it looks like a real companion poem, not simply a convenient gloss. As such, XIII appears the earlier of the two, though it comes later in the book. It begins with a mocking, promiscuous Gallus, like the Gallus of the definitely early XX, but then the poet claims to know that Gallus is really in love in the Propertian way. The proof is the way Gallus made love as observed by Propertius (line 15 ff.). This is all presented with the circumstantial detail, as for someone who did not know the story, or did not know he had been observed. In X, however, the depth of attachment, and Gallus's knowledge that Propertius knows about it, are taken for granted. So XIII, following X, is explicit to the point of redundancy: X virtually requires XIII in order to be fully understood. Moreover, XIII concludes by wishing Gallus success in the new kind of relationship he has ventured on. By X the relationship seems to have progressed further. Gallus now required advice for a later, more thorny stage, when the girl has quarrelled with him. The sense of sequence in both form and content is so strong that X must be supposed to have been composed as a kind of sequel to XIII.

But there is an important difference in the way the two poems present Gallus's night of love. In XIII Propertius indicates unmistakeably that he was

(1) Camps appositely refers to Catullus XLV "in which the poet is a witness of a friend's amour", but Catullus is comparatively reticent about the details.

(2) Williams pp. 524 ff. seems to have such doubts. Unfortunately however his discussion conflates poems X and XIII so it is not certain if his strictures apply to both or only to XIII.

(3) 13.5% of polysyllabic pentameter endings as opposed to 5.5% for XIII. See Introduction pp 5–15

137

not actually present.[4] The claim is a joke against Gallus, and should be taken as such by the reader. Propertius is urging a Propertian kind of love on his promiscuous friend, or trying to induce him to see a current attachment in that light, but the actual incident is a fiction, a prophecy described as a fact in order to bring about its fulfilment. Propertius was fond of such prophecies at his friends' expense.[5]

X carries the process one stage further. The incident, including Propertius's presence as witness, is offered as fact, with no clear giveaway details. The first impression must be that Propertius is a voyeur. XIII, which would weaken this effect, is deliberately placed later in the book. This gives the incident a highly equivocal status. We know from XIII that the incident is to be taken as a fiction, yet in X Propertius also encourages us to take it at its face-value.[6]

This allows Propertius to do something more interesting than to recreate the feelings of a voyeur. Essentially, he is admitting that the motives behind his interest in Gallus's affair make him akin to a voyeur. In XIII he had assumed an air of objectivity, as though his sole motive was good-will towards Gallus. This left him superior to his friend, who at moments appeared faintly ludicrous. In X Gallus is still slightly ridiculous, but now Propertius is far more so. A voyeur is a despicable form of erotic life, for a Roman as for a modern.[7] This makes the opening strongly self-critical. It shows he realises how far he has projected his own experience onto Gallus in order to satisfy personal needs. Prescribing to Gallus helped him to achieve a kind of objectivity and even resignation in his relations with Cynthia, although it also released emotions of troublesome intensity. The description becomes an insight rather than an emotional adventure insofar as it is seen to be an image, not (in terms of the poem) a "fact": that is, as long as the incident has an equivocal status, experienced with the intensity of a fact yet understood as an image conveying a judgement. The level of insight, the difficulty and complexity of the task, and the remarkable control with which Propertius has managed it, makes this poem a higher order of achievement than XIII.

(4) See the discussion of XIII especially at lines 19–20.

(5) E.g. poems IV 19 ff., V 4 ff., VII 26; in IX he again assumes as here that his prophecy has been fulfilled. See our discussion there.

(6) In case there is any doubt, we should insist that this account concerns the way the poems should be taken, not the historical Propertius or the historical Gallus. It is of course highly unlikely that the historical Propertius ever watched the historical Gallus make love, but that probable fact is entirely outside these poems and irrelevant to their meaning. For a fuller consideration of this question, see section I of the Introduction.

(7) This is a probable supposition, when one considers the ridicule of exhibitionism in Martial I xxxiv; this vice and voyeurism are two sides of the same coin.

'O iucunda quies!' the poet exclaims at the beginning of the poem. 'Quies' here is often glossed as equivalent to night[8] but with no justification. The word means serenity, rest, or by extension sleep, which often occurs at night but is certainly not happening on this particular night. Since the poet is exclaiming, we assume that it is he who is experiencing the feeling. 'Iucunda', however, suggests pleasure of an erotic kind.[9] So Gallus is making love but Propertius feels 'jucunditas' as well. From the beginning a strange kind of bond has been established between Gallus and Propertius. Gallus's feelings at this point, however, are characterised by tears. These could of course be tears of joy, but their mention sounds ominous. Certainly Gallus's emotion is not like the poet's own 'quies'. A contrast is also made formally: 'quies' is at the beginning of the first line 'lacrimis' at the end of the second, almost as far apart in the couplet as possible, as though to distinguish Propertius's response from Gallus's. The two main words describing Propertius's role in the events are also contrary in their implications. 'Testis', witness, gives Propertius a quasi-public role, as though he were an important witness on an official or ceremonious occasion, a guarantor but not otherwise a participant. The word has a precise legal flavour. But 'conscius' indicates much greater complicity, a close identity of feeling between the two men.

The main verb in line 2, 'affueram', is a pluperfect (lit. "I had been present"). It is usually normalised to the more common preterite,[10] but Propertius's choice of tense should·be respected. His purpose here is to insist on the pastness of the action, a common idiosyncratic use of this tense for Propertius. The effect is strongly distancing, a reminder that all this took place a long time ago, in spite of the impression of immediacy and involvement given by the opening exclamation. The result is an impression of great strain, as of a mind strongly moved but immediately reasserting control. A temporal clause following 'o iucunda quies', especially one of this kind, retrospectively forces the exclamation to behave more responsibly and rationally, transforming it into something more like "O what a delightful quiet I felt". The ejaculation comes to seem like a compressed, ellipsed main clause, forced out of the poet by the intensity of his emotion.[11] This is

(8) By e.g. Enk and Camps, neither giving any reason; Butler translates 'repose'.

(9) Cp. the use of 'iucunda' at I xix 7.

(10) E.g. by Enk; it can probably be assumed that the other commentators' silence implies that they also normalise.

(11) The contrast can be made illuminatingly with II xv, the only other poem where Propertius starts with such a burst of exclamations;
'O me felicem, o nox mihi candida et o tu
lectule deliciis facte beate meis!'
Here the only statement, that of the last four words, is attached so closely in syntax to the address to the bed that it does not disturb the relatively even rhythm of the exclamations.

tonally balanced by the temporal clause, whose cool objectivity offers an ironic counterpoint to the depth of feeling behind the exclamation. So the exclamation is balanced by a finite clause, subjectivity by objectivity, the not wholly unequivocal joy of observing another's love by a recognition of the wholly equivocal nature of that love.

The syntactic form of the first couplet, exclamation followed by temporal clause, is expanded asymmetrically over the next two couplets, into two exclamations and a rather longer temporal clause, with an increasing disorder in each element. The third line picks up 'iucunda', with the 'quies' now intensified to a 'voluptas' which engages more directly with the scene. The form is made more dense by the fact that the initial 'O' has to act through the whole line before it reaches its vocative. The intervening words are left in an equivocal syntactic state.[12] The 'quies' of the opening was no stable Stoic 'apatheia' or Epicurean 'ataraxia', and as this feeling of peace moves into the past and becomes memory it also becomes a keener pleasure that is more strongly sexual. In line 4 he invokes the night or his pleasure — 'illa' could strictly agree with either, so the night and the joy tend to float together in his mind. The imperative sense in 'vocanda' communicates a sense of urgency as the night with the memory of its joy assumes a talismanic importance for the poet himself.

The next couplet (lines 5–6) presents the scene more explicitly and vividly than did the first, with magnificent power and virtuosity. Every word does its work; he says here what was spread over six lines in poem XIII. The equivocal tone of the first line and the irony of 'lacrimis' becomes here more extended and more obvious. Commentators, being males to a man, have tended to be over-flattering to Gallus's performance in this couplet, and have allowed 'complexa', 'embraced', the less usual passive meaning.[13] But as 'vinctum' from XIII 15 makes clear, the girl is doing the embracing here with a suffocating comprehensiveness. The word order too has Gallus locked dying in this embrace, embraced as it were by the words for the girl and her activity. Words for dying in elegy normally refer to the debilitating effects of ungratified desire,[14] and so the words he forces out in the pentameter are not the relaxed murmurs of a satisfied lover, but strained words filling the

(12) Camps acutely notes 'There seems here to be a telescoping of two constructions: (a) 'o noctem quam meminisse est iucunda voluptas': (b) 'o iucunda voluptas meminisse illam noctem'. It is clear, though, that the second is the right construction and that the equivocation of the syntax is due to the disordering of the words.

(13) Enk, Camps, B & B, all allow the possibility of the active as well, but favour the passive; they ought to exclude the less usual meaning here.

(14) 'Morientem' here is well glossed by Shackleton Bailey with Ovid Amores III xiv 37 'mens abit et morior quotiens peccasse fateris'. 'Languescere' (Prop. I iii 15) has a similar force.

'longa mora' between desire and fulfilment.[15] Again XIII provides the gloss: in line 17 of that poem Gallus longs 'deponere animam verbis optatis', and only after this ('deinde') does he do what Propertius's shame bids him to conceal.

So Gallus's experience is a protracted ecstasy compounded of pain as well as pleasure, action and passivity, prolonged by the girl. Propertius's description is, however, no clinical account, but recreates his own activity as he describes that of Gallus. This can be observed in a kind of zeugma involved in 'vidimus' of line 6. This word syntactically governs the first part of the couplet, though the girl exists only in an independent phrase. The pentameter, though it seems also to be governed by the same word, "I saw", is in a different grammatical mood, the infinitive. It is possible to see somebody 'morientem', 'dying', but the proper term for perceiving words spoken is not 'videre', and the change in grammatical mood alerts us to a shift in the mode of perception. But one can see the action of producing these words, and it is this that comes across, conveyed through 'ducere' ("draw out with difficulty"). The elliptical construction gives a sense of strain to the lines which conveys something of the quality of the experience. The poet does this even more explicitly through his word order, where 'ducere verba' is placed between 'longa' and 'mora'. The movement of the whole poem up to this point has had the clogged rhythms of the experience itself; the poet's words seem also to be dragged out in the description.

The next two couplets are less exclamatory, the rhythms more leisurely than what has gone before, moving into a post-coital mood as 'sleep presses' the poet's eyes. There is here a very strong sense of identification between the poet and Gallus, which is underlined by the poet's powerlessness to withdraw ('non potui'). In this lack of power, Propertius seems almost to be simply an extension of Gallus, seems to have to give up some of his own ego to be the witness of the affirmation of another's.

Lines 7–8 give two reasons why he would be expected to leave the lovers. The first, in line 7, is obvious: he is tired. Line 8 gives a second reason. The usual interpretation of this, that it is a mere periphrasis for "the moon is at its height", i.e. the time is well into night, makes this a very weak line. This would not be a distinct reason for going home, apart from being tired. Midnight is a lover's noon. A line devoted to noting the fact would be at best a great drop in the density of the language. But 'ruberet' used of the moon is not an equivalent of "shine" ('luceret').[16] A red moon portended an

(15) Modern translators of this line take 'longa mora' to equal 'longis intervallis'; the silence of the commentators presumably indicates agreement with this interpretation. This is possible, but the singular 'mora' would be unusual and 'longa mora' largely repeats the sense of 'ducere' which implies slowness as well as difficulty. To take it as a temporal ablative, the period before the desire is satisfied, is then slightly preferable grammatically and yields much more satisfactory sense.

(16) As Rothstein and Enk argue on this passage.

approaching storm.[17] If Propertius stays, he is liable to get wet — a positive reason for going, and proof of how strongly he is held by the scene he is witnessing.

The details also have metaphoric significance. 'Mediis equis' personifies the moon as a charioteer in full course (the ellipsis of the otherwise conventional chariot[18] serves to draw attention to the metaphor and give it new life.) This is an image for energies at their height. Propertius's passivity and the vigour of the female moon, who has her blood up and half the night to run, reflect the contrasting roles of Gallus and his mistress in the preceding scene. As the poet comes to merge with the "dying" Gallus, the mistress conjures up for Propertius the symbol he has already used for his own Cynthia, the moon.[19] The redness of the moon could reinforce this, suggesting the glow of youthful vitality, but primarily it portends a storm, already foreshadowed by 'lacrimis' in line 2. A storm is soon to break for Gallus as it has already broken for Propertius. Because the scene is set in the past, this threat has already been fulfilled.

The first section closes with the lovers' ardour still burning, though not so fiercely that conversation is inhibited. Line 10 has something of the force of an exclamation, but the earlier intensity has gone, and the line with its repeated a's is like a sigh of fulfilment, the product of a more contented mood. So the change of mood between lines 10 and 11 is as sharp as possible, and must be felt as such. The reverie of 'tantus in alternis vocibus ardor erat' is rudely jolted by the rational 'sed quoniam', "but since". 'Sed' does not here have an obvious adversative function: it serves mainly to indicate a change of awareness, a shift in mood and time. Where the opening lines are all in the past tense, the following sixteen are predominantly in an imperative mood. The commands are offered in the present, to be laid up for the hypothetical future described in the last four lines, when, as the result of taking the advice, Gallus will be able to enjoy his felicity again.

The opening line of this second movement has caused some difficulty to commentators. Where the tradition reads 'concedere', about half the modern editors prefer the variant reading of one Ms., 'concredere'.[20] This would refer back to some strange kind of pact, by which Gallus entrusted his love-affair to Propertius, even to the point of inviting him to watch on the first night. But we do not need to invent such an improbable pact to explain

17) Cp. Verg. Georgics I 436 'vento semper rubet aurea Phoebe'. See also Aratus Phaen. 784, 795—7. Theophrastus Sign. 12, 31; Pliny N.H. XVIII 348. Dr R.O.A. M. Lyne first drew our attention to this significance.

18) Cp. e.g. Tib. I viii 21 'e curru Lunam deducere', Theoc. Idyll XXI 19; in Ov. Tristia I iii 28, the 'currus' is not mentioned explicitly but is strongly implied.

19) See E. O'Neil, and also our account of I i 19 ff.

20) Enk, Camps, Shackleton Bailey, Barber in the Oxford Test are for 'concredere'; Rothstein and B & B for 'concedere'.

either the opening or this particular word. The conspiracy-theory, however, colours the interpretation of the Mss 'concedere' for most of those who accept it. The object is taken to be (sc.) 'laetitiam' (though this would involve considerable syntactic strain). On this view Propertius will give gifts in return for the favour of having been allowed to be present. However, this takes 'munera' at its face-value, missing the clear irony of the whole of the last section. The gifts are hardly worth having: nor, by implication, is the concession they are a response to. The best interpretation of the word is Pasoli's. He reads 'concedere' as absolute. This does not refer to a pact in the past, but to Gallus's present submission to Propertius's wisdom. 'Concedere' is juxtaposed with 'non es veritus' in a mocking paradox. Gallus's courage consists in yielding to Propertius. Friendly rivalry is a dominant element in the Gallus-Propertius friendship in the other poems addressed to him. There is a note of triumph in 'concedere' that is entirely consistent with that sort of relationship, as Propertius pretends to have reversed Gallus's usual dominance. This, of course, is partly a pretence, like Propertius's claim that he was present at the night of love.

Out of this relationship grows the command 'accipe', "take", of line 12. Gallus has deferred to him, so Propertius assumes the mantle of authority, a mock elevation of himself that is to continue until line 18. And Gallus is given a similar mock dignity as Propertius assigns to him the 'munera' of his 'commissa laetitia', "the happiness he has entered upon". In a later poem, Propertius talks of 'venus commissa' (IV vii 19), the bond of love entered upon, the act initiated.[21] 'Commissa' in the present context suggests an engagement of a solemn kind, recalling Propertius's role as 'testis' in line 1.

The equivocal nature of Gallus's joy is immediately signalled in line 12. Here Propertius talks of Gallus's 'dolores', 'griefs', without a transition. The word stands at the end of the line, like 'laetitia', to make the connection clear. The relationship between the two men is ambiguous, but the only word which has strictly any ambiguity is 'munera'. In Propertius the word generally refers to the gifts of lovers, but the nature of the transaction being described here suggests a more elevated meaning, the rights and duties of a public office.[22] The ironic resolution of this ambiguity only emerges, however, as the passage progresses; the advice that follows, which gives content to 'munera', turns out to be trivial, banal and debasing. So the 'munera' turn out to be all duties, 'gifts' to open the beloved's doors.

(21) At line 21 of the same poem he goes on to talk of a 'foedus' arising out of the act. For the legal sense of 'committo' = to set in legal motion, to initiate, see Heumann-Seckel on this word, section 3.

(22) The basic meaning of 'munus' as "duty" or "burden" is easily perceivable from the standard dictionaries. Shackleton Bailey specifically rejects this interpretation of 'munera' here, proposing the meaning 'praemia'. This is only tolerable if 'commissa laetitia' is "the happiness you have given me". For 'munera' = the gifts of the lover. Cp. Prop. I ii 4, iii 25, 26 II viii 11, etc.

143

To establish the irony, Propertius begins with inflated claims for his powers in matters of love. He can not only passively conceal sorrows, but can actively alleviate them ('reticere' is opposed to 'quiddam maius fide') and there follows the sonorous list of the things he can do. The thrice repeated 'possum' echoes hollowly against the realities of his situation, without Cynthia, and with only the satisfactions of a voyeur. The irony is underlined at this point by the way that this verb picks up the 'non potui' of line 9. There the poet was enfeebled, a powerless figure held fast by the scene he was witnessing. Here it seems he can reassert a strongly male vigour in his advice to his new pupil, but the power is illusory and the poet is no more effective than Gallus in winning over his own mistress. The irony is especially evident in the contrast between his claims and his advice, but it is beginning to assert itself in line 17, where his third grand 'possum' is limited by 'alterius'. The word means one of two. Here it might mean Gallus as opposed to Propertius. However, such self-pity would be out of place here. More probably the pair referred to through 'alterius' is a pair of lovers, in which case 'alterius' would be the male partner. Propertius's power, as he goes on to show, can only change the man so that he no longer offends. It does not reach directly to the woman.

The main effect of the three couplets that follow (lines 21–26) is the ironic contrast between Propertius's grand claims and the trivial advice he offers. His "power" is his knowledge that a lover must be totally abject. Lines 19–20 had seemed to promise things to aim at as well as things to avoid, but the list begins with 'cave', avoid, and never mentions what the lover should do positively. In fact a lover can do nothing.

Despite the general form of this advice, it has an air of particularity, and implies a recognisable situation in some detail — Gallus's, obviously. He has been insensitive (line 21) arrogant, then sullen (line 22) ungracious (line 23) and unresponsive (line 24). She has been genuinely offended ('laesa') and is right to be angry ('justas minas'). Gallus may have hardly registered that he was offending her. The fact that he needs such advice suggests that he is several times less sensitive in such matters than Propertius. Yet the details are also sharpened to something close to caricature. This implicitly shares Gallus's view that her demands have been unreasonable, that the relationship she wants is absurdly one-sided. She is the only one who is to be offended, or who is to do any asking ('petiit'): and this itself is a favour, not to be refused with an 'ingrata frons', an ungrateful as well as ungenerous response.[23] The tone here is double-edged: she has magnified things out of all proportion, but he has been rather crassly insensitive.

Lines 25–26, which conclude this sequence, have a summatory character. The triviality of her reaction is implied through 'irritata' (as against irata') but this mood is intractable. Line 26 is not entirely straightforward.

(23) Enk, Shackleton Bailey, take 'ingrata' as "unpleasing" which reduces its force to practially zero.

'Nec meminit . . . ponere' essentially equals 'nec deponit', "does not lay aside"[24] but 'nec meminit' coming at the beginning initially leads the reader to expect exactly the opposite statement, that she does not remember past offences. The effect of this twist of expectations is to draw attention to the arbitrary way a woman's memory works. She forgets many things, but not her revenge. Yet the rest of the couplet concedes that she has a case. 'Iustas' is unequivocal.

The conclusion, lines 27–30, gives the only remedy, total servitude, but with 'efecto . . . fruare bono' it also recalls the positive that might have been forgotten.[25] The good that he has done, the commitment celebrated on that night, should not be wasted: 'fruare' indicates a return on an investment but is not nastily commercial in flavour. 'Saepe' insists that the pleasure is not confined to the single night, to be paid for by a lifetime of slavery.

The final couplet presents the ambiguous situation of a lover committed to a single girl. The ambiguity is concentrated on 'felix' in line 29. The word means happy or successful. Usually there is no need to distinguish between these two meanings, but here to be "successful" with such a girl is to seem unhappy most of the time, as happiness is conventionally counted. Yet there is happiness in such a relationship, inseparable from everything else in it. Propertius's irony here has no self-pity, not even the wish that things were otherwise.

It is a strong poem, never out of control. The fact that it is so firmly to and about Gallus helps here. Propertius never loses the kind of detachment the strategy allows. The different parts of the poem are held together by a wryly ironic wit, directed at Gallus and himself. Yet it remains a disturbing poem. There is a real break after line 10, a disjunction between past delight and present pain which cannot really be bridged. This gives its equivocal quality to the opening. The memory of satisfied love is evoked as strongly as possible to give meaning to the present, but resisted as too intense to be endured. The strategy of projecting his feelings onto Gallus has its own difficulties. The relationship with Gallus is a complex and significant one. It involves tensions analogous to those in his relationship with Cynthia, and the feelings have an erotic element. So Gallus's presence adds to the complexity of the experience that the poem must manage, as well allowing some measure of objectivity and detachment. The poem's unity finally consists in this kind of precarious equilibrium.

(24) As Rothstein implies in his note on this line. Camps tries to solve the difficulty of this line by reading 'minas' in an extended sense as "anger".

(25) This is the reading of the main Mss. Enk, Rothstein, Bailey, B & B, Barber, Camps all read 'effectu' with the 'deteriores'. The argument is that 'effecto'/'effectu' must be a noun, but since 'effecto' could also be adjectival, the unambiguous 'effectu' is preferable. (Prop. uses the phrase 'effectus bonos' elsewhere, III xxiii 10.) Shackleton Bailey further rejects 'effecto' on the grounds that there is no good evidence for its general use as a noun. If he is right, then there is no ambiguity; 'effecto' here must be the past participle. Since the sense this gives is preferable – Gallus wants to enjoy a good, not an effect – the Mss 'effecto' must be retained.

Editorial knives have fortunately left most of the poems in Book 1 in one piece. The two exceptions are poems VIII and XI–XII. The fact that an editorial decision has been made is much less obvious in the case of XI–XII, since variants in two manuscripts (N_2 & P_2) divide the poem at line 30. Perhaps as a result of this, no editor this century has thought it necessary to give any reasons for accepting this emendation, as it essentially is. So there is no case to answer for someone who finds the division unhelpful and unnecessary. The poem makes very good sense when read as the whole the tradition has transmitted.

Apart from lacking good Ms authority, a division at line 30 is unsatisfactory in a number of ways. It leaves XI with a lame conclusion, and "XII" with an implausible start. Who is the addressee? In every other poem in this book Propertius is carefully specific about the addressee. Here the candidates are either a hypothetical and unimagined friend, or Rome, but both are immediately forgotten. But Baiae has been invoked in line 30. It is much easier to carry the address straight on into the next line than to invent this faceless friend, or change the syntax to allow Rome to be conversed with. A division also ignores a number of key parallels between the two parts, 'crimen desidiae' echoing 'crimen amoris' across the proposed break, and more crucial, 'Cynthia causa fuit' (26) picked up by the last line, 'Cynthia prima fuit, Cynthia finis erit'. It would be very odd if Propertius had prepared for this punchline in a different poem.

It is no accident that poems VIII and XI–XII alone in Book 1 have attracted this treatment from editors, for they are difficult poems of a similar type. Both poems dramatise the process of coming to terms with painful emotions of jealousy and doubt. Both follow a tortuous course, responding to sharp shifts of mood. Both try to resolve the emotional conflict by disengaging from the dramatic situation, and projecting the poem into a situation where the poet can give vent to negative hostile feelings that he almost knows are not justified. Poem VIII is technically more daring, probably the later of the two, since it seems inconceivable without XI–XII as a predecessor.[1] XI–XII seems closer to an epistolary form, and the key to both poems is perhaps XI 19–20: 'ignosces igitur, si quid triste libelli/attulerint nostri: culpa timoris erit'. His anxiety generates such powerful images of perfidy that they are described as fact. His love has to devise ways of ignoring them, or at least allowing an affirmation of his total love to coexist with extremes of doubt.

The first 8 lines establish the situation of the poem. They also convey

---

1) Polysyllabic pentameter endings 36% for XI–XII, 21.7% for VIII, but this difference is hardly conclusive (see Introduction pp 5–15). The stylistic grounds are stronger, but they are not conclusive either.

its emotional quality, its characteristic movement. The first 4 lines are an elaborate structure, describing Cynthia's holiday resort in an elevated and allusive style. Lines 5–8 introduce a different note. They are a series of urgent, self-concerned questions, elliptical, moving rapidly towards extreme doubt, finally almost imagining the seduction taking place.

The poem's geography is probably accurate, though not all the details are now certain. Baiae lies on the Bay of Naples, midway between Misenum and the Bay of Locrine, 3 miles on either side. The kingdom of Thesprotus probably refers to the Plegaean mountains, so 'aequora' in line 4 would be the whole bay round to Misenum.[2]

The first two couplets describe daytime activities, while night has dangerously fallen in 5–8. These first two couplets are also contrasted to each other, through 'modo'. 'Cessantem', idling, reinforced by 'mediis', in the centre of Baiae, indicates one way Cynthia might spend her time. 'Aequora' refers to the sea. 'Mirantem' could mean "to look", as commentators usually take it. However, the word could also refer to sailing (like 'mare noscere' in 1 vi 1). If so, the first couplet would describe inactivity on dry land, the second the relatively greater activity of sailing on the bay.

The periphrases here are interesting. 'Herculeis semita litoribus' refers to the strip of land separating Lake Locrina from the sea, known as the causeway of Hercules. So 'Herculeis' has been transferred from 'semita' to 'litoribus'. The figure recalls the strained language of the early poem XX, and serves the same purpose, to eroticise the landscape. At this early stage in the poem the point of the figure is not clear, but 'litora' is to recur, increasingly personified (lines 14, 28, 29) as Propertius transfers the blame for Cynthia's supposed infidelity on to the place. Misenum is named from Misenus, the Trojan trumpeter, 'nobilibus' serving to recall the heroic original and the act of invasion he shared in. The significance of the allusion to Thesprotus is not clear, but it may recall another act of invasion.[3] These are all hints, very subdued at this stage, that Baiae has a history of acts of armed rape. The fears are more explicit in lines 7–8 with the mention of a 'hostis' (stronger than "rival") and the phrase 'sustulit e', the very word for the act of pillageing.[4]

(2) This is consistent with Enk's view on the topography. The Phlegaean mountains were near Cumae and 'subdita' here will have the general topographical meaning of 'below' without implying that the 'regnum' is actually on top of the waters; Cp. L. & S. A 1. The view that 'Thesproti regnum' is Avernus does not consider the unlikelihood of a young woman's visiting such a place, nor is a reference to the engineering works of Agrippa particularly appropriate.

(3) A specific legend connecting Thesprotus with this area has been lost. That he was a strong and vigorous ruler in legend may be inferred from his conquest of Theseus (Pausanias I 17 4); that Cumae was founded by a Greek influx in the eighth century is known, and there is some reason to connect a further influx with this particular area. For a full and interesting discussion see Enk on this passage.

(4) Cp. e.g. Cic. 'Div. in Q. Caec.' I 3 'simulacra sanctissima C. Verres ex delubris religiosissimis sustulisset'; Caes. B.G. VII 14 'ad . . . praedam tollendam', etc.

Line 5 gives the long-awaited question announced by 'ecquid'. But the question itself is elliptical and obscure. Scaliger's emendment 'ah! ducere' for 'adducere', is often accepted, but exclamations are always suspicious as emendations, and this one still does not solve the problems. 'Te' must be supplied from line 1 in the first clause: does love for us steal upon you? 'Adducere' commonly means "to persuade", usually in a good sense. Its direct object would have to be 'te' understood, with 'memores noctes' the action or state that Cynthia might be persuaded to. The expected form would be 'ad memores noctes', but the omission of 'ad' would be possible,[5] and easy enough with the positioning here. However, the elimination of Cynthia grammatically from the line is almost perverse. It is as though he doubts that she is there to feel concern, or to remember their love.

The doubts are even more acute in the next line. The question now is not whether her love might be fading, but whether there is any trace of it left at all. It carries an implicit accusation, like the famous "Have you stopped beating your wife?"; 'extremo' indicates an outer edge.[6] 'Extremo amore' is still slightly odd. It may have been formed by a process of inversion 'amor in extremo loco' (which describes Cynthia in Baiae as far as Propertius is concerned) becoming 'locus in extremo amore', the doubt like the mirror-image of the situation. 'Locus', following 'memores' in the previous line, might have a technical sense, recalling the 'loci' or memory places in classical arts of memory. These were imagined niches in an imagined room or house, in which the rememberer would mentally place images of what he wanted to remember.[7]

With 'atque utinam' a new movement begins. Again an elaborate structure in the first two couplets contrasts with strained and disordered syntax in the next two, mimetic of a disturbed mind. As in lines 1—4, there is a contrast between active and passive enjoyments, but as 'atque' signals, he has changed his mind. Now he would prefer her to be doing something rather than have time to do what he fears. The activity he wishes for her is ludicrously restricted. A 'cumba' is a small boat anyway. The diminutive 'parvula', and the description of the oars as 'minutis', is either absurdly excessive or more probably consciously ridiculous. The Lucrine lake was small anyway, protected from the sea of lines 3—4 by the causeway of Hercules. But 'confisa' contains the serious point of the couplet. She must trust herself to the smallest possible boat that relies on the smallest of oars — that is, she must trust as little as possible outside herself.[8] Propertius is willing to be ridiculous to make the point.

(5) See Woodcock Para. 17 'Transitive verbs implying motion . . . when compounded with a preposition, may have a second accusative . . .' Cp. Ov. m.3 598 'dextris adducor litora remis'.

(6) Cp. I xx 29, 50 and notes.

(7) Cp. Cic. 'De Oratore' II 351 ff. 174.

(8) Cp. I ii esp. line 6 and our comments.

148

She is allowed to swim in lines 11–12, probably in some hot pool[9] which would be smaller and shallower than Lake Locrine. The hexameter is given its character by the opening 'teneat clausam', which like 'confisa' in line 9 draws attention to the need for her to be carefully guarded. The guardian in this case is 'lympha'. This word has been castigated as an example of Propertian redundance, following 'in unda' in the previous line.[10] This, however, is to miss the whole point of the line. 'Lympha' is a water nymph, who is supposed to be a strict guardian in line 11, but reveals herself as distinctly erotic and far from severe in line 12. The image 'facilis cedere', easily yielding, has clear sexual overtones. In I xx the Dryads are conceived in this way far more extensively and unmistakeably. 'Facili liquore' in that poem (line 47) is perhaps the direct ancestor of the present image. The landscape here is on the way to being eroticised, a process begun with 'Herculeis litoribus'.

'Vacet' in line 13 recalls 'cessantem' of line 1. This is how she will use her leisure. The syntax recognises that this is just a possibility that he hopes will not eventuate, but the images are so vivid and particular that he almost seems to see it happen. The next couplet, lines 15–16, is a generalisation, less vivid but more certain that she must have lapsed. He has reached the point of excusing her perfidy — any girl will fall if left unguarded — still without any reason for suspecting her.

In line 15 the Mss have 'amota'. This is usually emended to 'amoto' on the grounds that a 'custos' would be a man.[11] However, that is not nearly certain enough to justify emendation here. The 'lympha' of line 12 was female and a guardian. Baiae is more bawd than 'custos', but is the only 'custos' Cynthia seems to have — hence Propertius's anxiety. In line 14 the beach is called silent. This is only worth saying if the beach should not be silent — if it should have called out like a good 'custos' to prevent the outrage. 'Litora' in lines 28 and 29 certainly refers to Baiae.

(9) 'Teuthrantis' is Scaliger's conjecture for the Mss 'teutantis', with one variant 'teutrantis'. To whom the name refers is now undiscoverable, but Enk points out that the name is associated with the area from which Cumae was founded and cites Silius Italicus XI 288 and Strabo XII 472 (Teuthras as a king of Mysia which is near Cyme the metropolis of Cumae).

(10) E.g. by Shackleton Bailey; Camps is also unenthusiastic about it. For the personification of 'lympha', cp. Hor. Odes III xiii 15–16 'loquaces lymphae'; the word is very closely related to 'Nymphe', and the identification is made by Hor. Sarives I v 97. Petronius seems to have had this passage in mind when he wrote (Baehrens 84 3–4) –

O formosa dies! hoc quondam rure solebam
Naiadas alterna sollicitare manu.

(11) 'Amoto' is given in some Mss, but is clearly not the main tradition: Enk accepts it because, he says, the guardian here is Propertius himself — but that seems extremely unlikely. Camps prints 'amoto' as 'we seldom if every hear of a duenna'.

In lines 17–20 he half apologizes for having gone too far. The disclaimer in line 17 is tangled, tripping over its double negative. The indicative 'es' is also surprising. Propertius is usually supposed to be denying that he is unaware of her spotless reputation. As a gentleman, of course, this is what he should be saying. But if his unawareness was being denied, 'non quia' would normally be followed by a subjunctive. The effect of an indicative after 'non quia' is to make the statement true but not relevant. So he is saying that he is not aware of her having a spotless reputation, but that that is not the reason for his doubts. However, this is not said with rude directness. One effect of the double negative is to obscure his meaning. Even then, he is not actually denying that she might have a good reputation. He does not know about it, but even if he did it would not stop him worrying.

The reason for this is given in the next line. The central idea here is the emotional paradox 'amor timetur'. 'Amor' is the object of love, Cynthia, who is also, in these dangerous circumstances, the object of fear.[12] That is the dilemma at the heart of the poem: his love generates his fear, so his fear is a sign of his love. 'Omnis' tactfully generalises this statement. 'In hac parte' refers to the place, Baiae,[13] already receiving most of the blame for her tendency to stray. 'Hac' signals that Baiae is felt as almost present now, available to be invoked directly in the outburst from line 29.

Lines 19–20 virtually ask her to ignore this poem/letter, but he continues to write it. Lines 21–6 attempt to be more positive. Now he declares how totally he is dependent on her. That may have been implicit earlier, but he had not actually said it. Line 21 is semi-humorous, but has generally been misunderstood. It is usually emended to give it an exactly opposite meaning.[14] The confusion arises over 'custodia'. This is usually taken as equivalent to 'cura', a protective love. Clearly it would be very odd for Propertius to say that he cares more for his mother than for Cynthia, and emendation would be justified to remove such nonsense. But 'custodia' does not normally indicate that kind of concern. It describes the action of a 'custos', a guard, sentinel, watchdog, never a lover. 'Custos' in line 15 makes plain the specific sense of 'custodia' in this context. For a Roman to act as 'custos' to his aged mother was a ridiculous notion, yet Propertius is guarding

---

(12) Camps in an additional note on this line illuminatingly cites Ov. Pont. II vii 35–7 and concludes that Propertius here means 'any love is object of anxiety'.

(13) So Camps; other editors propose various versions of an abstract 'under these circumstances', but the concrete meaning seems obvious and comprehensible. The difficulty really lies in 'omnis Amor timetur' and it is through misunderstanding this that a misunderstanding of the rest of the line arose; this seems clear from Shackleton Bailey's prolix note.

(14) Enk following Beck prints 'nunc' for 'non', a conjecture of such violence that one would expect pages of justification necessary. Camps follows this, B & B print 'a' instead of 'an' after Lachmann, with an equal subversion of the sense.

his mother more closely than the young, beautiful (and fickle) Cynthia.[15] No wonder he is worried, the joke implies. The hexameter and pentameter give the two justifications for his fear: Cynthia is dangerously unprotected, and supremely important to him, home, parents and every moment of joy. The poem moves towards a preliminary conclusion at line 26, ending on the strong note 'Cynthia causa fuit', which foreshadows the conclusion of the poem. These lines insist on the joy the relationship has brought and can bring. 'Laetitia' and 'laetus' occur in successive lines. But the point of the couplet 25—6 is that Cynthia is the cause of both sadness and joy, the bitter things he apologises for in line 19 as well as the pleasures of their love.

So Cynthia must leave Baiae. The repetition of 'litora' prepared for the address to Baiae blaming it as the chief culprit. These shores are not merely the scene of divorce and rape, they are an active agent, the subject of the verbs 'dabunt' and 'fuerant inimica'. Behind the accusation is the covert history of the early part of the poem. The tenses of 'dabunt' and 'fuerant' are important here. The paradosis 'fuerant' is often emended to 'fuerunt'.[16] But Propertius characteristically used the pluperfect to insist on the remoteness of an action in the past. So this line refers to a distant past when chaste maidens were in danger of rape from invading armies. That does not happen in modern Baiae. 'Dabunt' could have been a present, but is future. The effect is to leave Baiae of the present safe, but hedged by a brutal past and a dangerous future. The tenses represent a kind of wishful thinking: if only Cynthia left now she would still be safe!

Line 30 addresses Baiae directly, and Baiae continues to be the recipient of Propertius's complaints for the rest of the poem. The device of speaking ostensibly to part of the scenery, really for the mistriess to overhear, seems to have attracted the young Propertius. I xviii is addressed to the 'deserta loca'. I xvi is even closer to the present poem: there the lover blames the door for his mistress's excluding him. In each case the device allows the lover to express a degree of resentment that would antagonise the mistress if said directly. (Cp. especially 1 xviii 23—6.)

Line 30 is basically a curse. Contained in this is an obscure accusation, 'crimen amoris', obscure because the genitive could make it either a crime against love (true love like Propertius's) or love which is a crime.[17] Fortunately this accusation is picked up and explained by the clearer 'desidiae crimen' in the next line. This is evidently the crime of sloth. So 'crimen

(15) If Propertius's mother was dead at this time the notion is even more ridiculous. That she was dead by the time he wrote book II seems evident from II xx 15.

(16) By e.g. Butler and Barber (following Scaliger) and Camps.

(17) Rothstein, B & B, interpret 'an offence against love', Enk, Bailey and Camps 'a reproach to love'. But the failure to notice the parallel phrase 'desidiae crimen', which must surely recall this on any view of the break between XI and XII, vitiates their accounts.

amoris' is the love violently forced on Cynthia by Baiae, or at Baiae (literally, the crime of committing love, the crime of rape or easy acquiescence). Line 31 contains a countercharge, attributed to Baiae but presumably coming from Cynthia. He has indirectly accused her of making love in Baiae. She (Baiae/Cynthia) accuses him of being too slothful to come to Baiae. 'Fingere' immediately undercuts this accusation: even she could not really believe this. 'Cessas' is singular, Baiae plural, but the apposition of the singular phrase 'crimen amoris' has helped to prepare for the switch. Baiae is now thought of as a person, hence the singular verb.[18]

Baiae accuses Rome of causing Propertius's dalliance. This matches Propertius's accusation, that Baiae caused Cynthia's fall. Rome is called 'conscia', a witness. The word indicates complicity making Rome an accomplice (cp. I x 1—2). She is a flawed 'custos', according to Baiae, who is as concerned to condemn the city as the person.[19]

The next couplet explains why he cannot join her. The distance between two great rivers was one of the ways of indicating a huge distance.[20] It is this great distance, not 'desidia', that keeps them apart. 'Meo lecto' is used for "me", because a lover's bed is the reference point for all important measurements of distance.

The thought of this distance leads naturally to the thought of his loneliness and deprivation. There are frequent parallels linking this part of the poem with earlier images in it. (These parallels would be one of the casualties of a division at line 30.) 'Nutrit' Cynthia in line 35 recalls Cynthia 'sola parentes' (line 23) as well as insisting on his need for constant renewal of love. Line 36, her sweet voice whispering in his ear,[21] contrasts with 'blandos susurros', the insidious whisper of his rival.

By line 37, 'olim gratus eram', he is again sure that she no longer loves him, as he was almost sure in lines 5—6. 'Non illo tempore' perhaps echoes against 'omnia tempora laetitiae' of line 24. But his claim in line 38 is carefully guarded: 'simili posset amare fide' keeps to what he is certain of, his

(18) The 'schema Pindaricum', whereby a plural subject has a singular verb, may offer some kind of parallel to the syntax here, but it is in any case easy enough for a town name to be conceived of as a singular entity.

(19) None of this has any point if the poem is split into 11 and 12. Cp e.g. the difficulties Camps has in interpreting here and B & B's involved discussion of 'conscia Roma'.

(20) In Seneca Apocolocyntosis 6 the following phrase seems to be used as a kind of proverb 'multa milia inter Xanthum et Rhodanum interesse'. Camps and B & B emphasise 'meo lecto' as though the point was his celibacy, not the distance of Cynthia. This is the result of trying to account for the poem as starting at line 31.

(21) See Shackleton Bailey's note for the interpretation of this line.

own love and total trust.[22] By lines 39—40 he is tossing off reasons for the "fact" that she does not love him. In line 39 the inferior Mss 'num' is often preferred to the paradosis 'non',[23] but this misses the casual nature of Propertius's argument here. 'Non' makes the opposition of a god seem self-evident, yet he goes on immediately to suggest an alternative reason, some magic potion.

Line 41 divides mimetically in the middle, a changed Propertius on one side of the colon, a changed Cynthia on the other. As in 1 v 18, 'qui' instead of the more usual 'quod' makes Propertius's change a radical one, a kind of loss of identity. The plural 'puellas' for Cynthia generalises the case, as he did at line 15. 'Mutat' is a less drastic or disturbing change than the one Propertius has undergone. Some commentators suppose that Cynthia must be back from the long journey for Propertius to know that she has changed,[24] but 'praesenti' in line 45 indicates that she has not yet returned. 'Mutat via longa puellas' is a belief which is not yet substantiated, generated by his distress rather than actual experience.

Lines 43—4 echo lines 35—6. The earlier couplet was organised by a double 'nec', what no longer happens for him: this couplet gives his present situation. Instead of Cynthia nourishing their love by her embraces, he spends his nights alone. 'Primum' is slightly strange here. Literally this is not true: presumably Propertius had slept alone before. But this is the first time his new self, created out of love and pain, has had to endure the experience. Line 44 more obviously echoes line 36. For 'dulcis' (Cynthia) there is only himself, 'ipse gravis'; for 'nostra', 'meis'; and for 'sonat', only 'esse', mute and painful existence.

Propertius's love now seems hopeless. The next two couplets give the advice that an ordinary lover might take in such a situation. Line 45 echoes the famous line in Vergil's Georgics: 'felix qui potuit rerum cognoscere causas. (II 490), but Propertius's version is a lover's parody of the sentiment. The lover's supreme felicity and wisdom consists of weeping to his mistress when she is there before him. Even this remedy is not available to Propertius, because Cynthia is not in Rome. The other solution is to go to another mistress. This will still be servitude, but the process of change gives a kind of joy.

Line 49 contains a sullen, resentful affirmation of his continuing loyalty. 'Fas' contrasts with 'crimen' of line 30. She may indulge in illicit

(22) Camps finds great difficulty in interpreting these lines, since he assumes that 'the general sense required by the context is that Propertius's love for Cynthia was formerly requited'. But our interpretation here allows the lines to be taken in their obvious surface meaning.

(23) So Rothstein, Camps, B & B.

(24) So Camps, B & B.

love, but such treachery is forbidden to him. This part of the poem has descended into a kind of emotional blackmail. He displays his distress, and indicates what others would do about it. But the last line rises far above this level, proclaiming his total and unequivocal dependence on her. She is not only 'omnia tempora laetitiae', as in line 24: she marks the temporal limits of his existence. The line expands 'Cynthia causa fuit' of line 26: she is his arche and telos, essential beyond the possibility of unfaithfulness, beyond all considerations of pleasure and pain.

POEM XIII

Poem XIII is clearly a companion poem to X. Both are addressed to Gallus, and they have recognisably the same incident at their centre. XII is more explicit in every way, and is probably the earlier of the two,[1] but it is not simply a first draft that was superseded by the final version. It is a very attractive poem, successful in its different terms, conveying a quite different and no less valuable quality of feeling.

The poem opens dramatically, with Propertius responding to something that Gallus has just said. The situation behind this exchange is usually supposed to be that Cynthia has left Propertius, and Gallus is mocking him for his misfortune.[2] That would have been cruel and insensitive, not impossible for the Gallus of poem V, but hard to square with the tone adopted towards him in this poem, since Gallus is called 'perfide' not 'irrisor' in this poem, and 'laetabere' is a positive word, not usually used for mockery or scorn. It seems much more likely that Gallus here is genuinely congratulating Propertius on Cynthia's absence. 'Casus' normally referred to bad luck, but could be good luck as well. Gallus is 'perfide', so for him the absence of a mistress would be a chance to be used, a cause for rejoicing. Gallus is not being malicious here, just superficial. The poem that follows is in praise of 'fides', through an account of the kind of relationship to which 'fides' is natural. The relationship is then half-playfully attributed to Gallus, a game Propertius liked to pay with his friends (e.g. IV to Bassus, and IX to Ponticus).

So 'vacem' in line 2 does not indicate bereavement or loss, but freedom, leisure (like 'vacet' in XI 13). 'Vacuus' is used similarly of hearts of eyes by Propertius (e.g. 'vacuos ocellos', IX 27, 'vacuo pectore', of Gallus in X 30). Of course, this is Gallus's word for Propertius's situation, the subjunctive indicating indirect speech. 'Solus' of itself is neutral but would have other connotations for Propertius (see XI–XII 43). But 'abrepto amore' indicates a violent wrench, how the situation would seem to Propertius.

In line 3 he sharply distinguishes his attitude from Gallus's. But line 4 moves off in an unexpected direction, which is to determine the rest of the poem. Gallus has advised Propertius to be unfaithful. Instead of advising Gallus to be faithful, the obvious rejoinder, he says that he hopes that Gallus's girl will not deceive him. 'Puella' here might be general – any girl – but could as well be a particular girl, whom Propertius is claiming to know. All this required some explanation, since Gallus has never had the kind of relationship where this would matter. The wish implies that Gallus has entered upon a permanent relationship like Propertius's, and is now equally dependent on his mistress.

(1) See argument at poem X,

(2) So Enk, B & B.

So in line 5 Propertius begins the claim that Gallus has fallen deeply in love in this way, contrary to what everyone thinks. Gallus's reputation is acknowledged, but is already on the way to being subverted. Line 6 describes his amatory approach till now: self-confidently promiscuous, avoiding all involvement. But 'certus' at the beginning of this line makes an obvious contrast with 'perditus' at the beginning of the next. The cock-sure Gallus is now quite lost. 'Mora' is also a key word. The 'mora' he used to avoid in sexual relationships will become the essential quality in the new kind of love. The same word is used for it in X 6, and the idea of delight being protracted almost unbearably is the point of lines 15–17 in this poem.

His pallor in line 7 is a conventional feature, but line 8 is more unusual and obscure. The paradosis 'adire' has seemed so odd that most editors accept 'abire' from V2. But 'abire' is hardly easier[3] and in fact 'adire' makes much more apposite a sense. The juxtaposition 'lapsus adire' contains the paradox of Gallus's new situation, a fall that is also an advance, a lapse from his previous point of view but an initiation into the new state.[4] 'Abire' would have no point here. 'Primo gradu' is the first stage in this ascent that is achieved by falling. In X 1 it will be called 'primo amori'.

Lines 9–12 describe the power of the new mistress, in ominous terms. In lines 19–20 it seems she will make him pay for the distress he has caused all his previous mistresses. Over these couplets she seems to assume a near-divine status. 'Poena' with 'erit' instead of a verb like 'afficere' suggests that she is a Poena, an avenging goddess, not simply a punishment.[5] Line 10 contrasts her single power with the weakness of the others, 'multarum/una' (the idea is developed more effectively in poem V 12). The function of 'miseras' has aroused some contention. Enk supposes it has been transferred from 'multarum' to 'vices', a view which Shackleton Bailey rightly castigates as involving 'a monstrous enallage'.[6] There is probably no enallage here at all, monstrous or otherwise. The many are wretched, of course, but Propertius has said that in the previous line and does not need to repeat it. His point now is to insist that the recompense will be equally pitiable. So 'miseras' goes properly with 'vices', but is juxtaposed with 'multarum' to bring out the justice of the revenge.

(3) Both Enk and Camps have complex notes offering differing interpretations of the word – Bailey sums up the position " 'abire' has been generally adopted but variously explained". A departure from the paradosis ought to command more unanimity.

(4) A more elaborate Christian play with this kind of paradox can been seen in Donne
Then should I see a Sun, by rising, set,
And by that setting endless day beget.
(Good Friday, riding Westward, 11–12.)

(5) See also the transformation of Cynthia into the force Love in I i 1–4, and our comments on this passage.

(6) See Bailey. His own view, that the phrase means 'lamentable vengeance for many', is not far distant from ours. Camps thinks the enallagous meaning is possible.

Lines 11–12 still describe her absolute power, though now it seems slightly more beneficent. 'Compescet' is a strong word, but its object is his desires, not Gallus himself. Gallus will no longer even want to stray as he used to. 'Vulgaris istos' indicates the contempt he should feel for his unregenerate impulses, his undiscriminating affections. Line 12 is unclear. 'Amicus eris' could mean "be her friend", i.e. be in her favour: she will not like him if he continues his search for novelty.[7] But it could also mean "you will not like to", the restriction this time proceeding from his new state of mind.[8] The second is slightly more likely here, but both could be intended: he will not want to because she would not like him if he did, but really he will not want to anyway.

There are ominous hints in all this that will be developed at length in X but are muted in the rest of the poem. He now reaches the central episode of the poem, his eye-witness account of Gallus's night of love. The account is introduced by a prefatory couplet, lines 13–14. This ostensibly establishes the absolute truth of what is to follow, but it does this with a kind of over-assertive insistence that suggests the contrary. What follows is a joke, a send-up of Gallus, an outrageous piece of false evidence. This is not immediately evident, but lines 19–20 are high burlesque, where Propertius describes himself trying in vain to pull them apart, like copulating dogs, without either of them seeming to notice. If they had noticed, Propertius would not have needed to repeat his claim twice that he personally saw the whole business: 'vidi ego, vidi ego'. All this of course concerns the truth of the incident for the poem, not in historical fact.[9]

As in poem X, the woman takes the more active role. 'Toto collo' suggests that he is nearly suffocated by her total embrace. 'Iniectis manibus' in line 16 are the reason for his tears. 'Manus inicere' has a legal sense, of arresting a debtor or asserting a right of possession.[10] She is still the Poena of line 9, exacting her rights. But 'diu', emphasising how long her embrace lasts, gives another reason for the tears. These are the tears of an exquisite kind of pleasure, arising out of delay, as in X 2 and 5–6. 'Languescere' and 'animam deponere' both suggest, like 'morientem' of X 5, a weakness like death.

The paradosis 'verbis' in line 17 has seemed unsatisfactory to many commentators, who have been attracted by the emendation 'labris', her

(7) Enk supposes this phrase to mean 'nor will you be always dear to girls (who have not yet been deceived by you) as long as you search for novelty', but this seems a 'non sequitur' in view of the preceding line. Rothstein's view is similar.

(8) See Camps on this passage.

(9) See Introduction pp 5–15

(10) Cp. XII Tab. III 2 (Warmington). Rothstein and Enk think that the hands are his; but that is hardly consistent with the pictures of the previous line where 'vinctum' almost implies an inability to move.

physical lips instead of what she says.[11] But X 6 makes it clear that speech is an important part of the erotic experience for Propertius. (Cp. also XI—XII, 13 and 36, or II I 9—10.) 'Labris' here would be much more conventional and less interesting, the emendation of a male chauvinist, like the former Gallus in this poem, but not at all like Propertius. Propertius is trying to wean Gallus away from his kind of rapid and subvocal sexuality. The "longed-for words" he would die for will be a potent part of her power over him. In line 32 her speech will cause even Jove to love her. The relationship is not exclusively physical, but is no less erotic for that.

The next line, 18, begins to make the send-up obvious. He pretends to be suddenly overcome with shame and modesty ('pudor'), which the previous description has made seem unlikely. But this protestation only introduces the even grosser image of him tugging at their madly copulating bodies. Some modesty!

But the tone shifts entirely in the four couplets that follow. His aim is not to mock Gallus but to celebrate an experience. Lines 21—4 transpose it on to the mythic plane, where it is suffused with supernatural significance, dignity and splendour. Both myths describe a transformation. Enipeus was a river-god who was loved by Tyro, daughter of Salmoneus. But Neptune loved her too, and as she entered the river near the sea the greater god penetrated the lesser, the ocean mingling with the river, and made love to the willing Tyro.[12] The myth is seen erotically, a divinity permeating the lover in the act of love, the lover becoming a god. The transformation is not a destructive or violent one. It is described through 'mixtus', a mingling, and the love involved is yielding, easy ('facilis').

The second myth is more violent. Hercule's agony on his funeral pyre is presented as a first taste of his nuptial joys, the physical burning an image for the flames of love. Hercules having been consumed on the pyre at Cetaea became one of the immortals, the spouse of "celestial Hebe".[13] Propertius has given the myth an erotic meaning again: Hercules had to be destroyed in the fires of love to become a deity. Gallus is like Enipeus and Hercules but more so, ('non sic/nec sic'), transformed into a god by the intensity of his love. Such a love may seem like death (cp. 'animam deponere' in line 17) but is also a taste of immortality. This is the same paradox as 'lapsus adire' in line 8.

(11) Various emendations have been suggested; only 'labris' has gained general currency being adopted by Enk, Barber in the Oxford text, and Shackleton Bailey. Rothstein and B & B have retained 'verbis' but have interpreted it as his words. This is rightly criticised by Enk and Bailey, but the answer is not to emend, but to perceive that the words must be hers. This latter is the view of Camps.

(12) Cp. Hom Od. XI 235, Apollodorus I 9 8.

(13) Cp. Hesiod Theog. 953.

A single experience like this is worth more than the rest of a lifetime, which is why she is worth more than all other mistresses combined. Line 25 puts this argument, but in a compressed way that has proved obscure. 'Amantes' at the end is usually taken as a noun, lovers,[14] but this gives very strained sense. No lovers have been mentioned before, and they are irrelevant here. The point of the comparison is the superiority of this one act of love to all the other experiences that Gallus has known. Besides, if 'amantes' are lovers, we have, with 'praecurrere', the unlikely image of a race between a day and a line-up of champion lovers. With this reading of 'amantes', the line must mean "(by virtue of) this one day (you) have been able to outstrip all (other) lovers (except me)". This is just possible, but still not very relevant.

The essence of the line is contained in the initial juxtaposition, 'una dies omnes', one day against all. 'Dies' here is probably singular and probably recalls Lucretius's famous 'una dies infesta tibi tot praemia vitae (ademit)' (III 899). That single day in Lucretius is death, the end of all joys. Propertius's single day is a kind of death too, one which is the consummation of all joy. 'Potuit praecurrere' then gives the comparison in a more vividly kinetic form than, e.g. 'fuit melior'. The metaphor in 'praecurrere' recalls 'adire' in line 8. 'Amantes' is then a participle going with 'dies' (understood, with 'omnes'). 'Amantes (dies)' is for 'dies amoris', attributing quasi-human activity to the day as was done with 'praecurrere'. The day is identified with the girl whose love gives it meaning. In a sense she is that time (as Cynthia was 'omnia nostrae tempora laetitiae' for Propertius in XI—XII 24, by the same figure).

The torches in line 26 recall Hercules's funeral pyre. Gallus too is blazing, undergoing his transformation. Lines 27—8 move on to the period afterwards. As in lines 11—12, her control is exercised on his emotions, not just forbidding him to do what he still wants to do. She does not allow his old pride to reappear. 'Succedere' indicates a surreptitious approach: she will not allow even that. Line 28 is unclear. 'Adduci' of the Mss has seemed impossible to most commentators, and is usually emended to 'abduci',[15] a total change of direction as occurred with 'adire' of line 8. 'Adduci' is impossible if Gallus is the subject. However, if the emotion, 'fastus', is still the subject of the infinitive, then 'abduci' is exactly wrong, and something like 'adduci' gives the required sense. But this is not certain.

The next two couplets, lines 29—32, turn to the girl, and praise her beauty and attraction to the gods. She is compared to Leda and her daughters, and to "Inachian heroines". Leda's relevance is obvious. She was the beloved of Jove, and Gallus as the lover of such a girl almost attains to the same status. Leda's daughters, Helen and Clytemnestra, were of legendary beauty

(14) By e.g. Enk, Butler in the Loeb; Enk glosses 'you have loved for only one day, but on this one day you have surpassed all lovers'.

(15) 'Abduci' is the reading of a correction in one Ms. It is adopted by Rothstein, Enk, B & B.

as befitted the daughters of a god.[16] 'Inachiis' is usually taken as an equivalent of Argive, but the underlying myth has a closer relevance. The daughter of Inachus was Io, again beloved of Jove. From her descended the 50 daughters of Danaus, 49 of whom killed their husbands while one, Hypermnestra, remained loving to hers and spared him. This is the same pattern as in lines 10 and 30, superior to many. The "one" in line 10 was a Poena, this one is a redeemer: a mistress like this is both.

The closing couplets return to the tone of the opening. 'Tu vero' repeats the opening 'tu', but this is a totally changed Gallus, or so Propertius pretends. Line 33 claims that his "death" in love is imminent and inevitable. 'Utere' at the start of line 34 is surprisingly blunt and pragmatic after the mythic richness of lines 21–32. X 27–8 gives a similar impression. This is presumably a Gallus kind of thing to say, the sort of thing he might have said to Propertius before the poem opened, advising him to make use of Cynthia's convenient absence.

The rest of line 34 is doubled-edged. It should mean that he is worthy of exactly this mistress, but 'limen' for mistress is slightly ominous — the threshold is where a rejected lover waits — and the negative has pejorative implications, that he does not deserve anyone else. The implications of lines 9–10 lie close to the surface here.

The gnomic last couplet has its difficulties. 'Quae' is often emended to 'qui', to make 'felix' agree with 'error'.[17] But if 'quae' is retained the sentence is less awkward, and gives a better sense. Propertius's hope for his friend is that his mistress remains 'felix', propitious towards him, like a favouring deity. 'Error' here is wandering, a less hopeful version of the advance ('adire') of line 8, but recalling 'perditus' of line 7.

The last line returns to the idea of lines 11–12, a final statement of how the One can replace the many. At the end of X, fidelity is necessary for Gallus, but not obviously pleasant. In this poem, fidelity is offered as more effortless, a matter of finding everything one wants in the one mistress — though this is only advice, not a statement of how things are. This kind of basic certainty and delight is the poem's most attractive quality. The mockery of Gallus is good-humoured. There are hints of the painful side of love but they are carefully muted, and the celebration of the delights of love carries total conviction. It does not matter whether it was Gallus or Propertius who really experienced this delight on the night in question.

(16) Who are the three? It seems to us possible that they are Helen, Clytemnestra and their mother Leda, but commentators cite Eur. Iph. Aul. 49 which assigns three daughters to Leda. The third, Phoebe, is so obscure that it seems unlikely that Propertius should invoke her as an exemplar of beauty here.

(17) By e.g. Rothstein, Camps.

POEM XIV

All the signs are that this is an early poem, concerning a stage when Propertius's love was utterly satisfying.[1] But though it is pre-eminently a celebration, it is not simply an effusion. The elaborate form typical of his early poetry derives pleasure from its own performance, but the poem contains a carefully structured argument, not all of whose implications are immediately obvious or simple mindedly happy. So Camps, for instance, very properly compares it with its natural counterpart, poem VI, and then observes: 'There (in VI) the lover is contrasted with the man of action: here the pleasures of riches are contrasted with those of love, to the advantage of the latter'.[2] But the poem is in three eight line parts and only the first two are included in this summary. The third part describes love's power to make the pleasures of riches feel unattractive anyway, and stresses rather the pains than the pleasures of love.

But the poem's argument is less general than this kind of account might suggest. The first eight lines are not about riches as such, but about the very pleasant existence that is apparently available to Tullus. The poem concludes, not with a general proposition, that all men should prefer love, but with Propertius's particular decision,itself made provisional by 'dum'. In I vi, the natural pair for this poem, Tullus has apparently invited Propertius to go abroad with him, and the poet gives his reasons for refusing this invitation. Poem XIV is more formal in style, and cast in more general terms, so that its particular occasion is not so obvious, but the poem reads most satisfactorily, especially at certain key points in its development,[3] if it is seen as a courteous refusal to an invitation to spend a holiday at Tullus's villa.

The structure of the poem is unusually tight: it is organised in eight line sections, which contain considerable parallelisms of structure. There are parallelisms both within the sections themselves and between different sections. Each paragraph devotes three couplets to the qualities of the respective states of life, and concludes with a couplet arguing the claims of love. The first section is organised as a single grammatical unit, with 'licet' governing three couplets and picked up by the answering 'non tamen' of line 7. The opening 'licet' is concessive, introducing the list of things that Tullus can do. 'Abiectus' suggests a surprising loosening of moral fibre in Tullus, along with the adverb 'molliter' ('softly'): briefly it seems to be

(1) The percentage of long-word pentameter endings is high — 58.3%. See Introduction

(2) This is the standard view of this poem and is found in Rothstein, Enk and Butler and Barber.

(3) See particularly lines 7 and 23, discussed below.

161

Tullus who is reproved for unmanly weakness more expected of a lover. The periphrasis 'Tiberina unda' for the simple name of the river perhaps also suggests a kind of luxuriance.[4] In the next line, Tullus's activity has a similar quality. Lesbian wine was the smoothest in antiquity,[5] a very high quality product fetched halfway across the Mediterranean for the enjoyment of this Roman epicure. The silver cups of Mentor were the most valuable and refined 'objets de vertu' for Romans of the time. Pliny records that the orator Crassus had paid 100,000 sesterces for a pair of these, but was ashamed to use them in public.[6] This is Tokay Essence in a Cellini goblet. The lines do not imply mere vulgarity or ostentation; this is the best wine served in the most tasteful vessel, with all the panache of riches richly used. Even so, this description of the 'otium' of Tullus hints at a kind of slackness, the softness of Lesbos, a kind of reprehensible excess.

The next couplet, however, contains simple delight, a recreation of the pleasures of boat watching, or the pleasure of watching other people work. Both kinds of boat referred to here were working boats:[7] Tullus's villa was not withdrawn from all contact with the busy world of commerce, whose presence in this form was a source of pleasure to him in his leisure. The 'lintres' speed downriver (though 'celeris', speedy, is an amusingly incongruous epithet for a tub). They are probably laden with supplies for the city, while the 'rates' toil slowly upriver. The goods that come out of Rome would include imported luxuries of various kinds. These come towards the watcher, so that the wealth implicit here adds another layer of luxury to the scene.[8]

(4)   The phrase also occurs in Hor. Odes III xii 7 – 'simul unctos Tiberinis umeros lavit in undis' – where there seems to be some emphasis on the sensuality of the scene.

(5)   See Enk on this passage. Shackleton Bailey adds Pliny N.H. XIV 73 and Sil. VII 211. The latter suggests, he says, rather different qualities in Lesbian wines – 'Methymna ferox'.

(6)   N.H. XXXIII 147 quoted by Enk.

(7)   The first meaning of 'Linter' is a 'tub' of some kind: transferred it means a 'lighter' or something similar: cp. Cic. Mil. XXVII 74 'lintribus in eam insulam materiem, calcem, caementa, harenam convexit'. 'Rates' is a rather unspecific word in poetry, but the 'funes' makes it clear that some kind of barge is implied. The point is that this is commercial activity that Tullus is observing. Enk appositely quotes Pliny N.H. III 53 'et ideo quamlibet magnarum navium et Italo mari capax, rerum in toto orbe nascentium mercator placidissimus, pluribus prope solus quam ceteri in omnibus terris amnes accolitur aspiciturque villis'.

(8)   If Tullus's villa lay upriver, the commercial activity on the river would be the distribution of goods from the emporia of Rome to the hinterland. But it was possibly merely transTiberine (as Martial's was, IV 1 xiv 3 'longo Ianiculi iugo recumbunt (sc. horti)', in which case the activity would be Rome's, and the barges coming upriver would be coming from the port of Ostia with the goods of the world (see previous note).

The next couplet, lines 5–6, turns away from the river and observes the grove which was apparently part of Tullus's estate. The hexameter begins by referring to the grove as 'nemus', a word usually used of an uncultivated group of trees and which has a strong aura of the epic about it.[9] But this grove is entirely artificial and manmade. 'Satas' indicates planted by man, and 'omne', juxtaposed to it, insists that the wood is entirely the work of man. Some suppose that 'vertice' in line 5 refers to the tips of the trees. The singular here would be odd but not impossible, but this reading supposes a pointless and puzzling substitution, 'vertice', the part that reaches, for the direction it reaches, upwards ('caelo'). It is easier to take 'vertice' as a locatival ablative, along the crest.[10] Caucasus in the next line is also more apposite if Tullus's estate is on a hill. Then in line 6 the poet compares the trees in Tullus's plantation to the huge trees on the mighty Caucasian range. The effect suggested is a kind of studied wildness, epic grandeur in miniature. Tullus's villa expresses power as well as affording opportunity for the leisure described in the opening lines. There is inescapably a hint of the burlesque in this extreme hyperbole, though this is no Timon's villa:

> . . . . whose building is a Town,
> His pond an Ocean, his parterre a Down:
> Who but must laugh the Master when he sees
> A puny Insect, shivering at the Breeze.
>
> (Pope 'Mor. Ess.' IV 105–8)

Tullus does things well, and Propertius's description is collaborative, its own exaggeration and formality endorsing the similar qualities in what he sees. The mockery here and in the opening couplet is the banter of friendship, and is innocent of any general satiric intent.

But however attractive Tullus's villa and the way of life possible in it, it would not be able to outweigh Propertius's attachment to his love, as he states in the fourth couplet. Here the subjunctive mood of 'valeant' in line 7 is important; the 'would' needs an 'if', which is most easily supplied as 'if I were there to enjoy them'. 'Meo' here is also significant. It indicates that the statement in line 7 is not general. The struggle ('contendere') takes place inside Propertius.

The reason for the rejection is brought out in line 8, where the statement becomes more general, rounding off the section. 'Nescit' ('does not know how to'), the line begins, throwing the word into prominence. 'Amor' is the emotion, present in the individual but considered as an independent force, and it is this force that is said not to know how to yield to riches. One part of Propertius may recognise the attractions of Tullus's mode of life, but insofar

(9)   The word is a borrowing from the Greek and is frequent in Virgil; cp. also Ennius – 'in nemore Pelio' quoted in (Cic.) ad Her. 2 22.

(10) For 'vertice' as 'crest', see Pasoli on this passage. Enk, Shackleton Bailey and Camps disagree but without any very strong reason.

as his actions are determined by 'amor', he cannot even conceive of yielding to those attractions. This is subtly but importantly different from the general proposition (as dubious as it is conventional) that love is better than riches. Propertius's generalisation shows far more psychological insight: Love as an obsession overpowers the attraction of wealth, as he indicates more explicitly at lines 15–16.

However, the next three couplets set out to argue generally for the merits of Love. Retrospectively, they can be seen to answer point by point the desirable qualities of Tullus's villa. Lines 1–2 describe Tullus lying down; 9–10 describe the much more pleasant time Propertius as lover has when also lying down. Lines 3–4 describe a river busy with commercial activity, but 11–12 easily outgo this, as the legendary river Pactolus with its golden stream flows under his roof, and he picks up jewels from the Red Sea.[11] The 'quietem' is a genuine 'repose' for Propertius, as lazing on the banks of the Tiber is for Tullus, but it is not 'sleep': he does not sleep when he is with his mistress, and 'trahit' brings out the quality of effort involved in the prolonga-, tion of this kind of repose. In the following line, the flow is easier, since the lover has a less strenuous time by day than by night, and the word is 'ducit', a less intensive version of 'trahit', 'leads' for 'draws'. In the next couplet, the image of opulence that is used to convey the quality of his delight is more extravagant than anything that can be seen on Tullus's estate. The epic power of the grove of trees of Caucasian dimensions is answered by the lover's host of tributary kings, equally hyperbolic; but there is a change in the quality of the vaunt here, as Propertius indicates more specifically the subjective charac-ter of the vision, and its dependence on his love prospering. It is his joy ('gaudia') which is the guarantee of these conquered kings, who, with the imagery of opulence, are a projection of his delight in love. So he quickly safeguards this joy with a prayer for its continuance. This of course implies an awareness of its fragility.

The next couplet, lines 15–16, performs the same function for this section as 7–8 did for the first, opposing love to wealth, but the exact logical connection suggested by the opening 'nam' is not clear or straightforward. The regular progression 'nam – tum – tum – nam' suggests a simple balanced structure, but line 14 occupies an equivocal position in the argu-ment. The anxiety it expresses may be entirely parenthetical. Then 15 would substantiate the claims of 13, particularly, 'cessuros' – kings will admit Propertius's superior happiness because no-one can be happy when love is against him. But the words imply the problems of a lover rather than of a king, the problem the poet's brief prayer in 14 was designed to ward off.

(11) 'Gemma' is expansive in its vagueness, but it is probably best to see it as standing for 'pearl'. See Enk on this. The high value that the Romans placed on pearls is relevant: Enk quotes Pliny N.H. IX 106 'principium ergo columenque omnium rerum preti margaritae tenent; cp. also XXVII 62.

Line 16 reinforces these implications, since it is specifically concerned with the poet's own situation. 'Praemia' stands for the compensations or gratitications of wealth. But the MSS offer two readings for the copula here, of equal authority, 'sunt' (APDVVo) and 'sint' (N). All modern editors follow N, but without giving any reasons. Since they punctuate with an exclamation mark at the end of the line, it is difficult to think what good reasons they might have given. They must be reading this as a wish: "I want no riches if Venus frowns on me" (Camps). But this would be a foolish wish. If Venus frowned, riches might be better than nothing, and would at worst be irrelevant. It only becomes a plausible wish if 'tristi Venere' is equivalent to "If Venus would frown as a result of it": but that would be a very strained reading of the phrase.

So there should be no exclamation mark here. 'Sint' will then refer to a possibility, as did 'valeant' in line 7. The thought is similar in the two cases. This is the apodosis for a conditional protasis implied by 'tristi Venere'. The meaning then is: "There would be no compensation, for me, if Venus frowned (lit. with Venus hostile)". The line closely parallels the previous one. The difference between 'sint', in this reading, and 'sunt' is slight. 'Sint' however, must be correct, since it is clear that Venus is favourable to him, for the moment. It carries the right hint of threat, that love could turn sour for him if he offends, and prepares for the following description of love's power.

The force of both these lines, 15 and 16, would fit in very badly with the simple argument that the pleasures of love outweigh the pleasures of wealth. In fact he would have conceded the whole case, since he tacitly admits the other side of love, the pain that would cancel its pleasures. The real argument is that the lover could not enjoy the pleasures of wealth even if they were superior, if this were incompatible with his love; and this argument, which applies to Propertius rather than Tullus, is pursued in the final section.

The general point made in the three couplets 17–22 is that love has power to invade and destroy the pleasures available on Tullus's estate. The same three sources of pleasure are presented, this time in reverse order: first, the epic power of the heroes, expressed earlier through the images of the Caucasus with its mighty trees, and the tributary kings; then the conspicuous wealth of the Arabian threshold;[12] and finally the repose that is denied to the 'miserum iuvenem'. None of these three qualities, of course, is ever offered as excluding the others. Riches for instance are not absent from

(12) The editors with varying degrees of confidence identify the stone here as onyx; citing Pliny N.H. XXXVI 59. The most recent editor of Pliny considers that he contradicts himself in this passage and has misunderstood his sources (Eichholz; Loeb edition). But Pliny mentions a stone which is described simply as 'Arabus lapis' which is 'ebori similis' (N.H. XXXVI 153). This stone is unidentifiable according to Eichholz. Cp. also XXXVII 145. The same stone is described by Diodorus II 52, 9 (and not onyx as Rothstein, Enk and Butler and Barber say). The point is not of great importance, but it is worth removing a spurious note of confidence from the commentaries at this place.

Tullus's leisure activities. The Mentorean cup may also have depicted a heroic scene, and Propertius's contemplation of wealth in love is effortless as well as unlimited. The qualities of leisure, wealth, and power may dominate a particular couplet, but they are generally interwoven to create the rich fabric of a way of life.

'Magnas heroum . . . vires' ('the great strength of heroes') of line 17, with which the section opens, is not obviously applicable to Propertius – it recalls someone more like Hercules, whose strength was broken by Omphale, the Lydian queen – but the 'etiam "even" of line 18 allows a suitably depreciatory self-reference to be made. Even men of iron feel pains through love, so a 'mollis iuvenis' like the poet would feel it more and be less able to resist it.

An increasing sense of urgency can be felt over these three couplets, which makes itself felt as an inexorable and even faintly disturbing advance. The first two couplets are each syntactically self contained, their two lines parallel in form, but in line 21 Venus not only crosses the threshold and approaches the bed, she also goes over the barrier of the couplet, as she tosses the youth on his couch. Such a departure from the structural norm of the poem leaves an uneasy feeling, and there is something frightening about the silent and irresistible advance of this figure. The repeated denial that she fears ('neque metuit', 'nec timet') suggests a threat to her which is hard to locate in these luxurious surroundings, as though there is some magical power in the threshold to ward off ill omened spirits,[13] and some of the sense of threat is transferred to her. The form of her coming recalls the coming of that more famous despiser of riches, Death,[14] though the result of the irresistible visitation is relatively unfatal, a sleepless night. In the second line of this third couplet, Tullus's fine collection of silks ('variis serica textilibus' emphasises the number in the plural 'serica' and the range in the ablative 'variis textilibus') is looked at functionally as an aid to rest ('relevant') and found wanting, an amusingly perverse way of responding to such a collection.

(13) The threshold itself is a magic place. The superstition about stumbling there is well known: cp. e.g. Plaut. Cas. 815, Tib. I iii 19–20, etc. The 'limen' was also important in some magic rites; at the Feralia, the Feast of the Dead, an old woman 'digitis tria tura tribus sub limine ponit' (Ovid F. II 573): perhaps the intention is that the ghosts will then stop at the threshold? It is also interesting that Pliny reports a kind of prophylactic power as belonging to the 'Arabian stone': N.H. XXXVII 145 'hanc putant (sc. Magi) contra colores nervorum prodesse habentibus'. None of this is specific enough to give a reason why Venus might be expected to be afraid when crossing the threshold, though it does suggest the sort of power that might be involved.

There also seems to be some source of fear located in the 'purple couch'. Red was a colour of some power in magic. André p. 261 makes this point, citing Theocr. II 2 and A.P. V 205 6. But again this is not specific enough to explain the precise quality of this passage of Propertius.

(14) Cp. Hor. Odes. I iv 13 'pallida Mors aequo pulsat pede pauperum tabernas/regumque turris'.

166

The final couplet opens with 'quae'. This still refers to Venus but the form of the phrase could describe the girl as well, identified with Venus, implicitly of divine status.[15] 'Aderit', "as long as she remains with me", offers the reason for refusing the invitation. She is 'placata', which recalls 'adverso' of 15, the form of words suggesting a deity who has been won over for the present, but who could be offended at some later time. 'Dum', as long as, also implies this. The second half of the line sets out grandly: 'non ulla verebor' ("I will have no fear . . ") announces total fearlessness, and it is not until the end of the next line that we get the delayed 'despicere', the thing he will not fear to do. But fear is an ominous thing to say he hasn't got, as with 'neque metuit' and 'nec timet' in lines 19 and 20. It draws attention to the emotion, and makes one wonder what force he does fear, what he would be afraid to do.

'Ulla regna' and 'Alcinoi munera' are the desirable things he will courageously reject. There is initially something surprising about the order here. Kingdoms would seem grander than the gifts of one particular king, even Alcinous. But 'ulla' makes these kingdoms more vaguely conceived and therefore easier to reject than the gifts of Alcinous, who was an especially apposite figure to mention at this point in the poem. As Camps notes, his wealth, and particularly his garden and orchard, were proverbial in the ancient world, and the mention of his name perhaps retroactively connects with the description of Tullus's estate, especially lines 5—6. The gifts of Alcinous as described in the Odyssey (VIII 382 sqq.) were valuable, but not remarkably so. They were more remarkable for the unforced generosity of the giver. In the Odyssey, Alcinous's kingdom represents a brief haven, restful but not debilitating like the land of the lotus eaters, where the hero can recuperate his strength and from which he is perfectly free to leave, enriched by gifts. Even this, Propertius says, he is not afraid to despise. If the poem is a courteous refusal to an invitation, the implication is flattering to Tullus, but the refusal, though oblique, is unequivocal. Propertius cannot even allow himself a pleasant interlude if it put his love at risk. So the sense of the impermanence of love, or at least of good fortune in love, which made its first appearance just after half way through, is developed increasingly as the poem progresses, even though it coexists with a sense of the infinitely satisfying condition of successful love. In spite of the apparent opposition between the pleasures of love and those of wealth, both are lovingly and fully created in poetry with a delicate perfection of ornament. The shadows hinted at towards the close, which give a new depth to the mood of the poem, remain only potential. They make the pleasures of successful love more urgent, not more imperfect,than anything available in Tullus's luxurious retreat.

(15) Cp. similar effect in I i 3—4, where Cynthia becomes Amor, the obverse of this. For mistress as deity see I v 7—12, xiii 9—10 29—32 and notes.

POEM XV

The pentameter endings indicate that this is an early poem.[1] If so it is a startling production, technically far in advance of other things he was writing at the time, far more dramatic than for instance poem II, the closest analogue, though less controlled and successful than it.[2] The poem's meaning in this case is the drama it implies, and what is said reveals its full meaning only in relation to the central drama being enacted. Cynthia's responses are not given directly but are sufficiently implied in a series of what amount to stage directions, and these responses are crucial to understanding the dramatic exchange. It is this exchange which structures the poem, accounting for its sometimes curious line of development. Significantly, one editor has wished to divide the poem in two:[3] if the dramatic principle of its structure is not seen, this will be a natural response to a break as sharp as occurs at line 25.

The basic situation is clear enough. Propertius is about to go off on a journey, and he claims that Cynthia has seemed suspiciously unconcerned on his behalf. Surprisingly, this situation has not been evident to all commentators, some of whom suppose that Propertius is merely feeling unwell, and is peeved that Cynthia is rather late and overdressed when she visits him.[4] This interpretation involves giving an unusual sense to 'periclo' in line 3, and ignores the obvious storm-imagery there, and it is supported by nothing in the poem. So it is hard to see why these commentators want to argue for this account of the poem, against the obvious sense of the words. Perhaps they find it implausible that Propertius could have the initiative and energy to leave Cynthia and Rome, and prefer to think of him more pathetically as a flu-victim. But in poem VI he seriously contemplated leaving Rome and Cynthia, and in poem XVII he regrets having done so.[5] The mythic section in this poem is dominated by Ulysses and Jason, the two great voyagers of antiquity, and the reactions of the heroines there are not at all appropriate to the sickbed.

The poem opens with aggressive directness, accusing Cynthia of infidelity, but the reason that follows is strangely trivial. The discrepancy

(1) 66.6% polysyllabic. See Introduction pp 5–15

(2) Pentameter count on II is 43.7%, but the relationship between XV 1–8, and especially 6–8, and poem II makes II appear the earlier. See discussion below.

(3) Rothstein.

(4) Rothstein, Bailey and Camps choose the illness hypothesis, Enk and perhaps B & B decide for a sea journey. The case for illness is discussed by Bailey and with the myopia characteristic of traditional commentators, he confines this dicussion mainly to the single word 'periclo'.

(5) Our statements here refer, of course, to what he could write, not necessarily to what he actually did. See Introduction

between accusation and evidence is deliberate, and prepares for the resolution of the poem. The accusation was always unfair, and he knows it, but it proceeds from anxieties which are overwhelmingly real. The principle of this poem is similar to that of XI–XII, 'culpa timoris erit', though in XV his fears lead to real cruelty, and he capitulates in the end without real apology.

A key word in line 1 is 'timebam', which is picked up in line 4 by 'timore'. These are the two kinds of fear that lie behind the poem, his fears for her fidelity multiplied by his fears for the journey itself. 'Saepe' and 'multa' seem to reinforce his accusation, but in fact refer only to his fears. His fears have been frequent and multiform, but he does not say that they have ever been justified. 'Levitatis' is juxtaposed with 'dura', her frivolity with the pain it causes him, with an implicit contrast between her superficiality and his capacity for deep feeling.

Line 2 accuses her outright of unfaithfulness. 'Hac' apparently offers this as self-evident, something he can point to, but in practice it serves to limit the accusation. All he can point to is her lateness, as he calls it, and her over-careful attire, but these are only innocuous examples of the 'levitas' he claims is typical of her in line 1. Line 3 is much more rhetorical in manner, self-dramatising, but Cynthia in line 4 seems not to have taken it seriously enough. Either Propertius is taking himself ridiculously seriously here, or the self-conscious inflation of line 3 tacitly acknowledges that his demands are unreasonable.

Lines 5–8 give the catalogue of her offences. At first it is hard to see how they are offences. In line 5 she is criticised for doing her hair that morning before she came, surely an innocent enough act. Only later does it emerge why she is being criticised here. The contrast is with Calypso's unkempt hair. So 'potes' implies one criticism: she should have been so distraught that she could not attend to such matters. The point of 'hesternos' is not clear either till the Calypso passage.[6] Calypso's hair was unkempt for many days: Cynthia tidies hers up after only one night. The point of 'manibus' does not emerge till late in the poem, lines 35–38. Her hands were associated with her oath, and they especially ought not to be able to do anything so irrelevant.

But though the accusation is trivial the anxiety is real and the criticism is curiously important to him. The way he justified line 5 is an indication of that. Behind lines 6–8 is the argument of poem II, where he sees this kind of adornment as a worrying symptom of Cynthia's values. Line 6 is more sharply critical. 'Desidia' describes her sitting at her toilet in front of her mirror, but the word connotes slothful inactivity.[7] 'Faciem' could mean beauty, but

(6) The editors normally take 'hesternos' to mean 'yesterday's coiffeur' and cite Ov. A.A. III 153. Our interpretation differs in its understanding of the nature of that arrangement, or rather disarrangement, as 'componere' implies. 'Manibus' is passed over in silence but its prominent position requires an explanation – on our interpretation the tone is indignant as it should be here.

(7) The poet may be glancing at the word's root in 'desideo' = to sit; the word normally implies idleness.

could also refer to mere appearances. Poem II played at length with this kind of ambiguity.[8] 'Quarere faciem' here implies the superficiality of the beauty she is interested in. The length of time she spends in acquiring it ('longa') will be contrasted with the time Calypso spends in grief.

Line 7 refers to the jewellery she wears. Here the key phrase is 'pectus variare'. This will be picked up later, in line 31, 'nostro mutetur pectore', where it refers to Propertius's own constancy. As it refers to the jewels, 'variare' indicates the different colours these gems contribute, but the verb also suggests the impulse to emotional innovation that underlies the activity. Propertius will make this explicit in the next line. 'Eois', Oriental, points to the foreign source of these jewels, which makes them suspect in terms of poem II.[9] 'Formosa' in line 8 is also used in the strange sense that poem II has justified, as beauty of the surface. The line gives the only motive a woman could have for adorning herself like this: to get ready for a new mate.

Lines 9—22 then make his points implicitly through a series of mythic exemplars. Unfortunately the latent content of these myths has usually not been perceived, and editors have commonly not only missed the underlying argument, but deformed it. Lines 15—16 are usually shifted to near the end, for no good reason and without any attempt to understand the real principle of the progression here.[10]

The sequence given in the tradition makes an extremely intricate and satisfying pattern. It falls into two sections, the first introduced by 'non sic', the second by 'nec sic'. Each section refers to two stories, one longer and more famous (Ulysses, Jason), the other less well known, described in a single couplet. In the first section the heroine is active on her lover's behalf: Calypso gave Ulysses favouring winds, Alphesiboea revenged her husband by killing her brothers, though they had murdered him for her sake. In the second section the heroine is more passive: Hypsipyle pines away, Evadne dies on her husband's funeral pyre. In each section, the heroine of the couplet is the more extreme in her response. To murder one's own brothers, especially when their offence was only to try to avenge her honour, is more extravagantly loyal than to give favouring winds, and to throw oneself on a funeral pyre more so than to pine away.

The lines seem to focus on the heroines, but as with poems II and III, it is worth noticing the role played by the males. The heroines may be admirable, but the first three heroes are guilty of the same offence, desertion. This cannot be an accident, in a poem about Propertius's own departure. The message of the myths seems to be highly unfair: men can be unfaithful but

(8) Lines 21—22, and see our account.

(9) Cp. esp. lines 2—4 and 13, and our discussion at that point.

(10) 15—16 are placed after 22 by Lachmann and after 20 by Markland. B & B sum up the central point of the argument for transposition when they say 'As placed by the Mss the couplet breaks the train of thought; for clearly 'nec sic . . . thalamo' (17—18) must follow immediately after the previous simile (9—14)'. They strain at a gnat; there seems to us to be no difficulty in the suspension implied by the Mss arrangement, and the rhythm of the argument seems superior without transposition.

women must be totally loyal. Later he will insist on his own utter fidelity, so he is as unlike Ulysses and the others as she is unlike Calypso, but the myth seems to carry a threat as well as a criticism, or perhaps it acknowledges his own guilt. The last hero, however, breaks the pattern significantly. Capaneus was killed by Jove's thunderbolt on the walls of Thebes, in punishment for his arrogant boast that he could conquer the city without Jove's help.[11] So he died on this invasion of a foreign land. The male whose story closes the movement proved vulnerable in spite of his boasts, and is an image for Propertius's human fears, rather than his mythic pretensions.

The longest of these descriptions is of Calypso. 'Non mota' in line 9 makes an obvious contrast with 'ire' in the previous one. Two couplets, lines 9–12, emphasise how long she sat grieving. This of course is after Ulysses has left, so Propertius is obviously imagining Cynthia's behaviour projected into the future, after he has gone, supposing that she is behaving now as though he had gone already. Line 11 pictures her grief graphically. Calypso contrasts totally with Cynthia. 'Multos dies' contrasts with the brief time she will mourn him. 'Illa' is mimetically ⌐irrounded by this multitude of days, and 'maesta' is in the midst of 'incomptis capillis'. In line 12 she speaks to the sea. Calypso was a goddess, who could have asked the sea to destroy Ulysses: instead, in Homer's account, she won her departing lover a safe passage.[12]

'Fleverat' in line 10 and 'sederat' in line 12 are pluperfects. The reason for this tense here is probably to mark the two actions as prior to the action of the other main verb, 'dolebat'. Even after she finished mourning openly, weeping and watching the empty horizon, she continued to grieve. 'Dolere' is an inner feeling, where 'flere' describes the outward expression of grief.

The logic of line 13 is at first sight rather odd. Propertius seems to be saying "although she would never see him again, she grieved". We would expect that not seeing him again would be a reason for grieving, so 'quamvis', although, seems wrong.[13] But 'visura' is to be contrasted with 'conscia' in the next line. Her love does not need to be renewed by seeing him again: her happy memories of their love still nourish her grief. 'Longae' recalls 'longa' in line 6 to make a contrast again, between Cynthia's long, vain idleness and Calypso's longer shared happiness.

Alphesiboea is a strange example to have chosen. Alcmaeon her rene-

(11) Cp. Prop. II xxxiv 40, Aesch. Sept. 423–434.

(12) Cp. Hom. Od. line 268: his journey from the island was not in the end a safe one, but the goddess did her best.

(13) Rothstein notices the peculiarity of 'quamvis' and suggests that the morals of erotic poetry require that a lover should remain true if her gallant is going to return, but if not she is free to seek another. This is good rationalism, but bad psychology, though he is at least aware that there is something here that needs explanation whereas the other commentators are silent.

gade husband was murdered by her brothers.[14] Line 16 irrelevantly insists that love is stronger than familial ties. It is possible that there is an allusion here: perhaps Cynthia's relatives were hostile towards Propertius. But if there was an allusion it is now lost.

'Rapientibus' in line 17 echoes 'rapiat' in line 3, to connect Propertius's journey with the voyage of the Argonauts. Hypsipyle has an admirably total lack of interest in anyone else after Jason has gone. 'Hospitium', the act of welcoming or entertaining a guest, used instead of 'hospes', a guest, makes her seem even more selfless: once her function ceases, she just fades away. The form of phrasing does not value her at all as an independent person.

Evadne's sacrifice is the culmination of this process of feminine self-abnegation. 'Elata' refers to her physcially being placed on the pyre, but probably also has been chosen for its metaphorical significance as well, proud, lofty (cp. 'fama' in the next line).

Lines 23–4 predictably complain that she is not like any of these. 'Historia' implies that she should become a contemporary example of the quality: the word for legendary heroines would be 'fama' or 'fabula'.[15] What follows is much less predictable. In line 25 he seems to be telling her not to repeat her perjury. This implies that now at any rate she is swearing that she loves him, even if she was undemonstrative to begin with. But the description also shows Propertius rejecting her protestations. This is partly because — so he asserts — she has perjured herself. This will make her oaths dangerous. 'Parce' suggests the need for caution. The gods she swears by have been forgotten ('oblitos') or neglected by her, so she should be wary of rousing them. Lines 27–8 then imply that their fates are inseparable. 'Periclo' is Propertius's danger. Since the previous line describes Cynthia's dangerously perjured oaths. Propertius's danger seems to result from that. The offended gods may destroy him to punish her. But 'nostro' implies that his danger is hers as well (as 'nostro' in line 4 implied that she should share his fear). Line 28 then gives this idea explicitly. She will regret hs danger — caused indirectly by her — if something unpleasant happens to her with her natural protector absent.

However, he has not yet said that he is her natural protector. The myths have implied the opposite. Lines 29–31 imply this, but only indirectly, so their place in the sequence of thought is not easy to see. Lines 29–30 present two traditional impossibilities. The expression of both of these is unclear, which further complicates interpretation. 'Prius' signals the compari-

(14) For this legend Enk cites Apollodorus III 92 and Paus. VIII 24 8. That Alphesiboea killed her brothers is found in no other version of this story, except that of Propertius.

(15) 'Historia' usually means something which is actual or real: See TLL VI 2834 40 ff, and also Cic. 'de Or'. II 62. The equation of 'historia' with 'mythus' seems usually ironic, until Ovid at least; cp. TLL VI 2840 5 ff.

son to be made with these 'adynata'. The first impossibility concerns rivers. The manuscripts here have 'multa', which commentators have been unhappy with. It is often emended to 'nulla', so that the impossibility becomes rivers ceasing to flow.[16] But the common impossibility with rivers is their flowing upwards.[17] Ceasing to flow is not impossible enough, especially given the next line, where time runs backwards. So 'multa' of the Mss is probably right. Rothstein punctuates with a colon after 'prius': "many things will happen first". But this is weak. Besides, only two things follow, not many. 'Multa' seems odd if it goes with 'flumina', since "many" is weaker than "all". But a standard form of the commonplace named a single river,[18] and 'multa' is more than 'unum'. The expression here seems merely negligent, as though Propertius relied on the commonplace nature of the image to do his work.

Line 30 gives another impossibility, an inversion of the cycle of the season. The tense of 'duxerit' makes this second impossibility even more impossible, since it makes the completion of the anti-cycle the precondition for his breaking faith. These two images ally his love to forces of nature. It is as natural as the force of gravity, as inevitable as the progression of the seasons.

Line 31 contains the strongest affirmation in the poem, but it is curiously muffled in expression. The key word is 'cura', 'tua cura' his love for Cynthia. 'Cura' indicates a protective kind of concern, so the use of the word here makes the claim that justifies lines 27–8. He will never cease to love her, never cease to have the protective concern for her that she will value if she should suffer any hardship. That is why she will grieve if Propertius should come to harm. The rest of the line recalls line 7, to make a contrast between Propertius and Cynthia. She craves variety ('variare'), he will never change. She has jewels on the outside of her breast: his love is within. 'Sub' is significantly different from 'in' here. It implies subordination, protection, her love sheltering within his breast.[19] This whole line works in a curious way. Its basic meaning is clear, but apparently not related to its context. Why should he suddenly declare his undying love here, in the midst of his accusations? The relevance derives from an argument that remains entirely implicit. This argument would seem specious if stated directly, but it is important to Propertius. The line in fact admits his need for her, in a form which tries to pretend that she needs him. His sense of his own vulnerability is now closer to the surface.

(16) 'Nulla' is the reading of Passerat's Ms and is accepted by Enk and Camps; Bailey thinks emendation is probably necessary.

(17) Cp. e.g. Prop. II xv 33 'fluminaque ad caput incipient revocare liquores'; Eur. Med. 410, Dem. XIX 287, Hor. Odes I xxix 10.

(18) The Horace passage cited in the last note names the Tiber: Cp. also Ov. Her. V 29–30 (the Xanthus).

(19) L. & S. 'Sub' C 3. Generally the meaning is 'under the power of', but meanings of protection may naturally enter in – e.g. Hor. Epistles II i 99, possibly Prop. II i 26.

Line 32 now contains an important concession to her, in the first clause: She may be what she will. This presumably refers to her superficiality, vanity and indolence of the first 8 lines. So essentially he is retracting his criticism, or relaxing his demands on her. But 'non aliena tamen' is, as ambiguous as he is uncertain. Either 'eris' or 'sis' can be suppled.[20] If he is certain of her, 'eris' is understood. He may be absent, she may be dressed to kill, but essentially they remain united. 'Aliena' could refer to physical separation or to estrangement. There is something of a play on these two meanings here.[21] She is locked in his heart, 'sub pectore', so in a sense they will not be apart. But 'sis' might also be understood, and the clause becomes a plea. Whatever she does, may she not go so far as to break faith. But the difference between the two readings is more a matter of tone than grammar.

Lines 33–40 move towards the resolution.[22] He addresses her eyes, which she swore by in the past. The implicit stage directions now indicate that Cynthia is obviously distressed, claiming how much she cares. She raises her eyes upwards, appealing to the sun to confirm her truth. Her colour comes and goes, and she is weeping. This is the demonstration of concern that he wanted in the beginning, but now he is grudging and sceptical. In line 34 'saepe' echoes line 1 and 'perfidia' line 2, to suggest harshly and without evidence that he should not have trusted her on many previous occasions.

He continues in this vein, suspicious and ungracious about Cynthia's other outward signs of love and concern. Lines 35–6 recall an oath she swore, that if she was false her eyes should drop out. 'Suppositis manibus' here might be a grotesquely precise detail, her hands cupped to receive her eyeballs as they fall, even though that does not sound a likely form for an oath to take.[23]

The sun is an appropriate guarantor for her oath in line 37, as the source of light to the world.[24] 'Potes' implies that she should not be able to look up like this. 'Tremis' claims that if she does so, at least she should tremble. 'Admissae conscia nequitiae' recalls 'longae conscia laetitiae', to

(20) Camps points out the possibilities of ambiguity here, though he thinks one must supply 'potes esse' rather than 'eris'. The other editors are satisfied with supplying 'eris' only, and do not consider that any ambiguity could be present.

(21) For a similar play, cp. VIII 18 and our comments on the passage.

(22) In line 33 we print 'tam' after Palmer and along with modern editors. 'Quam' of the Mss might be justified as simply intensifying the adjective; it does seem to have merely this function sometimes in Latin comedy, cp. e.g. Plaut. Am. 541, Ter. And. 109.

(23) This is Enk's reading of the line, and he cites in support Prop. II xxxii 40 'supposita excipiens, Nai, caduca (poma) manu'.

(24) The sun is always a horrified witness of great crime, cp. e.g. Eur. Hipp. 601, Soph. Oed. Tyr. 1425 f.

reassert the total contrast between Cynthia and Calypso. Calypso remembered virtuous happiness, Cynthia ought to be aware only of her guilt. But this accusation is less absolute than it might be. 'Nequitia' is not utter depravity or deliberate infidelity. It indicates the negative moral aspect of 'levitas', culpable weakness of the will rather than deliberate evil. 'Admissae' is different to 'commissae' in a similar way.[25]

Her distress is evident in lines 39—40, but Propertius still refuses to accept these proofs of her sincerity. 'Quis' asks who is the cause of this passionate response. It must be Propertius, or Amor: 'cogere' is the normal word in Propertius for compulsion exerted by love.[26] But 'invitis' still accuses these tears of being forced, unwilling.

The conclusion that follows is equivocal. 'Quis' in line 41 refers to her eyes. 'Nunc pereo' claims that he is now dying, being destroyed. He could be saying that he is being destroyed now because in the past he trusted her oaths and those eyes, though it is not clear what 'pereo' here would refer to exactly. But the statement could be more dramatic, announcing that he is trusting them again, and now, as a result, is destroyed, lost. 'Moniturus' makes this second the more likely. This is a future, which would not be necessary if she had already betrayed him: he would already be a warning.[27] So he capitulates, absolutely sure that she will betray him, but this betrayal, and hence the warning, is in the future. The last line is the final implicit stage direction of the poem. He advises other lovers not to do what he is about to do himself. He has capitulated, but as grudgingly and ungraciously as he could.

Technically the poem is a remarkable achievement, but Propertius as a person does not emerge from it very admirably. The poem dramatises the process by which he has worked on Cynthia's feelings, to wring out from her a response that will allay his doubts. His anxiety breeds a kind of cruelty, as Cynthia is manipulated and abused. The underlying emotion he feels may be called love, but the predominant emotions in the poem are all negative, hostile, bitter. The drama does not make a pretty spectacle, though it is brilliantly realised.

(25) Cp. P. Africanus quoted in Gell. VII xi 9: 'omnia mala probra flagitia, quae homines faciunt, in duabus rebus sunt, malitia atque nequitia. Si nequitiam defendere vis, licet'. The word, as L. & S. indicate, is more frequent in the milder meanings than in the strong one of 'utter depravity'.
On 'admitto' and 'committo', L. & S. say '('admitto') expresses rather the moral liability incurred freely while 'committere' designates the overt act punishable by civil law'.

(26) For 'Amor' and 'cogo' see I 8, V 19, VII 8, etc. Camps translates 'What need was there for you to?', implying the opposite, i.e. that there was no compulsion. This strained reading is forced on him because along with all the other commentators he has not realised the nature of the drama taking place, or that it is a drama.

(27) This point about 'moniturus' is not generally noticed by the commentators, and the word itself receives scant attention, being glossed by Enk as 'after I die, I will be a warning to'.

POEM XVI

This poem has all the signs of being an early work.[1] It seems highly conventional, but its tone is cheerfully irreverent. It mocks the convention, but shares the convention's indifference towards the values of respectable Rome. It has a basis in the paraclausithyron form, a conventional lover's lament to the door of his cruel mistress, but the form is neatly inverted here, because this lament is set into the door's lament that the lover is lamenting. The device of having a door speak is not original: Catullus had used it earlier (Cat 67). But Propertius's use of this device is distinctive, a sophisticated reflection on stock attitudes and images of amatory convention. His response to these stock motifs is not merely clever, either. The poem does not feel like an expression of intense emotion. Propertius's technique at this stage seems in advance of the quality of his feeling. But the formal qualities he is exploring here are very interesting, foreshadowing some later developments of his technique. Poem VIII, for instance, insets a kind of paraclausithyron into a larger frame. XI—XII pretends to blame Baiae for Cynthia's guilt, as XVI blames the door. XVII and XVIII similarly talk to a landscape for the mistress to overhear. All these are descendants of poetic strategies first worked out explicitly in XVI. It may not be as passionately engaged as the great poems of his maturity, but it is still an intelligent and enjoyable performance, especially interesting for the light it throws on his artistic development.

The first 16 lines form a unit. Throughout this section an implicit contrast is made between elegiac values and the militaristic virtues of ancient Rome. The door means to uphold the ancient values, but she is personified as an ignorant and confused old woman, who more than half sides with lovers. So the opening seems intended to be ornate and impressive, referring to a magnificent past. 'Olim' and the pluperfect 'fueram' both seem to insist on the remoteness, and hence the gloriousness of this past. The diction of the second line is similarly lofty, but its content totally subverts the grand style. After the reference to ancient military successes in the first line, we expect a celebration of the virtues of ancient womanhood. The form promises this, ending with 'pudicitiae', but the legend of Tarpeia is rather different in character. Propertius tells her story at greater length in IV iv. Far from being a model of chastity, she opened the gates of Rome to an invading army because she was in love with the enemy general. It is as though the senile door is confused and has put 'Tarpeiae' for something like 'Sabinae'.[2] But this mistake is a kind of Freudian slip. Tarpeia's action may be treachery to a

[1]   The polysyllabic pentameter count is 58%; See Introduction

[2]   Commentators have been strangely humourless here and unwilling to accept Tarpeia as the betrayer of Rome. All wish to interpret 'Tarpeia pudicitia' as if it were real 'pudicitia'; both Camps and Bailey think that the legend which would make this explanation possible may have been lost.

patriotic Roman, but in the lovers' code it is high virtue for a mistress to open the door to her lover.

The next two couplets continue to contrast an illustrious past with a disgraceful present. Past and present are linked by transferred attributes, the process directed by common militaristic imagery. Lines 4 and 5 are closely parallel. 'Umida' describes the threshold wet with suppliant tears, but could apply to the door now, splashed with wine by the drunken revellers. The door is wounded in line 5, a casualty in the new kind of war. The sound of 'potorum' echoes the corresponding 'captorum' like a parody, to emphasise the contrast. In line 6 she is beaten by worthless fists, not shaken by the wheels of gilded chariots as in line 3. 'Supplicibus' also contrasts with this impudence. The word is repeated in line 14, applied to the faithful lover. The implication is that the lover is the only captive left who can conform to the ideal of line 4.

Lines 7–8 similarly contrast past and present. Line 7 does so fairly obviously. The suitors' or revellers' 'corollae' replace victors' garlands. They are filthy into the bargain. Line 8 makes the same kind of contrast, but it has caused some difficulty to commentators, and is often emended. 'Signa' is usually interpreted as "sign", and an elaborate deductive process is then supposed to be going on. If the paradosis 'exclusis' is retained, the torches are seen as signs to excluded lovers that other lovers are inside. Presumably the excluded lovers arrived too late to see their rivals' success. Lipsius's emendation to 'exclusi' is popular, but is still faintly ridiculous. The discarded torches in this reading reveal to some passing Sherlock Holmes that the lover has been there a long time.[3] But 'signa' can also refer to a battle ensign, a meaning which is much more relevant here. The torch is the emblem of a lover (see e.g. I xiii 26 and perhaps I iii 10), 'iacere' describes a prostrate figure. The word will be used by the lover of himself at line 23, to reinforce this connection between lovers and torches. The difficulty of the line arises partly because the metaphor is left implicit, partly because of a harsh ellipsis whereby 'exclusis' has replaced 'amantibus'. The reasoning in a more explicit form is: Torches are lovers' emblems: discarded torches are emblems of excluded lovers (where the mistress's door ought to be graced by the glowing torches of happy love). The thought may have seemed too banal to be made so fully explicit.

Line 9 has also proved troublesome. 'Defendere' is the difficult word. Commentators have tried to avoid its most natural meanings[4] but again the

---

(3) Enk, B & B print 'exclusis', Rothstein, Camps, 'exclusi'. The important point in our interpretation is the continuation of the dual reference of lines 3–6 in the metaphor of 'signa': the dative 'exclusis' should be taken closely with the following word.

(4) Postgate and B & B wish to translate 'to protect by concealing'. Camps is closer but thinks it means 'stop something already happening'. Enk takes the same view as ourselves on 'defendere', though he takes 'dominae' to be dative 'from my mistress' (citing Verg. Bucolics VII 47) rather than the more natural genitive.

177

problems resolve themselves when the military metaphor is allowed to work directly. The door sees herself as a heroic guardian, the scandalous nights as the enemy, 'noctes' standing for the licentious activities of those nights, 'infamis' for the 'infamia' which results. 'Tradita' in line 10 similarly has its strict military sense. The heroic door is betrayed by this new Tarpeia into the hands of scurrilous lampooners, instead of the fine poet she really ought to welcome (see line 41).

The mistress of course is deaf to all this. The general sense of the next two couplets, lines 11–14, is clear, but the exact constructions are not always easy to determine. 'Nec tamen' probably relates particularly to the vile verses of the previous line. Even these are not enough to recall her to her senses. 'Turpior' at the beginning of line 12 seems meant to attach the whole line' loosely to 'illa'.[5] The present age is vile, but she is even viler. Line 13 is also loosely attached to what precedes, through 'has inter'. 'Noctes' is usually supplied here from four lines previously.[6] This is strained though not impossible. But the immediately preceding 'luxuria' is also a possibility, 'luxuriae' summing up the marks of decadence that have been heaped up in the previous six lines, 'corollae', 'faces' and 'carmina'. Or 'res', again referring to these, could be understood. Certainly it would be poetically preferable if 'inter' here is spatial not temporal. It makes the image more vivid and concrete, and the immediately following 'gravibus' makes a more pointed contrast, between her heavy grief and the frivolity that caused it. But there is nothing very interesting going on here to justify this obscurity.

The lover's speech begins at line 17. From a common sense point of view he is obviously very foolish, blaming an inanimate door instead of the mistress who has shut it. This is a caricature of lovers' refusal to face reality. I viii contains a similar self-caricature. But by framing the speech with the speaking door's account of things, Propertius implies that the lover is wrong for an entirely different reason. The lover is not foolish to suppose that doors have feelings, in this poem: they do — but this door happens to be basically on his side. Lines 13–14 make this most clear. 'Cogor' in Propertius usually describes the constraining power of love on a lover. This door is constrained to weep in response to the lover's complaints. She claims she is sadder the longer he has to wait (line 14). The comparative 'tristior' here echoes ironically against the lover's accusation of 'crudelior' in line 17. If only he knew that the door cared! But of course, he does not want to know.

The lover is not entirely inept as a poet. The door describes his poetry with a graphic phrase, 'arguta blanditia', a brilliant piece of literary criticism,

(5) We follow Camps's account here; other editors, when they do not emend, take 'vivere' as dependent on 'revocatur' and not on 'turpior'.

(6) So Rothstein, Camps: Enk, B & B, following Passerat, read 'Haec'. To understand 'res' or 'luxurias' here has the same effect as Richmond's transposition of 7–8 after 11–12.

relevant to Propertian poetry in general. Charm may be an obvious quality for an elegiac poet to aim for, but 'arguta' refers to a more ambiguous quality: sharp, penetrating, touching raw nerves, not entirely pleasant, but impossible to ignore. In a similar vein the lover refers to his 'furtivas preces'. In the context this is stronger than "secret prayers".[7] These are prayers like thieves, the pick-lock prayers of an illicit love.

The first four lines of his speech punningly conflate the mistress and the door, exploiting a common strand of imagery in love poetry. If a mistress's heart can be as hard as iron, then metal doors can be supposed to feel. Line 17 establishes the connection. The line seems to say that the door is crueller than the mistress, but is open to another interpretation. 'Penitus' could intensify 'crudelior' — much more cruel — or it could subvert the whole comparison. It basically means within. But within is the mistress. So the door's soul, which is more cruel than the mistress, is the mistress herself. The door is the mistress, although the lover cannot admit this explicitly to himself. The accusations in the next three lines are ambiguous, overtly directed against the door, but covertly aimed at her. In line 18 the door is accused of being silent when really it is the mistress who might speak.. The door can only open or shut. Its hinges are metallic, and hence are inevitably hard, but 'duris' is the stock epithet for the heart of a disdainful mistress. In line 19 the lover says 'meos amores' for himself. But it is the doors of her heart that can properly admit his love, as the doors of the house admit his person. 'Mota' in line 20 is also ambiguous, the physical moving of the doors, and the mistress being moved by his pleas.

Line 21 contains an obvious plea, but the three lines following are more elaborately wrought. The thematic principle is a play with the opposites of heat and cold, stock opposites for conveying the vagaries of love. Line 22 uses these in an implicit way that has proved puzzling. The threshold is called 'tepide'. Some have wanted to read this as "chill",[8] but that would be very strained. 'Tepidus' is half-warm, neither as warm as a proper bed nor as cold as the stone would be without him. The stone is as cold as her love, while he is as hot as a torch. The result of the contact is an unsatisfying tepidity, an image of their relationship. In line 23 the main opposition is between 'sidera plena', the stars at their height, an image for erotic energies at full pitch, and the prostrate lover. 'Iacentem' is juxtaposed to 'plena' to point the contrast. It recalls 'iacere', used of the torches at line 8, to emphasise the symbolic value of the posture. The inferior Mss offer 'prona', but this entirely misses the carefully worked contrast.[9]

(7) Cp. Cat. VII 8 'furtivos amores', Tib. I v 7. See also lines 27–8 below.

(8) E.g. B & B. Enk, Camps, Rothstein, take the word in the same way as us.

(9) Most modern editors read 'plena', though Housman proposed to read 'prona'. Camps in his note seems to think that 'prona' gives the more satisfactory sound and sense. For the vigour of the night used as an image of the vigour of love, Cp. X 8 and our comments.

179

The hexameter describes mid-night, the lovers' noon, the pentameter refers to dawn. Coldness now is doubly emphasised, 'frigida' at the beginning and 'gelu' at the end. The line is carefully symmetrical, with 'me dolet' at the centre, and two adjectives at the beginning matched by their nouns at the end. It is not as formal as a golden line, but it has something of that quality. The construction here has affinities with I v 15, human suffering held within the static perfection of art. 'Dolet' is surprising on two counts. It is singular, yet the stars and the night in the previous line are also grieving. But a plural would have destroyed the self-contained perfection of the line, and the icy breeze can stand for the whole of Nature. But 'me dolet' would more naturally mean "hurt me" in this context, something that icy breezes are much more likely to do than sympathise.[10] However, 'tu sola' in the next line makes it seem that the breeze along with the rest of nature grieves, everything except the door. So 'me dolet' must mean "grieve for me". This is very strained and odd. Propertius may perhaps be arguing through a pun here: the icy breeze hurts, but because 'me dolet' can mean "grieves for me" this becomes a specious proof of its sympathy. This is still not highly satisfying, but then, logic is not this lover's strong point.

Lines 27–33 are the emotional centre of the poem. In lines 31–2 he at last imagines his mistress, beautiful and tender. Then he imagines his happy rival, and unable to endure the thought he falls to blaming the door again. The language here becomes much more interesting, urgent and economical. Lines 27–8 pick up the theme of 'arguta blanditia' and 'furtivas preces', but here it is fuller and more complex. 'Traiecta' describes a vigorously penetrative movement, but what is to penetrate is 'mea vocula', a diminutive of 'vox'. 'Mea vocula' nestles mimetically inside 'cava rima'. The process is vividly imagined, the voice seen in physical terms, contracted in size so that it can slip like a thief through a tiny crack. But 'percussas' at the beginning of the next line gives a disturbing sense of the power of this small voice once it has penetrated. 'Vertat', describing what it does once it has forcibly entered, conveys a more quietly purposive movement, working insidiously deep into her mind. Her ears are referred to by the affectionate diminutive 'auriculas', as he imagines his voice going in. A curious combination of tenderness and a kind of violence characterises the whole couplet.

The mistress is seen even more vividly in line 31. 'Ocellos' is a tender diminutive again, one that is central to the love convention. Her reaction is briefly but graphically described. 'Spiritus' is both a sigh and her soul. The implication is that her soul is revealed in this sigh: her true self must pity the rejected lover, in spite of her apparent behaviour. The offending rival's existence is briefly admitted in line 33, but a key word here is 'iacat'. This contrasts with 'surget' in the previous line, and recalls the other two uses of the word in the poem, at lines 8 and 23. The word has been given a symbolic

(10) The editors all take 'dolet' in the second meaning, even though this is by no means the more obvious, despite the parallel in Verg. Bucolics X 13 ff.

value for the poem which condemns her present state. The three verbs in these three lines form a counter-locking pattern reminiscent of 'plena iacentem' in line 23. Her soul should rise ('surget') but she lies despicably prostrate ('iacet') so his words fall ('cadunt').

In lines 35–44 the lover returns to accusing the door. The irrationality is now overt, since he has acknowledged the existence of the humans who in fact are responsible for shutting him out. In line 35 he either contradicts or corrects himself. If the door is 'sola causa' it cannot be 'maxima' at the same time. 'Muneribus' refers to lovers' gifts, but 'victa' at the start of line 36 recalls the door's military metaphors: again, a combination of aggression and bland persuasion.

The next couplet is the most difficult in the poem. Line 37 is clear enough. He protests that he has never said anything offensive to the door. The pentameter is usually obelized, and various suggested emendations have proved unsatisfactory.[11] However, most of it is comprehensible, if we accept the counterfactual premise of the poem, that doors can have feelings, and lovers can discourse with them. 'Quae solet irato dicere loco' will mean "the things which a man usually says to an angry place". In accordance with the logic of the poem the inanimate place is given the emotions of the person who lives there. 'Locus' might seem slightly strange here, since a door is not strictly a place, but it serves to generalise the meaning of the door. The whole house is the hostile setting which must be placated.

The exact force of the phrase will still be unclear, however, unless we know what is "usual" in such circumstances. If the whole line is in apposition to 'petulantia', as the run of the sentence would favour, it would refer to the heated response to a mistress's rate that makes the normal lovers' quarrel – see I x 21–26. 'Tota' remains puzzling, dropped into an already difficult construction. It can hardly agree with anything in the previous line except 'lingua'. The phrase 'tota lingua' must be formed by analogy from the commonplace 'tota mente' or 'toto animo', to refer to the extravagent, unrestrained speech which angry lovers usually indulge in, but which this lover insists he has carefully avoided. Elsewhere Propertius claims to be proud of his self-control in quarrels; see for example I xviii 13–16, and 23–26, where interestingly he says that he only complained to the silent door. This account of the line does not pretend that its meaning is straightforward, but it is more relevant to the poem's concerns than any suggested emendation, as well as retaining the reading of the best Mss.

Lines 41–4 describe the actions he performed, which ought to have worked successfully. The first of these couplets is predictable. He has com-

(11) This line is both obelised and emended by most editors; popular emendations are 'ingrato' for 'irato' (Camps, Enk), 'pota' for 'tota' (Camps) 'ioco' for 'loco' (Camps, B & B). But 'ingrato' merely weakens the force of 'irato' which is much more appropriate to this poem, and 'pota' and 'ioco' introduce an irrelevant drunkenness. For 'totus' meaning wholly engaged in something, see L & S 'totus' I B.

posed poetry for the door, implicitly better than the vile verses the door mentions at line 10. He has also kissed the steps. This line is highly sensuous and erotic. 'Nixa' is repeated from line 33. There it referred to her resting on her new lover. Here it is transferred to the excluded lover's kiss, as though his whole body was in the kiss, as though he were supported solely by his lips. 'Impressis' describes the same action, but from the steps' point of view: they are pressed down on, perhaps yieldingly like flesh, as the lips press upon them. 'Impressis' comes between 'oscula' and 'nixa' as though the sensation of lips and steps were intermingled. The intensely erotic feeling is unmistakeable. The fact that such eroticism must be wasted on inanimate stone is, of course, one of the ponts of the poem.

But the final couplet of the lover's speech is very strange. It has been suggested that the lover's curious behaviour, turning round in front of the doors, refers to some religious ritual, and that his hands are hidden, or veiled, again for ritual reasons.[12] 'Debita vota' certainly makes such considerations relevant. There may be some connection between his turning round in front of the doors, and his wanting the doors to turn around on their hinges. That is how sympathetic magic works. B & B object that "the interpretation is ingenious, but too far-fetched to be probable". The alternative, however, is equally improbable and much more banal – the lover must be supposed suddenly ashamed of his love, though he has given no indication of this before. It is natural for learned scholars to project onto the lover the embarrassment they would feel if they were caught in such an undignified position, but what is required here is a positive action, one that ought to have affected the door but has not.

After the lover has spoken, the door closes the poem with two couplets addressed to other lovers, inevitably 'miseri'. She complains of the 'vitia' of the mistress: but by this stage elegiac values have taken over so completely as to blur the conventional moral content of the word. Her vice is not simply her rioting with her present lover, it includes her neglect of her previous one. So this complaint merges with the second, the endless weeping of the faithful lover. His continuous weeping ('semper') is transformed in the next line into something grander, 'aeterna invidia'. So immortal disgrace, and hence by implication its contrary, immortal fame, is made the gift of this particular lover. This is because this lover is also a poet. The door does not emphasise the fact, but 'carmen' occurs three times in the poem. The power of poetry is one of the themes of this poem which seems at times to mock poetic conventions. This is the paradox of the Propertian lover himself: abject and ridiculous, yet strangely important and powerful.

(12) Vulpius suggested this account, citing Plaut. Am. 257. This is accepted by Rothstein, but not Camps, Enk, or B & B. Considering the fact that there is an element of sympathetic magic involved in all these paraclausithyra, Vulpius is likely to be right. Cp. Ovid Am. I vi with its refrain at line 24 etc. and cp. also F.O. Copley, Ch. I.

POEM XVII

The opening couplets of this poem seem to establish it as one kind of poem, but as it progresses it becomes another. It begins as a similar sort of poem to XVIII which follows it:[1] an ostensible soliloquy set in a vaguely conceived, conventionally solitary locale. As such it reads as a graceful apology, so indirect that the original cause for it lies entirely outside the poem. But the conventional images for solitude and danger lead by a natural progession to images of death which have a very different quality. The poem begins to tap feelings that are too intense and self-concerned to be appropriate for the original intention, feelings that a later poem like XIX will evoke more power-fully, and confront more directly. But the rest of the poem resists the morbid impulses, and moderates the images into a less frightening form. So the poem moves towards the macabre image of line 12, of Cynthia holding his dead bones, his nothingness to her loving breast, but shies away from this, to finish with images of peace and love, the appeal for reconciliation and reunion of the last two couplets. It is as though Propertius started to write a companion poem to XVIII, found something like XIX struggling to be born, but could not quite recognise or accept it.

The ostensible setting is not sharply focussed. It is uncharacteristically conventional in inspiration, remote from the precipitating experience behind the poem. But as usual Propertius has conceived the situation consistently but presented it indirectly. The first couplet makes the basic situation clear enough: Propertius has left Cynthia and is now closer to Halcyons and salt water than he would like. But it is not clear at this stage whether he is on a storm-tossed ship, or temporarily ashore on some inhospitable foreign coast. Most commentators seem to have assumed the first without discussion,[2] but by line 8 the second has begun to emerge as the more likely account. 'Haecine' is a pointing word, indicating close proximity. It is natural to take it as a gesture towards the desolate beach on which he is standing. Both accounts remain possible throughout the poem. With 'haecine' for instance, he could be pointing through the night (cp. line 10) at an ominously close shore, able to see the sand that will bury him rather than the rocks that will wreck his ship, and assuming that his body will be washed ashore not lost at sea. Such a reading is possible, but very strained. Similarly, lines 4, 17 and 18 can be explained on either account, but make easier sense if he is, for the present, landbound. A final consideration; some unreality is expected in such a con-ventional mode, but it is still hard to imagine the poet calmly penning these verses on a ship that is lurching in rough seas, dangerously close to a fatal shipwreck. At least if he were on land he would have the leisure, and stomach, to write poetry.

(1) It belongs to the same period as XVIII to judge by the percentage of polysyllabic pentameter endings (21.4% and 25%); see Introduction *pp 5 – 15*

(2) The boat at sea hypothesis is held by Camps, B & B, and apparently by Rothstein and Enk.

The opening couplet is an unusually frank admission of guilt by Propertius: implicitly, a full apology to Cynthia for his offence. 'Merito' is unequivocal. 'Fugisse' describes his conduct in the worst possible light, and the forces of 'potui' here is something like "had the nerve to".[3]

The second line continues to insist on the justice of his punishment. The line has usually been allowed to take its colour from 'desertas', interpreted loosely as "lonely", a piece of vague scene-painting, with the halcyons adding only a connection with the sea. But the traditional legend of halcyons gives 'desertas' a more literal sense. From Propertius III x 9 it is clear that the bird's cry is taken as a lament for its mate, and is accordingly a bad omen. But Halcyons were also famous for their power to ensure calm weather – the proverbial Halcyon days, seven days in winter when the seas are calm for its nesting period.[4] So Propertius addresses halcyons who have been bereft, and therefore cannot exercise a power that comes from satisfactory domestic love. Hence the logic of 'merito': he has abandoned Cynthia, so it is only right that the abandoned Halcyons, who are themselves female, should not help him with calm weather. The juxtaposition of 'ego' and 'desertas' helps to establish a superstitious connection between the myth and Propertius's situation, as though he has in a sense abandoned the Halcyons in leaving Cynthia. From this he can naturally go on to attribute to Cynthia a halcyonlike influence on the elements.

Line 3 has proved a difficult line. The paradosis 'solito' has had almost as many emendations as editors. 'Solito' for 'ex solito' is certainly hard to parallel in classical times, but this objection is not decisive.[5] The form of the word, picking up 'merito' in line 1, fits in with the rhythm of the poem's argument. 'Solito' only becomes impossible as a result of another decision, concerning 'Cassiope' immediately before it. This could be either a port in Corcyra, or the constellation Cassiopeia. Modern commentatores on the whole prefer to regard it as the port, [6] which makes 'solito' incomprehensible. The phrase 'Cassiope visura', for arriving at Cassiope, cannot intelligibly be qualified by 'solito'. But even disregarding 'solito', 'Cassiope' as the constellation is preferable. There is no apparent reason for the poet to name that particular relatively unimportant port as his destination, whereas he would be likely to mention a constellation in a poem about a sea voyage. Used of a constellation, 'visura', look down on, implies visibility. There are obvious conditions under which Cassiope will no longer see or be seen: most obviously, during the continual storm that has dogged Propertius's voyage.

(3) As in I xv 37.

(4) Cp. Ov. M XI 410–748 esp. 744–8.

(5) See Shackleton Bailey on ths passage, who cites parallels from post-classical literature.

6) E.g. Rothstein, B & B, Camps, but not Enk.

Two considerations may have suggested the choice of this constellation. Aratus talks of Cassiopeia's light as faint, so her presence in the sky would indicate good weather and high visibility.[7] He also talks of her protective care for the neighbouring constellation of Andromeda, a celestial extension of her maternal care for her daughter.

Line 4 raises for the first time in the poem the problem of whether he is on land or afloat. His 'vota', the promises and pleas he makes on his own behalf, fall uselessly on a shore ('ingrato litore'). If he is standing on this shore, the line is straightforward: the prayers are directed to gods of the ocean, like the Nereids he will invoke in lines 25—28, but these prayers fall on the shore, failing to reach their destination. The shore is 'ingrato', unpleasant and hostile, refusing to allow the prayers to pass. If he had been standing on a ship, the whole phrase would have been a strange thing to say. 'Litus' refers to the strip of land at the edge of the sea. If the prayer actually reaches land, how is it unsuccessful? But why is he addressing a prayer in this direction in any case?

With line 5, Cynthia directly enters the poem. Earlier she was referred to as 'puellam'. Now she is addressed as though she were actually present. By a nice irony this sense of her presence comes through a statement of her absence ('absenti tibi'). The point is that since the storm is serving her well, it acts as a reminder of her, and thence as an extension of her. Over lines 5—10 there is a growing sense of her identification with the storm. In line 5 he only points out that the wind is doing what Cynthia wanted it to do. The phrase implies that she indulged in the imprecations typical of an abandoned girl (or man: see e.g. I viii, 12—13). By line 6, the wind is behaving like an angry woman: 'saevas' recalls the 'saevitia' of the scorned or scornful elegiac mistress, and 'minas', threats, are strictly uttered by women and fulfilled by winds. So the questions of lines 7—8 are impersonal, but seem offered for Cynthia to hear and act on, if she will. Lines 11—12 then more directly attribute potency to Cynthia. 'Saevas querelas' echoes 'saevas minas' of line 6, as though for her to cease to complain against Propertius will bring the storm to an end.

Lines 11—12 in the first place give the reason why she should want to revoke her curses. The effect of these curses is to keep him marooned far from her, so that when he dies, she will regret both the fact of his death, and the fact that he has died so far away. But the lines show a new intensity of feeling, registered in vivid images and compressed language. At the centre of the line 11 are two savage puns, on 'fata' and 'reponere', so harsh that the words have caused difficulty to many commentaters.[8] 'Reponere' can

(7) Aratus Phain.

(8) Baehrens' suggested emendation, 'reposcere', is accepted by B & B and by Camps in his first edition.

mean, among other things, either to bury, or to repeat, or recall. The first of these is much more common, and ought to be apposite for this context, especially in the light of lines 20 and 22.[9] But in this case, there is nothing to bury, as line 11 will make explicit. One of the causes of her grief will be the absence of a corpse. So the dominant meaning must be her repetition of the story of his death, which she will not be able to do dry-eyed. But the other meaning of 'reponere' operates as a grim pun, in conjunction with 'fata', which could by extension refer to a corpse. Her repetition of the story of his unfortunate end is a way of reburying him, the only way available to her.

Line 12 gives an even more chilling image of death, in the process of describing the absence of a funeral. 'Tuo . . . tenere sinu' describes a loving act that recalls their happier days. This positive image generates its peculiar frisson by what amounts to a double negation. The key word for the effect is the surprising 'ossa', his bones, a vivid concrete to describe his dead body, giving an image which transforms his once living, now-dead body into the skeleton it will become. But this image is immediately cancelled almost before it has time to register, by 'nulla'. So the statement that she has nothing to hold is the end result of a process of dissolution of a positive image. It is as though in the space of two words his living body has been transformed first into bones and then into nothingness. But this means that we are left with an image of Cynthia holding a very specifc "nothing", an empty space that was Propertius, that was his bones, which still have a shadowy ghostly existence as an after-image. 'Nostra' here should not be simply reduced to "my". The bones are "ours" because they were his but he belonged to her, so she possesses them now of right. The word order similarly suggests their inextricable relationship. 'Tuo' and 'nostra' are juxtaposed, each word referring to a noun separated from itself by the other. Behind the image lies a primitive horror at the potency of an unburied corpse that would be worthy of Antigone.

'A pereat' immediately deflects some of the force of this on to the unknown and long-dead inventor of ships, and leads in to an expression of regret that he ever left Cynthia, an implcit apology again for his mistake, accompanied by a compliment ('rara puella fuit'). 'Dominae' and 'puella' both indicate a shift back into the reflective mood of the opening. Cynthia is no longer so vividly present that he can expostulate with her, and he rationally concludes that he has been a fool.

Line 17 reverts to his dramatic situation. Again the line works better if he is supposed to be on land. The shore is bounded on one side by the stormy seas. Now he looks in the other direction, towards the equally unfriendly surrounding terrain. 'Circumdata' is often used in a military context,[10] and suggests hostile forces lurking in these woods, reinforcing

(9) 'Ponere' seems almost to have a technical meaning in this poem; this constitutes strong pressure to take 'reponere' in such a sense.

(10) Cp. e.g. Caes. B.C. III 9 'circumdare oppidum quinis castris'; Sall. Jugurtha xxiii 1; Livy VI viii 9, etc.

the sense that 'ignotis' would give to a Roman, that the unknown is probably unfriendly as well.

The point of line 18 is an ironic contrast between the life of a lover and Propertius's present situation. This works partly through the verbs. 'Cernere' is the anxious, probing kind of perception demanded by his dangerous situation, very different from a lover's contemplation of his mistress. The phrase 'optatos quaere Tyndaridas' makes the connection more strongly. The Tyndarides are Castor and Pollux, the Gemini, stars used in navigation, and hence important to sailors.[11] But 'optatos' is a word from the amatory context, longed-for, desired, lovely, suggesting feelings much more appropriately directed towards the twin stars of his mistress's eyes. Propertius himself can use that metaphor, in his role as lover: he calls Cynthia's eyes 'geminae, sidera nostra, faces' (II iii 14). But to call real stars lovely and desired is deeply perverse for a lover, and this mocks the perversity of Propertius's foolish decision.

Lines 13–18 give an uneasy impression of Propertius scrambling back to the safety of the tone and situation of the opening, but from line 19 to the end, he returns to the negative feelings he had almost inadvertently aroused. 'Illic' makes a subterranean connection back to 'haecine' 11 lines earlier, switching the scene now to Rome. Propertius again envisages his death, but this time without the horror of a lack of the proper rites. The three couplets describing these rites themselves have a formal, ritual movement, oscillating between hexameter and pentameter. The hexameters have a pluperfect subjunctive as their main verb, the pentameters an imperfect. As usual in Propertius, the effect of a pluperfect is to locate the action of the verb as earlier than the other verb, and mark its action as complete, though here the syntax of the tense is a normal one.[12] The imperfect refers to a more open-ended action. So the pattern is a repeated movement from a completed action to a later indeterminate one.

Lines 19–20 are comfortingly vague and unphysical. 'Si qua fata' is dismissively uninterested in how he will die. The object of 'sepelissent' is not a physical corpse, but "my grief", a good thing to have buried. The pluperfect makes this act complete and final. In line 20 it is again an abstract, love, that

(11) It is surprising that most commentators (Rothstein, Enk, B & B, Camps) prefer a recondite and irrelevant interpretation of this image. There was a superstitious belief that Castor and Pollux could appear to sailors in a storm in the form of a luminescence round the mast ('St. Elmo's Fire'; cp. Pliny N.H. II 37 (101),cited by Enk). This was a sign of good luck and a presage of a safe journey. However if this had been what Propertius meant, 'quaere' would have been a strange verb to use; the phenomenon was of its nature unexpected, welcome when it came, but hardly 'looked for' (Camp's note recognises a certain amount of difficulty in the word). But in any case, the Tyndarides in a nautical context would much more easily refer to the constellation. For its navigational use, cp. Ov. F. V 720.

(12) See Introduction *pp 5–15*

image of fecundity: 'candida' has strong positive connotations, and is naturally used of the complexion of a beautiful girl.[15]

The last couplet explains why the Nymphs should help him: they should have good-will towards a lover. 'Amor labens' also suggests a successful voyage: 'labens' was used of boats skimming across the waves.[16] This serves to connect Love with the hoped-for easy voyage, almost identifying Propertius with Love. The final line is a plea for mercy and goodwill, ostensibly directed to the Nymphs but there for Cynthia to overhear. 'Socio' is usually taken as connecting Propertius with the Nymphs, as fellow-victims of Love, but it could equally indicate his new status as no longer the enemy of Love. The key word of this conclusion is 'parcite', a hope that his life will continue, though 'mansuetis litoribus' (by means of peaceful shores) equates life with being welcomed back by Cynthia.[17]

These final couplets are a triumphant affirmation, entirely convincing images of joy that are strong enough to dispel the morbid images of earlier in the poem. Such success may seem suspect. The poem contains two incompatible qualities of feeling, and achieves its final equilibrium only by renouncing one. It hints at depths that make it a more interesting poem than XVIII, but it lacks the unity and terrifying honesty of XIX. Yet it does not simply avoid intolerable thoughts. It successfully achieves a passage from shadows back into light and life. That is not an easy or negligible achievement.

(15) Cp. Prop. II iii 9, xxii 8, O.L.D. 'Candidus' 5 and 7.

(16) From Ennius onwards; cp. e.g. Enn. Ann. 478 'labitur uncta carina per aequora cana celocis', Verg. Aeneid VIII 91, etc.

(17) Most modern editors take 'mansuetis litoribus' as instrumental ablative as we do, but the past participle is slightly peculiar. It puts into the past something which is wished for in the future, namely the taming ('mansuescere') of the shores, and almost suggests that this taming has been the result of Amor's action; cp. IX 12.

lies buried. The stone that marks his end will stand above, the imperfect marking no end of its witness.

In the next couplet (lines 21–22) the focus is sharper. Cynthia is now seen, performing the rites. She cuts off her precious hair as an offering. (It is easiest to take 'funus' fairly literally, as the ceremony which is so important to Propertius. 'Meo funere' is then a temporal ablative).[13] The action she performs in line 22 is as beautiful as that in line 12 was horrifying, and its function is partly to allay the earlier image. 'Molliter' describes her action, 'tenera' the roses. The two qualities are similar, and the words come close together to suggest the affinity between her and the flowers. So the roses mediate between her and the bones of her dead lover, avoiding the shocking intermingling of living and dead of line 12.

The imperfect 'ponerat' here is surprising. It maintains the rhythm of tenses, of course, but that would not be sufficient justification. Its poetic effect is to extend this loving action indefinitely, as Propertius would want to imagine it, even though in reality this would be nearly as single an action as the offering of hair.

The last couplet of this sequence (lines 23–4) gently closes the scene. 'Extremo pulvere' works like 'ultimus lapis'; this is the dust that covers him at his end. The image is still discreetly vague, but the mention of dust comes closer to the reality of his dead body. In line 24 it is at last Propertius ('mihi'), not an abstract, that is buried, though the image is not strongly visualised. and the emphasis is on the lightness of the earth's weight above him.

In these 6 lines Propertius has given his imagined corpse a decent burial, but more importantly, he has laid his morbid imaginations to rest by allowing them formal and ritualised expression. This releases his imagination for the unexpected confidence and serenity of the conclusion. This invocation is a prayer for life, for calm seas and a safe passage back to Cynthia. It is addressed to the Nereids, but implies the change of mind indicated from the beginning. He deserved a storm because he fled from his mistress. Now he can hope for calm weather, since he longs to return to her. His first audience was the lonely halcyons; his last is the gay chorus of Nereids. 'Aequoreae' as a defining epithet suggests the natural connection of these nymphs with calm seas, 'aequor' being the undisturbed surface of the water.[14] The poem has returned to its starting point.

Line 26 is a delightful image, full of light and life. 'Solvite' suggests release, after the constrictions of the 'circumdata litora'. 'Felici choro' suggests the dancing waves around his boat, actively speeding him on his way. ('Felici' implies both happiness and beneficence.) The swelling white sail is an

(13) So Enk and Rothstein, though there is no need to suppose with the former that a future time is indicated, since the temporality in these clauses is all hypothetical anyway.

(14) Cp. Varro L.L. VII 23 'aequor mare appellatum, quod aequatum, cum commotum vento non est'.

The poem begins in a pastoral setting, seemingly a work in the pastoral mode. But pastoral was a highly artificial mode in the language and attitudes it deployed. Lines 9–18 and 23–26, the centre of this poem, work in a very different manner. They are obscure, analytic, argumentative, growing out of a dramatic situation conceived in realistic terms, and highly specific and complex in Propertius's mature manner.[1] So essentially the poem turns out to be in a more typically Propertian mode. But although there is a fundamental disparity between the two kinds of poem, Propertius has not simply used pastoral as a source of props and scenery. His relationship to pastoral in this poem is more interesting than that, if not always fully satisfying.

The scene of the first 4 lines is highly conventional. It can be paralleled in Vergil's Eclogues[2] and if Gallus's poems survived it might have even closer analogues. But the tone is surprisingly cool in the first line. 'Certe' is a prosaic word of emphasis. The absence of 'sunt' gives the line a casual, colloquial air. 'Deserta' seems vaguely used here, in contrast for instance with XVII 2. 'Taciturna' is not colloquial, but is intriguingly specific, and feels slightly odd. It gives the reason he can allow himself to grieve out loud, but we do not know that when we meet the word. It also comes over strangely because we are unsure at this stage of its relation to the convention. In realistic terms, all places are silent, hence 'taciturna'. In terms of the convention, all places can be personified, and potentially can talk – Propertius will ask these very trees to do just that, in line 19. How can he rely on the place to be silent, unless he is seeing it in realistic terms? But 'taciturna' implicitly personifies the landscape, which indicates that he is working within the convention.

He is much more guarded than the typical pastoral lamenter, much less indulgent and effusive. 'Impune' is a dig at Cynthia, slightly sarcastic: she cannot object this time as she has done in the past. 'Occultos' forshadows the defence he will make in lines 23–26: these griefs have been kept hidden till now, in spite of what she may claim. Line 4 pretends a doubt about the landscape which really reinforces his point about himself. A man who is anxious about trusting his secrets to rocks, which are symbols of trustworthiness, would hardly have been indiscreet. 'Sola', lonely or solitary, makes his caution even more ridiculously exaggerated, as though he is worried that rocks in company might tend to gossip a bit.

With line 5 he leaves the pastoral mode, and begins a parody of an epic

(1) The percentage of polysyllabic pentameter endings is 25%. This would place the poem in the latter half of the book; but see Introduction *pp 5–15*

(2) Verg. Bucolics II 1–5; for Gallus one may compare Eclogue X and see our note on VIII p. 142 note 3.

question, like Vergil's to Camilla.[3] Instead of the wrath of a goddess, he has Cynthia's arrogant disdain ('fastus') — the substitution another implicit criticism of her. Lines 7 and 8 contrast his previous happiness with his present shame. 'Notam' is a mark of disgrace: it is his reputation that has suffered, he insists, not hers.

Line 9 begins a direct defence. Why have I deserved this? he asks, and gives 4 possible reasons. The first possibility is magic spells ('carmina'). This is so fatuous that he does not bother to deny it. Some commentators have been so puzzled by its fatuity that they have accepted 'crimina' from the inferior Mss.[4] But this could not be right, since 'an' in line 10 indicates that infidelity is an alternative reason. But infidelity is the supreme crime, not an alternative to it.

This accusation of infidelity perhaps has a double-edged ambiguity on 'nova'. This could agree with 'puella', a new girl being the cause of her ill humour, or more subversively with the closer 'causa': a girl may be the most recent cause of her bad mood, but there have been other causes. He then denies the charge in lines 11–12. The image in line 12 is tender and complimentary, 'nostro' asserting that his threshold is still theirs, but 'levis' is directly insulting. This takes the offensive with her, implying that she might even be guilty of the same offence herself. The tone is aggressive, the undercurrent of hostility now coming to the surface to make a liar of him in lines 23–6, where he claims that he bore everything without a murmur of complaint.

The next 4 lines, 13–16, refer more overtly to a quarrel and mutual recriminations. 'Debet' asserts his right to be revenged on her for the suffering she has caused him. Line 14 does not say that he was not angry, just that he was not as angry as that. 'Furor' in line 15 is stronger, closer to insane than 'ira'. This is his own rage. Some commentators have tried to argue that it is her rage, not his, but that would be a near-unique usage, and does not fit the context so well.[5] In the next clause she is a weeping victim, not a righteous avenger. All this is the revenge he claims that he could have taken but did not. 'Merito' of line 15 insists that he has earned the right to even such extreme revenge.

(3) Aeneid XI 664 'quem telo primum, quem postremum, aspera virgo, deicis'; cp. also Hom. Il I 8. There are parallels for this kind of question in amatory poetry however; cp. Theoc. Id. II 64.

(4) 'Carmina' here still means 'poems' as well as 'spells': no-one could win her away with 'carmina' as potent as his, hence his confident dismissal of this reason. 'Crimina' is adopted by Enk, B & B, and Camps, but is dismissed by Bailey as a 'needless conjecture'.

(5) The dictionaries cite this passage for 'furor' meaning an object of rage, but no other. The only near parallel is Verg. Ec. X 38, but there 'furor' is an object of amorous passion, which would be an unsuitable meaning here. It is much more suitable to the context to take 'furor' as almost personified, a fury; for this usage the dictionaries offer several parallels of various kinds. On the difference between 'furor' and 'ira' cp. Hor. Epistles I ii 62 'ira furor brevis est'.

Line 17 introduces another reason. The line is slightly obscure, owing to uncertainty about 'parva' and the significance of the 'signa'. A change of colour could be a sign of guilt, in which case 'parva' would be defensive: "even though small". But that would make this accusation the same as the last, infidelity, whereas 'an' indicates a different reason. In any case, line 18 reinforces the second interpretation, that she has demanded absurdly gross outward signs of passion, a technicolour display to prove the intensity of his feelings.[6] So 'parva signa' means "only small indications", 'parva' perhaps echoing the form of her accusation. Again the statement of the charge has an aggressive, polemical note: even she cannot claim that he gives no signs of strong feeling, and the kind of demonstration she wants is vulgarly excessive. Line 18 brings this implication out more strongly: 'clamat', shouting out, indicates a crassly ostentatious manifestation of fidelity.

His reply to this is to invoke the trees. At this point he returns entirely to the pastoral convention, and claims to be acting in every way like a conventional lover. The poem's tone and conduct of its argument has made this stance seem an unlikely one for Propertius. The conventionality sits uneasily here.

At line 23 he reaches the last accusation, probably the central one, since it comes last, and most fully accounts for the poem's undertones. The accusation is obscurely put, so it is easiest to work back from his reply to it, lines 25–6. He contrasts his meekness ('timidus') with her outrageous demands ('omnia superbae iussa') as he has done throughout, but then insists, in line 26, that he has never complained out loud. The dramatic situation behind the poem is now revealed as fully as it will be. They have quarrelled, each accusing the other, (Propertius still refusing to admit that he was much in the wrong) but Cynthia seems especially incensed at the thought that he might have publicised his wrongs.

So in line 23 'tua iniuria' must be her wrongs against him. The question seems innocent, but its innocuousness masks a subtle hypothesis about her real motivation. On the face of it is a question about his state of mind: has her treatment of him caused him distress? But he knows it has, so the question really articulates her own anxious reasoning. She knows she has been unjust, and has hurt him, so she assumes that he must have expressed his resentment. This is the unfair logic behind her obstinate cruelty: she is sure he must have offended, because she knows that she has. Her obduracy comes from a guilty conscience. He does not want to say that she should not have a guilty conscience, just that she need not worry. He has effectively

(6) Camps has 'too small' which is almost the same as our interpretation, though his citation of line 25 to support this is wrong, since 'parva' there means 'the very least'. Bailey's note is helpful and though not explicit on 'parva', consistent with our reading. The opposite of 'parva signa' is given in XV 39–40, where the changes of colour are sure signs of the real feelings of the supposedly indifferent Cynthia.

denied the charge by the way he describes his grievances ('curas') in line 18, very circumspectly as "things known only to the silent door-posts".

He then turns back to the pastoral landscape again, which now provides images for his distress and his attempted recompense. 'Divini fontes' is vocative, a feature of pastoral landscapes and also poetic inspiration.[7] 'Frigida rupes' is a stock image. 'Dura quies' is slightly more interesting as an image for his state of mind.

The last four lines use the pastoral mode much more effectively. Image after image repeats others from the rest of the poem in a haunting echo-effect: 'querelae' ('querenti' line 8, 'queri' 26) 'cogor' (line 8) 'argutas' ('arguto' line 26) 'solus' ('sola' line 4) 'resonent' ('resonant' line 21) 'Cynthia' (lines 5, 6 and 22) 'deserta' (line 1) 'saxa' (line 4) and 'vacent' ('vacuum' line 2). The landscape is like an echo-chamber, which emphasises his real loneliness, and mocks his attempts to justify himself. So the solution is not further argument, but the humble submission of a pastoral lover. The debate about rights and wrongs reduces to his repetition of the single word, Cynthia.

The last four lines echo most often with the first four, to express his new relation to the pastoral landscape. He began by being suspicious of it, hoping that the place would be silent and empty. By the end the woods ring with Cynthia, and the rocks contain her name, 'tuo nomine' placed as though incised between 'deserta' and 'saxa'. This is a oneness with the convention too. The landscape expresses only his love and need, and can now be eloquent. His peace-offering to Cynthia is to become as egoless and unintelligent as a pastoral poet. The renunciation is moving: fortunately it seems not to have been permanent.

(7) 'Divini fontes' is obelised by Enk, B & B, and considered dubious by Bailey. But it is not so very surprising to address divine waters in this way and in these circum-stances: Vergil's Eclogue X, which has some similarities to this poem begins with an address to Arethusa, and the Naiads are also addressed in line 10. The 'et . . . et', which Enk finds too emphatic if 'divini fontes' is vocative, will then be indignant. For 'fons' addressed as divine cp. Verg. Aeneid XII 181.

POEM XIX

This is obviously a good poem, one of the most immediately impressive in the book. It is one of the latest poems to be written for the book,[1] but unlike most of the others composed at that stage it is curiously unspecific about its ostensible cause. It implies no particular event that causes the feelings expressed, no actual threat of death or loss. This gives its concern with death a disturbingly motiveless quality. It is irrational, objectless, appearing suddenly with horrifying vividness, seemingly in the midst of a tranquil phase of the relationship. The morbid feelings are not indulged, but present themselves more powerfully for his attempts to resist them. He finishes with an affirmation of the need for love, the 'carpe diem' motif, but it is an extremely sombre version of the theme. Love is an urgent necessity, something that might allay his irrational terrors, not a pleasure to be enjoyed.

The poem opens with the phrase 'non ego nunc . . . vereor'. This phrase is always puzzling and equivocal where it occurs in Propertius, but nowhere more so than here.[2] It seems to deny that he is afraid. 'Nunc' then limits this claim, but in a way that remains unclear. Either he is not afraid now, but used to be: or, he was not afraid in the past, and is still not afraid, in spite of what others may think. It is especially hard to decide between these two in this case, since both are so clearly untrue. He is terrified of death to an unusual degree. The phrase indicates his unwillingness to admit his fear directly at this point, or understand its source. The ambiguity here comes from his being uncertain which of two false denials to insist on: hardly a promising route to self-knowledge.

The object of the fear he denies is 'manes'. This is exactly what he is afraid of, in all its imprecision. The word refers to either ghosts, the gods of the underworld, or the realms of the dead. The context does not indicate which of these he means, or does not mean. 'Tristis' agrees with 'manes'. These are not so much sad themselves, as the cause of sadness in others, gloomy. But the word is juxtaposed with 'ego', Propertius pretending to be unaffected by them. Some of its colour rubs off on him, hinting at his real feelings.

'Nec moror' in the next line initially seems more nonchalant. Its idiomatic meaning is: "I do not worry about". But a more straighforward meaning for it would be "I do not delay my fate". This gives an almost opposite sentiment. So the phrase at one level pretends that he is unconcerned about his fate, while at another level it sees it coming irresistably. The related phrase 'remorentur fata' in line 17 makes this second meaning seem likely, as an undermeaning, revealing the real doubts beneath his asserted

(1) Percentage of polysyllabic pentameter endings is less than 8%; see Introduction

(2) Cp. I vi 1, ii 25.

nonchalance.. The rest of the line describes death, but in a roundabout way. It is not mentioned directly, or visually realised, so its impact is neutralised. 'Extremo debita rogo' is a bland euphemism, like the English "Nature's debt". 'Extremo' refers to death, but only obliquely. This is the pyre that marks the outer limit of his life, the edge of his days. Only 'rogo' in this phrase is not a euphemism. It refers to the funeral pyre, which allows an image of the corpse being consumed in fire. It is a less comfortable word than e.g. 'sepulcrum'.

'Fata', however, is slightly difficult to construe in conjunction with 'debita'. 'Fata' can mean something like fate, or doom, which would be an appropriate sense here. But strictly it is his body or life which is owed to the grave, not his "fate" which is owed in any sense: in fact it is his fate that this is so. So the line must probably be read with 'debita' loosely attached to 'fata', almost like an equivalent phrase: "my fate, what I owe to the grave". 'Nec moror fata' is the kernel of the line, but it is uncomfortably direct, so 'extremo debita rogo' serves to soften its force and cloud the construction.

In line 3 he gives what he says is his real fear. 'Timor' in line 4 is stronger than 'vereor' of line 1.[3] At first reading this fear seems an innocuous one. 'Funus' commonly means funeral rites, 'ne' indicates a possiblity that is feared, and 'forte' insists that it is only a possibility. The line seems to be saying that he is afraid that she will not love him at his funeral. But 'funus' can also mean a corpse. The next couplet indicates what his real fear is: that his dust will still desire her. So under the surface of this line there lurks already the grisly image that becomes explicit in lines 7–10: his corpse will still crave her love, or will not receive it.

The comparison in line 4 is an unexpected one. 'Exsequiae' refers to the funeral procession, or by extension the whole ceremony. This was a painful business for mourners, (cp. 'durior') but not for corpses, who were meant to be comforted by it. The effect here is to see the process from the point of view of the mourners: so Propertius effectively becomes a mourner at his own funeral.[4]

Lines 5–6 give the underlying belief that makes his vision plausible. Line 6 gives the basic premise. This is similar to the notion 'conscia terra sapit' of a later poem (II xiii 42) but it is more ambiguously put here. 'Vacet' could be used either of lands, where it means without an owner, or of persons, where a common meaning is to be at leisure, at rest. The ambiguous status of 'pulvis', still Propertius yet only dust, brings out this ambiguity in 'vacet'. His dust belongs to Cynthia, so it cannot lie at rest. 'Oblitus' more directly .

(3) L. & S. 'vereor' quote several egs. which reveal the distinction between 'timeo' and 'vereor'; e.g. Cic. Phil. XII 12 29 'Veteranos non veremur? nam timeri se ne ipsi quidem volunt'; Livy XLI 37 17 'veramur vos, Romani, et si ita vultis, etiam timemus'.

(4) 'Exsequias' is usually taken as a rhetorical synonym for 'death' (e.g. by Butler in the Loeb, by Enk); for the critical principle of this practice, see Introduction

suggests that this dust can think and feel since it cannot forget, though we do not know as yet that it can also walk.

Line 5 gives the reason for this state of possession, Cupid. The consensus of the Mss gives 'noster' here, but the majority of editors have preferred to follow the Ms which reads 'nostris'.[5] But the reasons for this preference are mainly metrical, which is not sufficient, since 'noster' is possible, better attested, and makes better sense. 'Nostris' would make the eyes his. But the commonplace image that seems to lie behind this is of Cupid trapped in the eyes of the beloved.[6] 'Noster puer' indicates the mutuality of the love. 'Haesit' stresses how strongly this love clings to the lovely eyes of Cynthia, whch is why he cannot lie at rest in the grave.

The next two couplets, lines 7–10, have a macabre power hard to match even in Propertius.[7] 'Illic' is immediately startling. The preceding couplets have circled round Hades: now we are suddenly there. Protesilaus, newly wed, was the first to land at Troy and the first to die . As a result he was allowed to return to see his bride. She killed herself after the visit, so that they could be re-united.[8] His wife Laodamia is not referred to by name, but through a periphrasis that makes a maximum contrast between living and dead, love and death. 'Iucundas' means joyful, with erotic overtones, especially when used with 'coniunx', a spouse, a bride. These words describing her nestle mimetically between 'Phylacides' and 'heros', referring to Protesilaus. 'Non potuit immemor' draws its significance from the image in line 6. Protesilaus too is incapable of forgetting and being at rest, even in a place described with such frightening vagueness, 'caecis locis', blind places, or an obscure realm. Again it is not clear whether the place is being personified, and would want to see but cannot, or whether like the dust it is inanimate, and merely cannot be seen or allow sight.

Not only memory survives in this bleak realm, but also love, disembodied lust which reaches out for its joy, with hands that have no existence ('falsis') and so can never attain it. Propertius plays a grim game with genders in this couplet. 'Cupidus' is a masculine adjective, agreeing we think at first with 'Thessalus' in the next line, the Thessalian. The word can be either a noun or an adjective. But after the verb we have 'umbra', unequivocally a

(5) Only P and a variant in V give 'nostris' which is printed by Enk, Barber (OCT), Camps. Enk says that 'saepissime' the word before the caesura agrees with the word at the end of the line; but that is a trivial and inadequate reason for choosing the inferior reading.

(6) The commentators refer to the 'bird-lime' image in Meleager A.P. XII 92 and elsewhere. Though the connection is not absolutely clear, it seems that this trapping image lies behind 'haesit'.

(7) IV vii has some strong images but they are less subtle and so finally less disturbing; cp. e.g. IV vii 11–12 and 94.

(8) Cp. Apollodorus III 30, Ovid Her. XIII.

noun, with strong claims to being the subject to the verb. So restrospec-
tively 'Thessalus' seems to transform back into an adjective like 'cupidus',
both agreeing with a masculine noun that no longer exists. The frisson this
produces has evidently been missed by commentators, who usually eliminate
the effect in their defence of the anomaly. 'Thessalus' could be seen as masculine in form, but really feminine, agreeing with 'umbra'.[9] This would be
just possible, but leaves 'cupidus' isolated. Or 'Thessalus' could be a noun
in apposition to 'umbra'. This is the account of it which probably finally
establishes itself, as a grammatically regular way of juxtaposing the two
incompatible modes of existence, but the status of 'Thessalus' remains
uneasy.

Thessalus refers to Protesilaus in terms of his birthplace. This, along
with 'antiquam domum' in the same line, implies another motive for this
ghost, one which is often attributed to them. It is his home he haunts, as well
as his wife. 'Antiquam', ancient and venerable, implies his respect for it.
This makes Protesilaus less specifically a lover's ghost, a more comprehensive
image of ghostly psychology.

The tone changes with the next two couplets (lines 11–14), as Propertius recovers himself, indulging a complimentary wit to populate Hades with
more congenial company. The opening 'illic' is not a surprise this time. Line
11 distinguishes between what he will really be like ('quidquid ero') and his
reputation there. 'Imago' here must be close to 'umbra', a shade, but its use
is jocular: on earth he was known as her lover, so here he is known as her –
ghost. It is still faintly disturbing, since 'tua imago' ought to be herself as
ghost.

Line 12 is less troubling, a comforting restatement of the power of love
in death. Instead of a ghost crossing over into the world of the living, Love
crosses into the world of the dead. This makes Hades more pleasant, and the
world of the living safer from ghostly visitors. 'Fati litora', the shores of fate,
recalls the image of fate in line 2. The pyre seemed absolute and final then:
now he has passed beyond, and 'fata' does not seem so terrible after all. The
mention of shores begins to give Hades a landscape, in contrast to the
frightening indeterminacy of 'caecis locis' of line 8.

Hades becomes positively enjoyable in lines 13–14. He is immediately
surrounded by a host of legendary beauties. These are ostensibly mentioned
only so that he can compliment Cynthia, by saying that he will prefer her,
but the thought of them remains to sweeten his image of death. There is
grammatical oddity here, analogous to 'Thessalus/Umbra'. This bevy starts
off feminine and in the plural, 'formosae', but after the plural verb they are
referred to by the singular 'chorus', as though he has already lost interest in
these beauties as individuals, and lumps them all together in a group term,

(9) Rothstein sees no difficulty here; B & B think that 'Thessalis' (fem. adj. agreeing
with 'umbra') might be the correct reading but Enk points out that in that case
'cupidus' would have nothing to agree with.

which happens to be masculine. The joke, by repeating the kind of grammatical oddity that made line 10 so disturbing, helps to allay the feelings it aroused. The juxtaposition of 'Argivis' and 'Dardana', however, brings out a connection between this image and the story of Protesilaus. He was an Argive, loyal to his mistress. Propertius rejects the women Protesilaus's comrades were unfaithful with after their victory, and waits like a Protesilaus for his Laodamia to rejoin him.

Lines 15–16 contain the compliment that the previous couplet has prepared for. But in line 16 this begins a transition into morbid images again, imagining first her death, then her reaction to his death. The movement is begun by a prayer to Tellus, the Earth, the place where the dead are buried. This prayer is usually taken as being on Cynthia's behalf, but 'iusta' would then be odd. Cynthia would want the Earth to be kind, not just. Commentators suggest it has that meaning here.[10] But the expected object of such a prayer would be long life. However, something like long life is introduced by a concessive, as something undesirable. It is then seen as old age, which is not desirable to a woman, something that did not happen to Laodamia and which Cynthia should not want. So 'iusta' has its normal meaning, "just". The justice he wants is the right to meet her when she is dead, in the way line 18 goes on to describe.

'Remorentur fata' here is reminiscent of 'nec moror fata' in line 2, but inverts it. There he was casual about the approach of death. Here she should be resentful that it is so slow to come. Old age will interfere with her union with her lover. This inverts the meaning of 'fata' from line 2, where it meant the sentence of death. Here it is the sentence of not dying. The text here is uncertain, the tradition dividing between 'te longae' (PDVVo) and 'longe te' (NA). Both would mean much the same, though 'longe' is slightly the better attested. It would emphasise 'remorentur' more, while 'longae' stresses the regrettable length of her old age. But the order 'longe te' seems rhythmically unlikely.

'Cara' at the beginning of line 18 contains another unpleasant surprise, like 'Thessalus' of line 10. We naturally expect that this will be feminine singular, referring to Cynthia, part of a protestation how much he will love her when she is old. 'Ossa', when it comes, is a shock, neuter plural for her dead bones. At the beginning of the line we supposed she was flesh and blood, now we find she is only bones. This is not at all ungrammatical, but exploits a transient ambiguity.[11] Even when we find out what 'cara' agrees with, the effect is still unsettling. 'Ossa' is shockingly physical here, so much so that commentators have uneasily wanted to suggest that it should be taken

(10) Cp. e.g. Camps ' . . . 'Tellus' is 'iusta' because thought of as not claiming Cynthia sooner than is kind or right.'

(11) See M.W. Edwards, art. cit.

vaguely, as "ghost" or "ashes".[12]

The line also involves a complex interweaving of present and future, living and dead. The chronological ambiguity of 'futura' is crucial here. It seems that Propertius now is alive and weeping for her, as though he has survived her in spite of her long old age. But 'ossa futura' could also be,"the bones you will be". And Propertius seems to be dead, waiting for her to join him, (cp. 'remorentur'). The tears he is weeping for her death could be of the present, when the poem is being written, grief at the thought of her death. Or Propertius could weep though dead, as he can love in Hades. 'Cara ossa' provides the focus for this temporal paradox 'Cara' is her present, 'ossa' her future: she is dear now, and will be bones. This is used to claim that she will still be dear when she is only bones, but the image has the effect of seeing her as bones while she is dear, and living. Eliot's description of Webster applies even more forcibly to Propertius here: "he saw the skull beneath the skin".

This superimposition of present and future, living and dead, is extended in line 19, seen this time from Cynthia's point of view. 'Sentire' describes an act of perception, to see, feel or intuit. 'Quae' is the thing to be so perceived by Cynthia. This is a neuter plural. It is usually taken as referring generally to what has gone before. Commentators normally give it the most innocuous meaning possible, "a love like mine".[13] It is not clear how it could mean this, though it is obvious why this meaning should be favoured: it makes the poem less disturbing.

But if 'quae' refers back generally, it most naturally refers to the whole scene, the lament of the living/dead Propertius for the bones that are his mistress. One cannot pick and choose till one finds the nicest meaning. This then is the image she must see as she gazes on the ashes of the dead Propertius: her mortality, and his love. The sentiment is not surprising or unusual, but the vividness of its realisation is. But 'quae' could also qualify the nearest neuter plural, 'cara ossa'. This would give a more vivid version of the same meaning. As she looks in the ashes she is to see her own bones, her own death. The order of the words then becomes a significant image: 'tu viva', her living, between 'quae' and 'mea', her bones and Propertius's ashes. This is reminiscent of line 7, where Laodamia is similarly placed. 'Tu viva' juxtaposed with 'mea' is certainly part of a life-death contrast. The ablative 'mea

(12) Camps paraphrases as 'ghost', Enk suggests that 'ossa' stands for 'umbra' (or something similar), B & B suggest something similar. This is a typical example of the assumption that poetic vocabulary consists mainly of rhetorical synonyms. See Introduction . The feeling of the word is much more macabre than the notion 'ghost' or 'shade': cp. IV vii 11–12 and 94 cited above (note 7); cp. also Lucian Mort. Dial. I 334.

(13) So Camps, B & B, Shackleton Bailey; Enk assumes it means 'the same as I will feel for you when I am dead'. Typically, the commentators do not argue for their view but simply assume that any other is unthinkable.

favilla' is a straightforward locatival: this sight is to be seen in the ashes themselves. (In the usual interpretation of the line, this ablative causes difficulty — see e.g. Camps.) 'Favilla' continues the living-dead paradox. These are properly embers, still glowing, an image of life in death.[14]

Line 20 draws an apparent resolution out of this: death will not be bitter for him, whatever it is for her. 'Ullo loco' is not entirely clear here. It may mean "wherever I die", but that seems weak. It more probably alludes to his dual existence, his ashes in the earth and his ghost in Hades.[15]

This has allayed his fear of death, the fear he started by saying he did not have. He now returns to the fear he acknowledged in line 3, the fear that she will not love him. Lines 21–4 maintain the fiction that though she will probably be unfaithful, it will be in spite of herself. The ablative construction 'contempto busto' leaves it unstated who is doing the despising, though it is obvious that it must be Cynthia. In line 22 an evil Amor pulls her away from the tomb. The Mss here have 'abstrahat e', but 'e' is usually emended to something like 'ei' or 'heu', The reason offered is that 'e' is "impossible" (Butler & Barber), by which is presumably meant ludicrous and indecorous. However, the slightly grotesque image may well be what Propertius wrote. It carries the fiction of Cynthia's loyalty even further, picturing her actually in the dust, and Amor dragging her out. The image has a certain morbidity, but this does not make it less likely in this poem.

The fiction is continued in the next line, with 'cogat', love's comulsion, and 'invitam', her unwillingness. The final 'cadentis' again adds a touch of exaggeration. 'Siccare lacrimas' would mean, to dry her tears, cease crying. 'Cadentis', "while they are falling", speeds up the process. They are to be dried up in the act of falling. He pretends to believe that she will mean to be faithful, but he describes her getting over her grief with comic rapidity.

Line 24 then provides an excuse for her now-certain unfaithfulness. 'Assiduis' leads us to expect 'precibus', the normal method of a lover.[16] Cynthia should be able to resist those, but threats ('minis') are another matter, and make her capitulation less culpable. It is Amor not her who is to blame. Although this all seems certain of what was only feared in line 3, the tone now is much lighter.

Lines 25–6 contain the second conclusion. 'Quare' is a prosaic causal conjunction, which gives the appearance of dry logic to this last couplet, though the actual connection is not at all clear. The conclusion is a commitment to joy and love, the antithesis of the feelings that have dominated the

(14) See TLL and Cp. Verg. A. III 573 and Lucr. II 676. Propertius uses the word in I ix 18 and in IV iv 69 with the meaning of 'live ash'; in II i 75 ('mutae favillae') the meaning is apparently 'dead ash'. But there may be a kind of oxymoron in the juxtaposition of 'mutae'.

(15) See Camps on this passage.

(16) As at viii 25.

poem. The command is 'laetemur', let us delight. 'Inter nos amantes' refers to the mutuality of their love, but the poem has made such love and mutuality not necessarily a matter for delight. The vision of love in death has made the need for living love seem more urgent and necessary, but simple delight hardly seems able to coexist with the intense morbidity at the poem's centre.

The last line is enigmatic. It seems to have been formed by inversion out of a commonplace: no time is long enough for love. Initially that commonplace might seem a suitable sentiment to close the poem, regret that the time for love is not eternal. It is interesting that Butler translates the line like this: "Eternity itself is all too brief for love." Propertius, however, has written exactly the opposite: love is not long enough, is too brief, for any time. Love hardly lasts a minute. This gives an even more frenetic urgency to the "delight" of the previous line. It makes the period indicated by 'dum licet' fearfully short. It justifies his fears about Cynthia's fidelity in lines 21–4. It also denies his central fear in the poem, that love will continue beyond the grave, but this denial does not carry much conviction. This is the last of his unsuccessful strategies for exorcising his fear. In place of insight and control he can only offer this strained paradox, cast in pseudo-logical form, a desperate attempt to reason about the unreasonable.

POEM XX

This is probably one of the earliest poems in Book I.[1] It is the longest, but the least controlled, sometimes needlessly obscure, over-luxuriant, awkward. The point of departure is the tale of Hylas.[2] The moral is applied to Gallus, but the relation between the mythic narrative and the dramatic situation involving Gallus is not well worked out, as it would have been in a later poem. We are not always sure what Gallus's situation is, nor when it is relevant. The centre of the poem is not this dramatic situation, but the mythic narrative, or more exactly, certain poetic effects the young Propertius wanted to explore through the narrative descriptions. In later poems he was to exploit these effects with far greater control and assurance, but the interest of this poem comes from its immature extravagance. Some of the individual images may be impenetrably obscure, but their very extravagance helps to illuminate his poetic technique. It is close to a poetic exercise, almost a parody of his distinctive style, an interesting, revealing poem rather than a successful one.

The tone of the first couplet is direct and conversational, very different from the main body of the poem. The plural 'monemus' give Propertius's warning a more general character, but 'amore' is a strong word for the relationship between Propertius and Gallus — stronger than 'amicitia', for instance, which Propertius uses for his relation to Tullus in I xxii 2.[3] Line 2 reinforces the warning, in a way that reflects unfavourably on Gallus's intelligence. 'Vacuo ex animo' could be proleptic, if we are charitable to Gallus: his mind will be empty if the warning flows out. But its use suggests that such vacuity is a normal state for Gallus.[4] 'Defluat' prepares for the images of watery enervation of later in the poem.

The advice, when it comes in line 3, is banal yet vague in its application to both Gallus and the myth. In the story that follows, Propertius concentrates on Hylas's imprudence, though Hercules was also careless. Who is Gallus in terms of the myth? Lines 5–6 seem to cast Gallus as Hercules, his boyfriend as Hylas, but over lines 7–10 he becomes increasingly like Hylas.

1) 53.8% polysyllabic pentameter endings; see Introduction

2) The obvious parallel is Theocritus XIII which deals with this story, but one may compare also Id. XI which recounts the story of the Cyclops's love for Galatea and is introduced by a section addressed to a friend of the poet. The experimentation with Hellenistic models may have been typical of Propertius's first poetic attempts — likely enough in the cultural climate of the time — and the epitaphic XXI and 'seal-poem' XXII bear witness to this.

3) See Enk's comments on this passage.

4) Our view coincides with that of Postgate who translates 'idle, unthinking'. Enk wishes to translate 'free from anxiety': if this is right, it seems to us impossible to read the line aloud without a note of sarcasm, in which case the result is tonally much the same.

The uncertain identification is probably the result of the myth's preceding its application to Gallus, but it leads into the diffused kind of sexuality that increasingly characterises the poem.

Lines 4—6 introduce the myth itself. But line 4 is unsatisfactory and unclear. 'Crudelis Ascanius' begins the process of personification, by which rivers will be more active than people, but Ascanius has no particular role to play, and is masculine. If he is to be related to anyone in Gallus's story, it must be to Propertius, who is giving the advice to Gallus that Ascanius gave the Argonauts, and would be the recipient of Gallus/Hercules's laments as at line 16. But Propertius is not obviously cruel or wild, the epithets used of Ascanius. In this line the tradition divides evenly between 'dixerat' (APV) and 'dixerit' (N). The hypothetical note introduced by 'dixerit' seems gratuitous here, so 'dixerat' is preferable. A pluperfect would serve a normal function for Propertius, of insisting on the remoteness of the action in the past.[5] 'Minyis' is sometimes taken with 'crudelis', cruel-to-the-Argonauts,[6] but Ascanius was not specifically cruel to the Argonauts, and needs someone to talk to, so 'Minyis' is best taken as an indirect object with 'dixerat'.

Lines 5—6 seem an extremely strained way of saying that Gallus's boyfriend is almost as good as Hylas. The language is so tortured that it may even be a kind of joke at Gallus's expense.[7] In line 5 the accusative 'speciem' is left in the air by the change to an ablative, in the apparently parallel phrase 'non nomine dispar'.[8] Line 6 is even odder. 'Proximus' slightly undercuts the exact equation established by the previous line, since it indicates that Gallus's love is only the nearest thing to Hylas. The whole construction also relates uneasily to the previous line. 'Ardor' is used unusually for 'amor' as the object of love. The figure is functional here, part of the consistent shift of attention from distinct persons to generalising abstracts.

Lines 7—12 then switch to Gallus, describing him in terms which connect him with the myth. This movement begins with 'hunc tu', Gallus and his boyfriend juxtaposed, but the action that relates the pair, 'defende', is mimetically delayed for four lines by a description of Gallus's self-indulgent wanderings. The paradosis 'hunc' is odd here: 'huic' would go better in a

(5) The modern vulgate is 'dixerit', but the editors do not argue the case.

(6) Ascanius was not so much cruel to the Argonauts as Enk says but to Hylas and Hercules, since it was there that Hylas was lost; cp. Strabo XII 563 3, cited by Enk.

(7) Cp. Krokowski (quoted by Enk) who considers that the whole poem is a sort of joke at Gallus's expense.

(8) With most of the modern commentators we take 'nomine' to mean 'fame'. There is not need to suppose that it means 'name', an unlikely enough coincidence. Bailey's objection that if 'nomine' is not taken in the latter sense, 'Hylan' in the last line would need 'tuum', will not stand. By the end of the poem, Propertius has almost turned 'Nymphis credere Hylan' into a proverb.

construction with 'defende'.[9] If 'hunc' is right, it may be an accusative of respect, perhaps also imitating the Greek habit of placing an ordinary accusative at the beginning of the sentence in which it is the most important notion.

Lines 7–10 describe Gallus's leisurely and aristocratic version of the voyages of the Argonauts. The repeated 'sive' seems to promise syntactic parallelism, but each line has a different construction, no doubt to avoid any easy symmetries. The lines all describe Gallus, but the hexameters cast him in a more active, heroic role, as a Hercules-figure, while the pentameters see him more as a Hylas. 'Spatiabere' in line 9 suggests motion on a grand scale, especially with 'gigantea' in the same line. This may allude to the shores of Baiae, with its causeway named from Hercules.[10] Line 7 does not refer specifically to Hercules, but 'leges' is often used of ships[11] and hence could look forward to a heroic voyage like that of the Argo. The shadows here ('umbrosae') seem pleasant but in this context are not without menace.

The descriptions in lines 8 and 10 in contrast have Gallus passive, the rivers active. In line 8 the Anio washes his feet in a foreshadowing of the nymphs' seduction of Hylas, and the relationship between Gallus and the river is even more intimate in line 10. This line is the only one of the four with no distinct verb to describe Gallus's activity. 'Ubicumque' leaves the place indefinite. 'Vagus', wandering, is transferred from the river to the welcome by an extremely effective hypallage, "the winding hospitality of the river", so that the welcome becomes as serpentine as the river's characteristic motion, or as unstable as a reflection. Gallus is clearly threatened with the fate of Hylas as well as Hercules, seduction as well as loss. He has become a sexually ambiguous figure in this eroticised landscape. Was he Hylas to Propertius, and Hercules to someone else?

Line 11 describes the ceaselessly lascivious attacks of nymphs which he must ward off. But the picture of Gallus beating off these importunate nymphs is strongly in the foreground, and the boyfriend has almost disappeared from the scene. We have to recall 'hunc' from four lines earlier to remember that it is not Gallus himself who is being attacked, although we cannot even be sure of that. 'Hunc' instead of 'huic' makes it uncertain, since the accusative is less clear than the dative would have been about the relation of the youth to the assault.

(9) 'Huic' is printed by Enk, B & B, Camps, but not by Rothstein, who suggests that the construction with 'Hunc' is forgotten or ignored by the time the poet comes to completing it.

(10) Cp. I xi–xii 2.

(11) See O.L.D. under 'lego'. From the examples, the word seems to be epic in its reference to ships.

Line 12 then closes the section with a joke about the sexiness of Italian girls. The last word of the line is given as 'Adriacis' by all the Mss, which is usually emended to 'Adryasin', following Struve. This would be a coinage, its effect being to describe Italian girls in a high-flown and inflated fashion, as Dryads. The joke is that the girls of Italy are as promiscuous as they nymphs of the myth.

Gallus is unequivocally Hercules in the next two couplets, lines 13—16. The hard mountains and icy crags are the stock landscape for a rejected lover. The pools he is doomed to visit are described by 'neque expertos', for 'inexpertos'. This is probably both active and passive. The active is the more common meaning, and pools in this poem are quite capable of knowing, or not knowing, where Hylas is. But 'ignotis oris' in the next line also glosses this one: these are obviously pools that Gallus/Hercules has not known before.

The difficult opening section closes with an extremely highly-wrought construction. Hercules's wanderings ('error') rather than himself have first to endure, in line 15, then, even harder, in line 16 this wandering has to weep for the fact that it is to exist. No explanation should try to make the expression seem other than very strained. But the effect has some poetic justification. As with 'ardor' in line 6, and 'hospitio' in line 10, attention is displaced from the persons to a quality in the narrative that is not specific to anyone. The individuals dissolve, lose their separate identity and merge in the common quality. So Gallus would have his wanderings, and 'error' is used of Hylas at line 42, and the quality applies to the waters as well. Man and water, hero and lover can be interchangeable.

The retelling of the myth now begins, formally introduced by 'namque ferunt olim', suggesting a narrator conscious of the dignity of his office.[12] The couplet proceeds in a grand style. 'Argon' is a Greek form, the genitive 'Phasidos' after 'viam' is an unusual form.[13] The ship is the subject of 'applicuisse', a surprising personification, again attributing unusual activity to inanimate things. The periphrasis used for the Hellespont ('Athamantidos undis'), the waves of the daughter of the Athamas, is relevant to the poem's central concern, drawing attention to the tutelary nymph of the waters.

The Argo then beaches near the rocks of Mysia.[14] The rocks stand

(12) Cp. Cat. LXIV 2. Fordyce notes on this '... 'dicuntur' emphasises at the outset the traditional source of the story. So 'fertur' (19) 'perhibent' (76, 124), 'ferunt' (212); the Alexandrian scholar-poet stresses his dependence on tradition, though the tradition he follows may be an unusual one ...'

(13) The word 'Phasidos' seems to have been first used by Cat. LXIV 3. The genitive after 'viam' is unusual; see Enk of this passage.

(14) 'Scopulis' is probably dative. Enk notes that 'adplico' normally takes 'ad' in prose, and the dative is a common substitute for 'ad' in poetry. Shackleton Bailey cites Postgate 'not on the rocks, but they are the most prominent feature of the country', and compares Soph. Aj. 720.

ominously close, but the heroes have found an amenable stretch of coast for their camp. The image is one of softness surrounded by hardness. This quality is to dominate the rest of the poem, a multi-layered effect of things within things. It comes over strongly in line 22, through what seems like intensive repetition. The shores have already been described as 'placidis'. Now their sands are described as soft ('mollia'), then covered with leaves.[15] These heroes have a refined sense of comfort, and relish such softness on softness. The two phrases are mimetically woven into each other, adjective-adjective, noun-noun.

While these hardy Argonauts are engaged in this luxurious activity, Hylas goes off, but the object of the quest is another luxury. 'Raram' in this context suggests preciousness,[16] and 'sepositi', secluded, connects this water with the dominant motif of the section. The word-order is again carefully worked and significant. It gives an image of things enclosing things, but interestingly it exactly inverts the order of the things described. So 'raram . . . aquam' is at the centre of the fountain but encloses the line. Inside these two words, adjective against adjective and noun against noun, is 'sepositi . . . fontis', while at the centre of the line is the verb 'quaerere', describing an action that takes place outside both the fountain and its waters.

The next eight lines describe the first assault on Hylas, by Zetes and Calais. The whole story seems to be Propertius's own invention. The two brothers were hostile to Hercules according to traditional accounts, but had no particular interest in Hylas.[17] When Hercules was absent searching for Hylas they urged that the Argo should leave, in revenge for which he was later to kill them. Propertius is here elegizing the heroic narrative, by assuming that their motive must have been sexual jealousy. The episode also generalises the threat to Hylas: men as well as nymphs and rivers might assault him.

The details of this assault have proved difficult to determine. Line 26 is clear, the two symmetrical phrases giving a vivid image of the two poised menacingly above Hylas. It is evident that kisses are involved in lines 27–8, but the rest of what is going on is confused.[18] 'Suspensis palmis' in line 27 is a problematic detail. If these are the brothers' hands as is usually supposed, they are hanging down, with the psychological sense of 'suspensus' also rele-

(15) Modern commentators generally take 'mollia' as proleptic, but there is no need; the obvious interpretation is the right one.

(16) Enk thinks it means water is scarce in the region and imagines he has controverted Rothstein, who thinks it means 'exquisite', in contradicting him. Camps, who cites first Enk's view, sees its absurdities and suggests something approaching Rothstein's and ours.

(17) For Hercules's quarrel with the Boreads, cp. Apollonius I 1300–1309.

(18) See the bizarre and conflicting accounts of the various editors.

vant, anxious, eager. The thematic quality is important here. 'Suspensus' connects with 'pendens', of Hylas in line 29, and 'pendebant', of the Hylas-like apples in line 35. Hylas's hands are also mentioned later, at line 43 in the analogous phrase 'demissis palmis'. So the brothers have a surprisingly Hylas-like erotic enervation and passivity here. But it is more satisfactory to suppose that these are Hylas's hands, put up vaguely to ward off the brothers' assault. 'Palma' is then being used precisely, for the palms of his hands, their inner surface, hovering above him like the dewy apples of line 35, being kissed by his ravishers, a means of defence that only arouses them more. If these are his hands there is more point to the juxtaposition 'suspensis instabant', his passivity with their urgency, and the whole picture is easier to visualise if it refers to Hylas as well as to the brothers.

They are kissing him again in the next line, apparently swooping in alternately. But 'fuga' emphasises their movement away. This is not a violent act of rape, more a teasing assault. 'oscula supina' has proved obscure to commentators. It must mean kisses given or received in a supine state. Some have though that 'supina' refers to the brothers[19] who must therefore be supposed to turn over on their backs like sharks to kiss the youth. But this is a grotesque image, with no justification in the poem. It is much more likely that 'supina' refers to Hylas. It conveys his kind of passivity even as he resists the attack, and the picture is readily visualizeable, Hylas looking upwards as would be natural, and receiving kisses on his temptingly upturned mouth.

Lines 29—30 describe this method of self-defence. This too is unclear. The obscurity partly comes from Propertius's obsession here with certain formal and thematic qualities, 'pendens' ('suspensis' 27, pendebant' 35), 'secluditur' ('sepositi' 24, 'desertis' 36) and 'extrema'. The phrase 'extrema ala' has been interpreted in a variety of very different ways.[20] But 'extrema' is repeated at line 50, and connects with a key imagistic concern of the poem, the sense of multi-layeredness. 'Extrema' refers to an outer edge, the wings which are the edge of the space.[21] The picture Propertius seems to have in mind is static and formal but physiologically possible and thematically relevant: Hylas crouching, shielding himself with himself, framed by the wings of his assailants.

Hylas however beats them off with a branch, which makes the pair seem ludicrously ineffective. Lines 31—2 describe their departure, in language so elevated as to seem like parody. But the description that follows is magnificently sensuous and erotic, a satisfying culmination of the experiments of

(19) So Camps, though he offers an alternative explanation.

(20) Camps interprets as more or less = armpit, B & B as 'where the wing joins the shoulder', Enk as the extreme tip of the wing.

(21) Cp. esp. 'extremo amore' XI—XII 6. The number of parallels in general and in detail between the two poems suggests that XX is the direct ancestor of XI—XII. See our discussion of that poem.

the earlier parts of the poem. The scene is set first in lines 33–6, developing the qualities latent in line 24. Again there is a multi-layered effect. The fountain is under a mountain, but above it are trees, down from which hang apples. The apples are 'roscida', dewy, suggesting a youthful quality they share with Hylas, and dew, like water in general in this poem, has an erotic value.

The images of lines 37–8 are heavy with the distinctive eroticism of the poem. Moistness by now has strong sexual connotations, so 'irriguo prato', a meadow drenched with water, swamped, suggests almost total enervation. But this is juxtaposed with 'surgebant', the lilies thrusting up, as active as the nymphs. The next line has its vivid contrast, a botanically unlikely mingling of poppies and lilies, whiteness and purity stained with purple. 'Candida' was often used of the colour of delicate skin, a girl's or a youth's. 'Candor' will be used of Hylas's shoulder at line 45. The purple of the poppies is rich but ominous, the colour of death, though poppies suggest a langorous loss of consciousness.

Hylas then performs the ominous symbolic act of plucking some of these startling flowers, as he will be plucked in his turn. But Propertius does not underline this obvious symbolism. In line 39 he seems more interested in the sensuous quality of the act, the mixture of softness and hardness, Hylas as destroyer and victim. He plucks the flower, but does it like a boy: his nail is tender but is still a nail. Line 40 presents this as a kind of irresponsibility.

In the next couplet, lines 41–2, he proceeds even closer to a delightful loss of consciousness ('nescius'). The water is described as 'formosa' a word more usually used of the beauty of girls. But an element of narcissism comes through in 'blandis imaginibus', which are presumably images of himself. 'Errorem', his wandering return to the rest of the crew, recalls 'error' used of Hercules in line 15, but he puts this off, captivated by his own beauty.

In lines 43–4 he briefly returns to a sense of his duty. Line 44 suggests great effort, as he prepares to draw a full draught, though the action of leaning ('innixus') may be due to his continuing lassitude rather than the need to support his shoulder to draw a full draught. 'Demissis palmis', his hands lowered, also describes a necessary action for someone who wishes to draw water, but again could suggest slackness. Certainly he offers negligible resistance, when the nymphs grasp him and pull him under, as line 47 makes clear.

As he falls, Hylas makes a sound. Whether this is a cry or only the splash of his body entering the water is not clear. 'Sonitum' does not usually refer to speech, but this may be an inarticulate cry which Hylas manages to utter as he sinks into the water. The point of the next two lines, 49–50, recalls the effects he was concerned with in lines 22–30, of things within things. Hercules is far away ('procul') from the unreachable inwardness of Hylas. 'Extremis', as in line 29, indicates an outside edge. Hercules calls Hylas's name, but the sound comes back, carried by the wind from only the fountain's outermost edge, quite unable to reach a Hylas unconscious in its secret centre.

The poem finishes by returning to Gallus, with a disappointing admonitory couplet. This banal warning seems external to Propertius's real interests in the narrative, and his moral sense does not seem to have been continuously awake throughout. The final line is slightly obscure. 'Visus' could have one of two meanings, either that Gallus has been seen to entrust Hylas to the nymphs, or that he seems to have done so.[22] The first is less satisfactory, since Hercules did not trust Hylas to Nymphs. But the warning is not important. Whatever it is, Gallus would not have known better how to "preserve his lover" from having read this uneven, experimental, interesting but self-indulgent poem.

(22) The second is favoured by B & B, the first by Enk.

POEM XXI

This is a short but difficult and perplexing poem. It is usually seen as a funerary epigram, of the kind collected in the Greek Anthology,[1] but it is far more enigmatic and strange than any to be found there, hardly related in its qualities of form or feeling. These funerary epigrams were highly literary productions. Propertius of course is also a self-conscious artist, but the literary inspiration for his poem seems to come from another source, not funerary epigrams but actual tomb inscriptions. Out of the simple motifs of this sub-literary genre Propertius has developed this curious little piece, and some of its oddities of thought only become explicable when its relation to the genre is realised. But some of its force, its power to disturb, comes from these roots. It is a sophisticated poem, yet it still has something of the elemental quality of actual inscriptions that were chiselled on the gravestones of men who had really died.

Characteristically in these grave-epigrams the dead man is felt to be speaking the verses which are inscribed on his tomb. The epitaphs frequently begin with 'Heus', indicative of the extent to which a real if one-sided conversation is thought to occur with the passerby.[2] A recurrent theme of these conversations, or cries from the grave, is the affinity between the dead and the living established by death, the common fate of all. These two conventional qualities are brilliantly recalled and used by Propertius's opening. 'Tu' is normally part of an intimate address. In the three other poems in Book I which commence with this word it refers to an addressee who is well-known to Propertius, as though picking up a continuing relationship from outside the poem. There is nothing intimate about this Tu, however, juxtaposed to the explanatory 'qui properas . . . miles', which is strongly reminiscent of a common motif in grave-inscriptions.[3] The pronoun reaches out for a 'miles' who remains nameless throughout. This nameless soldier, however, is immediately drawn into a disturbingly close relationship with the dead man through 'consortem casum', a conjoined fate, a brother-death. 'Consortem' always implies a very intimate connection. The paradox is common in the convention: Propertius has merely expressed it more forcefully, though he explores the notion with a tortuous ingenuity not to be found on the average tombstone.

Propertius departs from the convention in line two by suggesting a particular soldier, who had been wounded in the same battle. The impulse to present a scene with dramatic particularity is typical of Propertius. Here

(1) Book VII of the Greek Anthology; cp. esp. 337, 180 as good examples of the type.

(2) Cp. Anthologia Latina 55, 119, etc.

(3) See Anth. Lat. 1950, 1943, 1451, etc. The first of these says 'Ego Antoninus umbra tenus 'have' tibi dico, meator, quamvis festinanti gradu carpas iter.' Haste is a constant characteristic of the passerby addressed in these epigrams.

it does not cancel out the universal bond established by man's common mortality. However, the dramatic form here has misleading implications, especially in a rationalist age like ours which does not believe in ghosts. We naturally assume that both men must be alive, even if one is dying. But the last line makes it clear that the speaker is already dead, as he always is in grave-epigrams. So he is not simply dying, as some commentators have thought.[4] Certainly he seems to be speaking, but this is the necessary convention of the genre, without which there would be no poem.

Line 3 still has its difficulties. It is clear that the soldier is troubled by the address, but not so clear what his eyes are exactly doing. 'Turgentia lumina' are always associated with strong emotion, usually of a negative kind. Some commentators see the movement of the eyes as towards the speaker, others away from him.[5] Probably both are right: the soldier's eyes roll to and fro as he is torn by fascination and fear. Groans from a wounded man might not result in such anguished indecision: groans from a dead man would. So the opening question, 'Quid', which suggests that there is something inappropriate and excessive in the soldier's reaction, is really ironic. Gallus knows that the 'miles' has good reason to be alarmed.

The next line presents even more difficulties. The difficulty centres especially on 'militiae'. Until that point in the line the natural sense of the words left a single straightforward meaning for the line still possible. But 'militia' normally refers to a kind of activity over a period of time, whereas here it is related, through 'sum' and 'pars', to 'ego', a person, hence a different kind of entity. The word placed as it is at the end of the line is clearly meant to startle the reader into a new appraisal of either itself or what precedes it. 'Militia' certainly could have a concrete sense, and refer to a troop of soldiers, but this would be unusual, and the oddity is multiplied by the construction with 'proxima pars', all this with no apparent justification from the poem itself. There are further difficulties at the level of meaning. The opening line seems to refer to the soldier as a chance passerby. If the two men were close comrades, Gallus would surely have called him by name. If Propertius meant it as a surprising revelation that really the two knew each other well, he has certainly placed it oddly and been pointlessly obscure. 'Ego', however, while strictly meaning "I", could easily refer to Gallus's condition by a figure common in Propertius, who often identifies a speaker with his fate.[6] The reduction of the person to the general lesson to be learnt from his mortality is a grimly apt figure in the present poem, justification for the tortuous expression. The speaker's condition is the next point in the

(4) Enk, B & B, Camps, but not Rothstein who takes the same view as ourselves, that the man is already dead.

(5) See Enk's discussion. He comes to the same conclusion on this question as ourselves.

(6) Cp. I xx 15 'error Herculis' and I xix 11, the latter of which is rather closer to the example here.

soldier's military progress. The 'casus' is 'consors' in an uncomfortably close sense. The underlying thought has the grinning-skull quality of all the best tomb-epitaphs. One may compare the clumsier ironies of

Heus tu, viator lasse, qui me praetereis,
Cum diu ambulaveris, tamen hoc veniundum.

where the coming of death is described in terms of the present physical action of the passerby.[7] The convention commonly uses the metaphor of a journey for this sentiment, and it is probably significant that a word like 'viae' is needed to complete the natural sense of the line. The intended effect may be a kind of παρα προσδοκιαν, relying on the surprising substitution of 'militiae'. 'Proxima', also tellingly delayed in the line, draws the speaker and the addressee more closely together, locating the death in a fully-realisable near-future, not the vague "sometime" implied in a grave-epigram.

The speaker then switches to the imperative, wishing the 'miles' well on behalf of his parents. This is again part of the funerary formula.[8] But Propertius again intensifies the formulaic sentiment to emphasise the poem's concern with the relationship between the living and the dead. The result in line 6 is a request so odd that uneasy editors have wanted to emend it.[9] The first oddity concerns the appearance of a sister. If the poem has been read to this point as a dramatic encounter it is natural to ask: whose sister? But no particular answer to this question sounds at all convincing. The run of the sense in the paradosis would make her the soldier's sister, since they were his 'parentes' in the previous line. But if this sister is going to be so upset about Gallus's death as it appears, she would seem to be very closely connected to Gallus — most probably his wife. So the 'miles' turns out to be someone like a brother-in-law, rather a coincidence, which makes the oblique opening even odder. If the sister is Gallus's sister, the soldier would have to know Gallus very well to identify her without her name. But all such speculation sounds irrelevantly ingenious and inconclusive. None of these difficulties arise if the relationship is a generic one, following the fiction of the grave-convention already encountered in 'consortem casum' and 'pars proxima'. Gallus takes pleasure in the happiness of the nameless soldier's parents because the brotherhood of death makes them his parents too. Out of this relationship he can create a generic sister — the soldier's sister in the first place, as the run of the sentence suggests, but also his sister, everyone's sister — a female mourner to pay her respects at Gallus's grave.

The request has puzzled commentators for other reasons, centring chiefly on the opening negative 'ne'. The difficulty here, however, comes

7) Anthologia Latina 119; cp. also 83.

8) Cp. Anth. Lat. 62, 63, 64, 76, etc.

9) Enk prints the Mss text: others variously have 'haec', 'nec' or 'me' for 'ne' and 'Acca' for 'acta'. See Camps on this passage.

from taking 'acta sentiat' generally as "to learn the news", as though Gallus did not want her to know of his death. Such a request would be highly unlikely in the grave-epigram convention, and in any case is incompatible with line 10. The words must refer not to the bare fact of his death, which she will inevitably know, but to the way she ought or ought not learn them. 'Sentiat' implies an emotional, intuitive mode of apprehension: and 'e lacrimis' would be the worst way to break the unhappy news, the way most likely to inflict the greatest grief on her in the telling.

Part of the cause for grief is not just the fact of death but the manner of it. 'Ereptum per medios enses' is almost epic in diction, recalling the Homeric hero being snatched from the dangers of battle by some deity.[10] So in line 7 Gallus sees himself cast in an heroic role, an object of special concern to the gods. His actual end in line 8 is a total contrast: 'ignotas manus', no Achilles but ordinary soldiers killed him, perhaps even after the battle had been lost. This was not a noble way to die, though he was not actually disgraced.

The final couplet converges wholly on the grave-epigram. The sister or female mourner is imagined coming to the mountains and seeing all the scattered bones. The 'miles' is to mark Gallus's. The following poem, XXII, suggests that this hope was not to be fulfilled, but given the generic status of the soldier this was not to be expected. The final 'haec sciat esse mea' points directly to the spot: the bones are speaking and announce themselves in the normal manner of tombstones — 'Hic est Gaius'.[11]

But the poem is not simply a literary exercise, putting new life into a simple popular genre. The subject of the poem is Gallus, a real person, probably a kinsman of Propertius. This poem is followed by XXII, where an unnamed 'propinquus' suffers the same fate as Gallus. The two poems read as glosses on each other, and it is difficult to believe this is not intended. XXI gives the dead man's name and dramatises the circumstances of his death: XXII indicates his importance, and the significance of his death to Propertius. The juxtaposition makes certain biographical facts poetically relevant, and brings the poem into contact with an actual death, and with the kind of poetry that normally went with it. So the nature and intention of the poem becomes clearer. It really is a kind of epitaph, designed for a tomb that the poem itself explains does not exist.

The dramatic narrative and the animated tomb-stone fuse in this expression of Propertius's grief, in his attempt to give meaning to that death, and to death in general. Out of this comes the central and puzzling effect of the poem. Its strange combination of remoteness and familiarity is achieved by expressiong the notion of the brotherhood of the living and the dead in terms of a particular close family tie, but this general truth is conveyed in a

(10)   E.g. Hom. Iliad V 318, 445, etc. cp. also Hor. Odes II vii 13.

(11) Cp. e.g. Anth. Lat. 58, 59, etc.

poem about the death of a real person who was in fact closely related to Propertius. The poem fulfils the dead man's request in the only way that is still possible. When the poem is read like this, with an awareness of the kind of poem it is and where its roots lie, it not only becomes easier to follow without recourse to emendation, it also emerges as a very fine and moving poem.

POEM XXII

This is the last poem in the book, and superficially seems to have the characteristics of a σφραγις or seal-poem.[1] Such poems generally conveyed a potted biography of the poet, performing something of the function· of a publisher's summary on the dust-jacket for a modern writer. But there are two reasons for doubting that this poem was simply composed after the rest of the volume, as a seal-poem. One is its dating, on the basis of pentameter endings. This gives a very early date for its composition.[2] But another reason is its tone. It has a kind of muted aggressiveness which is quite uncharacteristic of the genre. It more or less conveys the information that would be wanted from a seal-poem, hence perhaps its position in the volume, but it is a poem in its own right, much more evasive and personal than such poems usually were. Either Propertius has once again transformed a stock form, or this was not originally designed specifically as a seal-poem.

The poem starts with three questions about Propertius which Tullus is always asking. Propertius does not in fact answer two of these, so it has been suggested that really they all mean much the same. The poem would have been a better seal-poem if he had answered all three, however, so Propertius's inattentiveness here has deprived us as well as Tullus of information we would have valued. Assuming that Propertius knew that there were three distinct questions, he clearly did not want to tell Tullus the answers, and is not over-concerned to give us a satisfactory dust-jacket poem.

The questions themselves, about Propertius's status and origins, are standard, but the line has an awkward feel to it. 'Qualis' relies on 'sim' understood, 'genus' on an unstated 'sit', and between these and the next question is a suppressed 'et'. The effect of all this ellipsis is to break the movement up into a series of staccato questions, and the line as a whole seems to go on and on.

The sense of uneasiness this gives rise to is crystallised by 'semper' in the next line. This would go most naturally with 'quaeris', to suggest a persistance in this questioning which is slightly ludicrous, as Camps points out. It would imply a resentment of Tullus very unusual in a poem of this kind. But 'semper', with its hostile note, is enclosed by 'nostra amicitia', as though to indicate that this irritating questioning is enclosed by their friendship, accommodated within it. Camps suggests that 'semper' goes with 'amicitia' in an adjectival fashion, for 'continua'. As a primary meaning this would be strained, but the placing of 'semper' here may be intended to suggest something of this kind, that their friendship is as continuous as this persistent questioning.

(1) On this see Enk, who cites in comparison A.P. XII 257 (Meleager), and other examples of the type.

(2) See Introduction *pp 5–15* The percentage of polysyllabic pentameter endings is 60%, though the sample is too small to be really conclusive. However, the poem can hardly be late.

The answer, when it comes, is oblique. Perusia was the nearest large city to Assisi, where Propertius probably came from, so Perusia is a natural preliminary indication of the place. But the hypothetical form of the question is strange. The family of the Volcacii Tulli was Perusine.[3] The if-form ought to be an insult to his knowledge: "If Perusia's graveyard is known to you . . .". It ought to be known to a Perusine noble, unless he has entirely forgotten its origins.

But Propertius is more interested in history than geography. It is the graveyards, not the city itself, which he uses as a marker. 'Sepulcra' is defined by two words, 'Perusina' and 'patriae'. So Perusia is not set against 'patria' but included with it. 'Patria' is picked up by 'Italia' in the next line. The troubles referred to are the Perusine war of 41 B.C., an unhappy episode in Roman history in which Propertius's family seems to have been on the wrong side. In the present poem he laments a relative who died then. In XXI someone who appears to be the same man fought against Caesar. In IV i 127–30 it appears that Propertius's inheritance was reduced, presumably in the distribution of lands to Octavius and Antony's veterans. The indirect point of this history lesson is that Propertius's family was a casualty in this war. It indirectly answers the first two questions, 'qualis et unde genus'. His ancestry is more noble than his present situation might indicate, though in this poem he makes no claims of this kind. 'Romana discordia' might be intended to make a contrast with 'Italia' in the previous line, implying criticism of faction in Rome, contrasting the city with the country. The indirection of all this suggests a slightly touchy pride, perhaps a measure of resentment.

The poem changes direction sharply at line 6. The edgily aggressive construction of the 'si'-clause is abandoned, and overcome by a new intensity of emotion he forgets Tullus, as Tullus had, perhaps, forgotten his birthplace and its sufferings. Now he addresses the earth of Etruria. 'Pulvis' is a surprising word here. Its associations were with dry, powdery dust, with the ashes of the dead. 'Solum' would be much more natural here, while 'pulvis' would be preferable at line 8 in place of 'solum', so Propertius has probably crossed over the terms to suggest a connection between the two kinds of earth, the rich Etruscan soil and the dust that covers the dead.

The transition to this address is made through the opening 'sit' of line 6. This is commonly emended to 'sed' or 'sic',[4] but this is to misread the tone entirely, and make it cool and explanatory, not the sudden outburst it is. There is a contrast intended here between the coolness of 'nota' and the merely hypothetical relation to Tullus, and Propertius's own intensity of feeling. By the next line Tullus is completely forgotten, and 'tu' is the

(3)   For the Volcacii Tulli see Poem VI note 1. This family had managed to come out on the right side in the civil wars, whereas Propertius's family was clearly not. See Introduction

(4)   Rothstein, B & B, Enk, have 'sic', Camps has 'sed'.

Etrurian dust, which feels vividly the outrage of the unburied body of Propertius's relative. 'Perpessa' is a strong word, to endure with great fortitude, which implies that what is to be endured must be correspondingly hard to endure.

'Propinquus' leaves the exact nature of the relationship vague, but 'mei' makes it seem important to Propertius. But the fact that these bones are unburied makes the memory even more distressing to Propertius. Bones exposed in this way were a continuing affront.[5] They are also an image for something unresolved in the conflict. So line 6 is an instruction to himself to continue to mourn for this relative. The paradox of line 8, 'pulvis' being addressed instead of 'solum', because of the lack of 'solum' instead of 'pulvis' to cover the scattered bones, is another sign of something continuing to be wrong.[6]

Lines 9–10 pick up the syntax and tone of lines 3–4 as though the outburst of lines 5–8 had not happened. But the effect of such a neutral tone now is to suggest a tightness and reserve. In line 9 he fixes the position of his birthplace. It is in Umbria, not Etruscan Perusia, though very close to the border. 'Supposito campo' is a curious ablative,[7] but clearly it must indicate the precise situation of Propertius's family estates. 'Campus' is strictly a field, but this martial context could bring out its secondary meaning, as a field of battle. 'Suppositus' primarily refers to its low-lying situation, but the poem's concern with the bitterness of the civil war could bring out another meaning, subjected.[8] He comes from a low-lying plain, the scene of the struggles just described, the memory of which it retains, within it.

All this gives resonance to the final line. 'Genuit' picks up the questions of the opening, and makes the apparent digression of lines 3–7 relevant at last. He is now identified with the land itself, which is his true ancestor, with its rich lands. The double insistence on fertility and natural riches in 'fertilis uberibus' makes a contrast with the account of the suffering and death of the war. Propertius's wealth is Umbria, as his distress was due to his concern for her fate in the war, and his sense of wounds not fully healed. But this last image implies healing, reconciliation, the natural fertility of the land re-asserting itself.

(5) Cp. e.g. I xvii 8, 11–12; cp. also Cic. Pro Milone 13 33.

(6) See Postgate on this line, cited by Enk; 'An expression like 'pulvis solo contegit ossa' makes the same thing a personal agent in an action and then the instrument with which the action is performed.'

(7) On this see Enk. It is a somewhat difficult line, but Enk and Camps agree in thinking that it describes the plain from which Assisi rises.

(8) This is possible even though all the examples of the meaning 'subject' for 'suppono' are later than Propertius; Ov. Tr. IV viii 48, F. I 306, Pers. V 36. The point is that unless we are to assume that Propertius is being obscure for the sake of obscurity here then one must suppose that 'supposito' has some function further than the topographical, since in that function it is difficult to decipher.

So the way the questions are not answered points out something unsatisfactory about their terms. The poem implicitly challenges the narrow and rather complacent assumptions that lie behind them. It brings out some of the strains in 'nostra amicitia' which the well-meaning Tullus was unaware of, and indicates why the constant question was as much an irritant as 'semper' hinted. The friendship is real, and Propertius does no more than hint at his criticisms. Nor does he want to revive the war. But the past remains alive to nourish his somewhat touchy pride, and Tullus's questions are made to seem annoyingly facile. The poem may be an opaque entry for a contemporary "Who's Who" but it is a revealing little poem about Propertius's sense of the foundations of his own position, and his relation with the noble Tullus.

Note on the Text

We have used the apparatus criticus of Enk's edition of book I for information about the Mss readings. Our text differs from the Oxford Classical Text of E.A. Barber in the following respects:—

Our text	O.C.T.
I i 2 A colon	A full stop.
i 24 'Cytinaeis'	'Cytaeines'.
ii 7 'tua'	'tuae'.
ii 13 'persuadent'	obelised.
iii 16 'et arma'	obelised.
iii 18 full stop	semi-colon.
iii 27 'duxit'	'duxti'.
iv 14 'dicere'	'ducere'.
iv 26 full stop	colon.
iv 27 'nostri maneat, sic semper adoro,'	'nostro. maneat sic semper, adoro',
v 9 'ruis, non est contraria nostris,'	'tuis non est contraria votis',
vi 10 'irato'	'ingrato'.
vii 16 '(quod nolim nostros eviolasse deos)'	'quo nollem nostros me violasse deos',
viii 13 'tali sub sidere'	'talis subsidere'.
viii 15 'patiatur'	'patiantur'.
viii 19 No commas	comma after 'te' and 'remo'.
viii 26 'Hylaeis'	'Hylleis'.

At this line, the O.C.T. closes inverted commas and begins a new poem. Our text continues the inverted commas.;

ix 4 'quaevis'	'quovis'.
ix 30 'aufuge'	'a fuge'.
x 11 'concedere'	'concredere'.
x 28 'effecto'	'effectu'.
xi 5 'adducere'	'a! ducere'.
xi 15 'amota'	'amoto'.
xii 1 We read this as a direct continuation of xi.	

xii 2 No commas	commas after 'nobis' and 'Roma'.
xv 15–20	Arranged by Barber: 17–20, 15, 16.
xv 29 'multa'	'nulla'.
xvi 11-12	In parenthesis.
xvi 38 'irato ... loco'	Obelised.

vii 1 Comma   exclamation mark.

vii 3 'solito'   'salvo'.

viii Comma in 23, question   question mark in 23, full stop in
ark in 24;   24.

viii 27 Commas after 'quo'
1d 'fontes'.

ix 5 'noster'   'nostris'.

ix 22 'e'   'a'.

x 4 'dixerat'   'dixerit'.

x 13 'sint duri'   'sit duros'.

x 50 'fontibus'   'montibus'.

xi 5   'ut possint'.

xii 6 'sit'   'sic'.

Bibliography

Commentaries and editions of Propertius:

Sexti Properti Carmina, ed. E.A. Barber, Second Edition, Oxford 1960.
Propertius Sextus Elegien, ed. Max Rothstein, 2 vols., 1898 and 1920, reprinted, 1966 Dublin/Zurich.
Sex. Propertii Elegiarum Liber I, ed. P.J. Enk, Leyden 1946.
Elegies of Propertius, ed. Butler and Barber, Oxford 1933 (cited as 'B & B').
Propertius Elegies Bk. I ed. W.A. Camps, Cambridge 1967.
Propertiana, D.R. Shackleton Bailey, Cambridge 1956.
In Properti Monobiblon commentationes, A. Pasoli, Bologna, 1957.

Other works referred to:

A.P. Allen, 'Sunt qui Propertium malint', pp. 130 ff. in *Critical Essays on Roman Literature: Elegy and Lyric*, ed. J.P. Sullivan, London 1962.
J. André, *Etude sur les termes de couleur dans la langue Latine*, Paris 1949.
B. Axelson, *Unpoetische Wörter . . .*, Lund 1945.
H. Bardon, *La litterature Latine Inconnue*, Paris 1955.
E. Burck, 'Römische Wesenszüge . . . ', *Hermes* 80(1952), pp. 163–200.
F.O. Copley, *Exclusus Amator*, Madison Wis. 1956.
E. Courtney, (On the symmetry of bk. I of Propertius), *Cl. Phil.* 1968 pp. 251 ff.
L.C. Curran, 'Vision and Reality in Propertius', *Y.Cl.St.* 19.
M.W. Edwards, 'Intensification of meaning in Propertius and Others', *T.A.P.A.* 92(1961), pp. 128–144.
E. Fraenkel, *Horace*, Oxford 1957.
J. Fontenrose, 'Propertius and the Roman Career', *Univ.Cal. pub. in Cl. Phil.* XIII (1949), pp. 371–388.
G. Krokowski, 'De Propertio Ludibundo', *Eos* XXIX (1926), pp. 81–100.
R.O.A.M. Lyne, (On poem III), *Proc. Cam. Phil. Soc.*, N.S. no. 16(1970) pp. 60 ff.
R.O.A.M. Lyne, (On poem VIII), *Proc. Cam. Phil. Soc.* 1972.
L.A. Moritz, 'Well-matched lovers (Prop. I vi)', *Cl. Phil.* 62(1967), pp. 106–8.
E. O'Neil, 'Cynthia and the Moon', *Cl. Phil.* 53(1958) pp. 1–8.
Brooks Otis, (On the symmetry of bk. I), *H. St. Cl. Phil.* 70 1965.
A. Otto, *Die Sprichwörter . . . . der Römer*, Leipsig, 1890.
E.H. Sandbach, 'Propertius I 21', *Proc. Cam. Phil. Soc.* 1937 p. 12 f.
O. Skutsch, (On the symmetry of bk. I), *Cl. Phil.* 58(1963).
E. Solmsen, (On the symmetry of bk. I), *Cl. Phil.* 57(1962).
J.P. Sullivan, ed. *Critical Essays on Roman Literature; Elegy and Lyric*, London 1962.
R. Syme, *The Roman Revolution*, Oxford 1951 (2nd. imp.).
H. Tränkle, *Properz und . . . Dichtersprache, Hermes Ein.* 15(1960).
P. Wilkinson, *Golden Latin Artistry*, Cambridge 1963.
G. Williams, *Tradition and Originality in Roman Poetry*, Oxford 1968.
E.C. Woodcock, *A new Latin Syntax*, London 1959.

CPSIA information can be obtained
at www.ICGtesting.com
Printed in the USA
LVOW01s1715201216

518129LV00015B/248/P